AN ARGUMENT FOR A NEW

NATIONAL CENTRIST PARTY

Or

let's clean up our own backyards

Michael Bajek

An Argument for a New National Centrist Party
or
let's clean up our own backyards

First published in 2018 by Completely Novel in the United Kingdom.

ISBN: 9781787232792

Printed in the United States of America and the United Kingdom by Lightning Source

.

Contents

OUR DYSFUNCTIONAL TWO-PARTY SYSTEM

"Complaints are everywhere heard from our most considerate and virtuous citizens, equally the friends of public and private faith and of public and personal liberty, that our governments are too unstable, that the public good is disregarded in the conflicts of rival parties, and that measures are too often decided, not according to the rules of justice and the rights of the minor party, but by the superior force of an interested and overbearing majority....

By a faction I understand a number of citizens, whether amounting to a majority or minority of the whole, who are united and actuated by some common impulse of passion, or of interest, adverse to the rights of other citizens, or to the permanent and aggregate interests of the community....

A zeal for different opinions concerning religion, concerning government, and many other points, as well as speculation as of practice; an attachment to different leaders ambitiously contending for pre-eminence and power; or to persons of other descriptions whose fortunes have been interesting to the human passions, have, in turn, divided mankind into parties, inflamed them with mutual animosity, and rendered them much more disposed to vex and oppress each other than to co-operate for their common good.....

It is in vain to say that enlightened statesmen will be able to adjust these clashing interests and render them all subservient to the public good. Enlightened statesmen will not always be at the helm. Nor, in many cases, can such an adjustment be made at all without taking into view indirect and remote considerations, which can rarely prevail over the immediate interest which one party may find in disregarding the rights of another or the good of the whole."

Federalist Papers No. 10 (Madison)

The Republican and Democratic Parties

The actions of both major parties during the 2016 campaign and following the election were bizarre, showing the very worst of the U.S. political system. It's embarrassing at the best, and certainly dangerous if it is to continue. I could almost call it a double suicide - slow, and admittedly not final yet - but the parties are on life support, and will require intensive care to recuperate, if it is even possible at this late stage. Several national polls now show that over 40% of voters now consider themselves independents. This figure was less than 10% at the time of the 2012 election. It is clear that a significant number of Americans are troubled by the current state of political affairs in the country and believe we can do better.

The Republicans had seventeen candidates going into the primary. Sixteen of whom were relatively qualified, lackluster and not stellar, but not objectionable people by any means. The seventeenth, Donald Trump, was the least qualified, least suitable but had a message that resonated, and he won. The sixteen losers did not have their fingers on the pulse of the Republican constituency. And they were too arrogant and self-serving to band together and stand behind just one or two of the most likely candidates. If they had done so before the primary, the numbers in the anti-Trump camp would have probably been enough to prevent Trump's victory. But, he divided and conquered his opponents, and no one saw it coming.

Now, one year after the election, we have a government mired in an investigation into possible collusion with Russia to meddle in the election. We have a President who is so inflammatory and divisive that he has one of the lowest popularity ratings in our history. Even though the Republicans hold both houses of Congress, the members are so divided among themselves that they can't push legislation through. And bipartisanship among the two parties, is just a bad joke.

And the Democrats! Hear all that whining now about Russians meddling in "our democracy"? What did Hillary Clinton and the Democratic National Committee do? They locked Clinton in as the one and only candidate at the beginning of Barack Obama's term. They took significant steps to prevent Bernie Sanders, the unanticipated late starter, from competing on an even playing field with Clinton. And Clinton herself, destroying 33,000 emails after they were subpoenaed by Congress might have committed a serious, actionable offense. Classified documents were among those emails not destroyed and released to Congress. That alone was grounds for legal action. But, what was contained in the missing 33,000? Many Americans, including myself, would like to know.

So here was the playbook presented to voters in the 2016 election:

Vote for a nasty man, or
Vote for a nasty woman.
Vote for a lying man, or
Vote for a lying woman.
Vote for a corrupt man, or
Vote for a corrupt woman.
Vote for an election meddling man, or
Vote for an election meddling woman.

And what was the deciding factor? Having a clear message and communicating it effectively.

The twit with the most tweets won.

In 2016 there were an estimated 235 million eligible voters, but only 129 million actually voted. Donald Trump won the election by electoral votes but lost the popular vote to Clinton who received 66 million to his 63 million. So, Trump won with the votes of only 27% of the American voting population. It would be a hard stretch to say that Trump is now governing with a national mandate. If Clinton had won, with 28% of the vote of the eligible voting population, what's the real difference? 72% of the eligible voters would not have voted for her versus the 73% who would not have voted for Trump. The bottom line is that the majority of our population is not represented by our President now, nor would it have been if the election outcome had swung the other way.

The 106 million eligible voters who did not vote (some estimates have this figure at 90 million, but that is not really relevant in this context) are a huge potential voting bloc that a third party should pursue. We do not really know why they did not vote, but it is safe to assume that a significant portion were not happy with either of the two major candidates, or with the minor third-party candidates, or in general felt that the whole election process was pointless, not relevant to them personally. A new third party, centrist and with new directions, could make significant in-roads into enfranchising the disenfranchised, which I think would be very good for the country and a patriotic thing to do.

The Royal Court of Washington D.C.

"And all the little Oysters stood
And waited in a row.

"The time has come," the Walrus said,
"To talk of many things:
Of shoes--and ships--and sealing-wax--
Of cabbages--and kings—"

The Walrus and The Carpenter
Lewis Carroll
(from Through the Looking-Glass and What Alice Found There, 1872

"If we resort for a criterion to the different principles on which different forms of government are established, we may define a republic to be, or at least may bestow that name on, a government which derives all its powers directly or indirectly from the great body of the people and is administered by persons holding their offices during pleasure for a limited period, or during good behavior. It is essential to such a government that it be derived from the great body of the society, not from an inconsiderable proportion or a favored class of it; otherwise a handful of tyrannical nobles, exercising their oppressions by a delegation of their powers, might aspire to the rank of republicans and claim for their government the honorable title of republic."

Federalist Papers, No. 39 (Madison)

Our Aristocracy

"We have heard of the impious doctrine in the old world, that the people were made for kings, not kings for the people. Is the same doctrine to be revived in the new, in another shape – that the solid happiness of the people is to be sacrificed to the views of political institutions of a different form?"

Federalist Papers No. 45 (Madison)

We Americans just can't seem to shed our love for monarchies and aristocracies. We declared independence from England in 1776, but we still look upwards to our leaders in Washington, not as high-level public servants, statesmen, and representatives of we, the people, but as special people imbued with divine rights, sometimes hereditary. We therefore excuse them their foibles, their whims, their arrogance. We look to them for the solutions to all our problems and feel powerless to take steps to solve our own.

Our President is our king (or maybe someday our queen). Their children are the princes and princesses who may someday inherit the throne. Our senators are the dukes, our representatives the earls. We hang on their every word as if it came from above. Then there are the barons – the feudal lords who dominate commerce in the United States, accumulate wealth and power to extraordinary levels, then pass them on to their children. Sometimes the "barons" might enter public service as a reward for supporting the winning presidential candidate, but do they really have the same definition for "public" and "service" as we do?

We believe in dynasties. We've had Roosevelts and Kennedys. We've more recently had the Bushes and Clintons. President George H.W. Bush to President Bill Clinton to President George W. Bush. Twenty years out of twenty-eight between just two families. Then in 2016 there was almost a President Jeb Bush and almost a President Hillary Clinton.

I have little doubt that Hillary Clinton has given up. After two tries at the Presidency, I expect she will try again in 2020. She would be counting on the unpopularity of President Trump, and she very well might win this time. Or,

13

maybe it's time for Bill and Hillary's daughter Chelsea to enter the fray. After all she is now 37 years old, and eligible for the Presidency. Or maybe Chelsea will first take a congressional seat in 2020, build up some creds like her mother did, then enter the general election in 2024. And which Bushes wait again in the sidelines? We accept all of this. We accept hereditary monarchies and aristocracies, while touting our democracy. Something is missing here. Out of 327 million people we must have equivalent or even superior talent out there to what has been offered us of late.

"We need leadership!" A constant refrain we hear in media from the political pundits. To me this is a whiny lament that we do not have a strong king or queen to inspire us, command us, charge forward over the hills ahead with us loyally trotting behind. Too many people seem to want one person, or a small set of persons, to solve all their problems. And for whatever reasons - inability to put solutions to problems, or maybe just laziness - such complainers do not want to take "leadership" in the areas in which they can make a positive contribution. Or find a responsible person to take charge in that area. Most people are content to take the easy way out and just keep on voting in the same old aristocracy.

Everyone has the capability and should take the responsibility to be a leader in their own "backyard". No need to be the world's expert on every matter under the sun. In our own environments, each of us has skills and abilities possessed by no other person, and we can apply these talents not only to improve our own lot, but also to be a significant asset in "grassroots" efforts to improve the lot of the group, be it small or large.

All of us must also be followers. It is nonsensical for any one of us to believe that we have all the answers, skills and abilities to take charge of solving everything for everyone. Somehow, too many have become convinced that they must be "boss" to have any validity. Rather than leading in areas they are strong and following in areas where weak, many believe they must lead in all, even when ignorant on the issue.

But, for the higher levels of government we do need enlightened statesmen who are responsive to the needs of those they are elected to represent. We have not seen that very often in recent crops of Presidents, Senators and Congressmen. We need new faces, identified not by themselves but sought out and chosen by us in the rank and file. Those persons of superior intellect, courage, and ethics are out there somewhere. We need to find them.

What a Third National Party Can Do

"Let us not seek the Republican answer or the Democratic answer, but the right answer. Let us not seek to fix the blame for the past. Let us accept our own responsibility for the future."

John F. Kennedy

A strong, third party can serve as a bridge between the two, currently major parties. Resting squarely in the center of national, state, and local politics, this "middle-of-the-road" party would provide stability and solidity in the U.S. process of governance. Extremist views to the left or right would have difficulty in dominating the platforms of either of the two current parties. There would be a natural tendency for the staunch but moderate adherents to the Republican and Democratic parties to steer their platforms towards the center, knowing full well that the third party would have both a significant membership of its own and also be capable of drawing moderate members of the two other parties to it if their own party platforms tilted to the extremes of the parties. The Republican and Democratic parties will want to remain relevant and to preserve their place in the electoral process. They will have to re-brand, seek to represent mainstream America, or risk becoming minor parties, focused on a narrow set of partisan issues.

In the current two-party system, there appears to be a phenomenon for each of these parties to swing towards the extreme factions of their parties to present a countervailing force to the extremes of the other. Imagine a pendulum, with the Democrats being at the nine o'clock position and the Republicans being at the three 'clock mark. The majority of members probably prefer to be at the seven and five o'clock positions respectively. However, Newton's Third Law has some conceptual applicability here - each force has an equal and opposite reaction. In today's politics, there is a reactive impulse to move further to the extreme to neutralize or counter the extremes of the other party. As with physics, with a zero-coefficient of friction the policies of the Nation swing wildly back and forth following each election in which one party takes over from the other. Both feel that they need the non-mainstream factions in their parties to have enough votes to overcome the combined moderate and extremist factions of the other party. The mainstream elements do not object, they provide no friction to slow or stop the swinging.

With a strong, third party this is less likely to happen. I believe most Americans are naturally more centrist in their political thinking. They want a strong, prosperous, and positive-thinking country with governments at all levels working from foundations of ethics, representation, pragmatism and the higher precepts as outlined in the Constitution. As phrased in the Pledge of Allegiance: "With Liberty and Justice for All." A third party, and the moderate elements of both other parties, will provide the "friction" to slow or even stop erratic swings in the political agenda.

American thinking has been focused most pointedly on the executives of each level of government – President, Governor, Mayor. While these positions are important, I believe it is the legislative branches in which a significant third-party representation will be the most effective. I would like to see a third centrist party hold one-third of the seats in the U.S. Congress, State Houses, county and city councils. Why not more? Why not 51% of the seats? Because I believe the value of a third-party will be in modulating the power of those bodies, not taking all powers from them. Otherwise, the third-party could well become just another major party, most likely vying with the strongest of the other two for preeminence and the back and forth cycle like we have today would just resume.

So, assume the third party holds one-third of the seats in the U. S. Congress, both House and Senate. No party by itself would be capable of passing a bill or law without the support of 18% of members from one or both other parties to reach the magic 51% to pass the action; or 34% of members from the other parties to reach the two-thirds vote needed to overcome a presidential veto, impeach the president, amend the Constitution (for referral to the States for ratification) and other Federal actions requiring the highest level of Congressional consent. A centrist third-party, understandably composed of both slightly left and right-leaning members would be well placed to formulate bills, laws and policies that would be acceptable to the moderate members of both other parties – an effective tri-partisanship in other words quite different to how it works today with the dominant party in Congress holding 51% of the vote and thus capable of ramrodding an action through over the unanimous objection of the other. Bipartisanship, in today's toxic political environment, has not proven possible as good as it sounds in theory. At the present time, policies of the Republican and Democratic parties appear so black and white to their respective constituencies that representatives are fearful of crossing over to the other side and incurring the ire of their voters. A centrist third-party, if it adheres to Constitutional principles and a minimalist agenda that has broad appeal across party lines, would have significant flexibility to present its own legislation, support legislation of another party, or negotiate with both parties to develop actions that would have broad agreement among those in the American populace who are not comfortable with the fringe elements of either party.

At the Executive level, and here I am speaking specifically of the Presidency, having three choices in the national election would, I believe, have great appeal to most American voters. For one, the pressure would be on all three candidates to tone down the divisive rhetoric and stop vying to be the most inflammatory in support of the fringe "alt-right" or "alt-left" agendas. Voters, whether Democrat, Republican or third-party, will exert pressure on their parties to present the most qualified, statesman-like candidates. Members of all three parties will want their own party candidate to win. That is the competitive nature of Americans. However, with a three-party slate of moderates from each, it is much more likely that members of the losing parties will be less angered if the winning President is someone who they can respect and support regardless if not the first choice of the individual.

Obviously, with such a three-way split in the national popular vote, it is much more likely that the election would be decided in the House of Representatives. Many Americans fear this, assuming the final decision would not represent the will of the country, but the arbitrary decisions of the House members. I do not share this fear as the composition of the House is the representation from the disparate Congressional Districts around the U.S., and thus reflects the will of the voters at the lowest regional levels. Obviously, the House could have a Republican, Democratic, or third-party majority and thus vote in their party candidate. More likely, is that without any party having a deciding majority, the members will have to vote not on party lines, but in the best interests of the country. They will have to work among each other to reach a decision in a mature and statesman-like fashion.

Most members are that type of people. It is only the current, corrosive atmosphere of the greatly divided two-party system that seems to bring out the worst qualities of these otherwise superlative senior public servants.

AREAS FOR REFLECTION – THE "ELEPHANTS IN THE ROOM"

We are Divided

Yes, very much so. Why is this such a surprise? We always were, and we always will be. It is an impossibility that all Americans will agree on all subjects all of the time. Look at this.

Historians estimate that the population of the United States at Independence was about 2.5 million. The first census was conducted in 1790, counting just under four million people, including an estimated 700,000 slaves. The Union was comprised of 13 states on the eastern seaboard of the continent.

Our population at the last census in 2010 was just under 309 million. Here at the beginning of 2018, the Census Bureau estimates the population at 327 million. We now have 50 states and five continuously occupied territories, plus the District of Columbia.

In 1776, the population of the United States derived from English, Welsh, Irish, Scottish, German, Dutch and Scandinavian origins.

In 2018, our population includes people who came from, or whose roots can be traced back to every country and region in the world. This list of independent countries and semi-autonomous or disputed territories should fully illustrate how important our cultural and ethnic diversity is to political equations.

Afghanistan, Albania, Algeria, American Samoa, Andorra, Angola, Anguilla, Antarctica, Antigua And Barbuda, Argentina, Armenia, Aruba, Australia, Austria, Azerbaijan, Bahamas, Bahrain, Bangladesh, Barbados, Belarus, Belgium, Belize, Benin, Bermuda, Bhutan, Bolivia, Bosnia And Herzegovina, Botswana, Bouvet Island, Brazil, British Indian Ocean Territory, Brunei Darussalam, Bulgaria, Burkina Faso, Burundi , Cambodia, Cameroon, Canada, Cape Verde, Cayman Islands, Central African Republic, Chad, Chile, China, Christmas Island, Cocos (Keeling) Islands, Colombia, Comoros, The Republic of the Congo , The Democratic Republic Of The Congo, Cook Islands, Costa Rica, Cote D'Ivoire, Croatia, Cuba, Cyprus, Czech Republic, Denmark, Djibouti, Dominica, Dominican Republic, East Timor, Ecuador ,Egypt, El

Salvador, Equatorial Guinea, Eritrea, Estonia, Ethiopia, Falkland Islands (Malvinas), Faroe Islands, Fiji, Finland, France, French Guiana, French Polynesia, French Southern Territories, Gabon, Gambia, Georgia, Germany, Ghana, Gibraltar, Greece, Greenland, Grenada, Guadeloupe, Guam, Guatemala, Guinea, Guinea-Bissau, Guyana, Haiti, Heard Island and McDonald Islands, Holy See (Vatican City State), Honduras, Hong Kong, Hungary, Iceland, India, Indonesia, Iran, Islamic Republic of Iraq, Ireland, Israel, Italy, Jamaica, Japan, Jordan, Kazakhstan, Kenya, Kiribati, Korea, Democratic People's Republic Of Korea, Republic of Kosovo, Kuwait, Kyrgyzstan, Lao People's Democratic Republic, Latvia, Lebanon, Lesotho, Liberia, Libyan Arab Jamahiriya, Liechtenstein, Lithuania, Luxembourg, Macau, Macedonia, The Former Yugoslav Republic of, Madagascar, Malawi, Malaysia, Maldives, Mali, Malta, Marshall Islands, Martinique, Mauritania, Mauritius, Mayotte, Mexico, Micronesia, Federated States Of Moldova, Republic of Monaco, Mongolia, Montserrat, Montenegro, Morocco, Mozambique, Myanmar, Namibia, Nauru, Nepal, Netherlands, Netherlands Antilles, New Caledonia, New Zealand, Nicaragua, Niger, Nigeria, Niue, Norfolk Island, Northern Mariana Islands, Norway, Oman, Pakistan, Palau, Palestinian Occupied Territory, Panama, Papua New Guinea, Paraguay, Peru, Philippines, Pitcairn Island, Poland, Portugal, Puerto Rico, Qatar, Reunion, Romania, Russian Federation, Rwanda, Saint Helena, Saint Kitts And Nevis, Saint Lucia, Saint Pierre And Miquelon, Saint Vincent And The Grenadines, Samoa, San Marino, Sao Tome and Principe, Saudi Arabia, Senegal, Serbia, Seychelles, Sierra Leone, Singapore, Slovakia, Solomon Islands, Somalia, South Africa, South Georgia and The South Sandwich Islands, Spain, Sri Lanka, Sudan, Suriname, Svalbard and Jan Mayen, Swaziland, Sweden, Switzerland, Syrian Arab Republic, Taiwan, Province Of China, Tajikistan, Tanzania, Thailand, Togo, Tokelau, Tonga, Trinidad And Tobago, Tunisia, Turkey, Turkmenistan, Turks And Caicos Islands, Tuvalu, Uganda, Ukraine, United Arab Emirates, United Kingdom, United States, United States Minor Outlying Islands, Uruguay, Uzbekistan, Vanuatu, Venezuela, Viet Nam ,U.S. Virgin Islands, British Virgin Islands, Wallis And Futuna, Western Sahara, Yemen, Zambia, Zimbabwe

And religion! At Independence, the population of the United States was basically Christian Protestant from these denominations: Methodist, Presbyterian, Baptist, Anglicans, Quakers, Lutherans, Congregationalists, and vestiges of smaller sects such as Puritans, Moravians, Mennonites and others. There was a relatively small population of Roman Catholics in Maryland, and a few Jews in port cities.

Look at the religions and distinct denominations (which have further sub-denominations not listed!) present in the country today.

Christian: Roman Catholic, Eastern Catholic Churches, Syriac Catholic, Independent Catholic Churches, Greek Orthodox, Russian Orthodox, Coptic, Ethiopian Orthodox, Assyrian Church of the East, Indian Orthodox, Mar Thoma Church, Anglican Communion, Amish, Brethren in Christ, Church of the Brethren, Hutterites, Mennonites, Old German Baptist Brethren, Baptists, Brethren, Catholic Apostolic Church, Charismatic Movement, Christian Israelite Church, Unification Church, Christian Science, Children of God, Peoples Temple, Esoteric Christianity, Lutheranism, Methodism, Messianic Judaism, Most Holy Church of God in Christ Jesus, New Thought, Pentecostalism, Pietism, Puritans, Presbyterianism, Congregational Church, Religious Society of Friends, Spiritism, Unitarianism, Universalism, Adventism, The Church of Christ of Latter Day Saints, Jehovah's Witnesses.

Judaism: Conservative Judaism, Orthodox Judaism, Reform Judaism, Progressive Judaism, Alternative Judaism, Humanistic Judaism, Jewish Renewal, Karaite Judaism, Reconstructionist Judaism,

Islam: Kalam Schools, Kharjite, Shi'a (Ismailis, Jafari, Zaiddiyah), Sufism, Sunni (Hanafi, Hanbali, Wahabbi. Maliki, Shafi'i).

Buddhism: Nikaya Schools, Mahayana, Zen, Vajrayana, New Buddhist Movements.

Hinduism: Agama Hindu Dharma, Hindu Rivivalism, Lingayatism, Reform Movements, Shaivism, Shaktism, Tantrism, Smartism, Vaishnavism, Samkhya, Vaisheshika, Vedanta, Yoga.

Sikhism: Khalsa, Namdhari, Sahajdhari.

East Asian Religions: Cao Dai, Chongdogyo, Confucianism, Falun Gong, I-Kuan Tao, Jeung San Do, Legalism, Mohism, Oomoto, Shinto, Taoism, Tenrikyo

Native American Religions/Mythologies: Abenaki, Anishinaabe, Blackfoot, Cherokee, Chickasaw, Choctaw, Creek, Crow, Eskimo, Ghost Dance, Guarani, Haida, Ho-Chunk, Hopi, Huron, Inuit, Iroquois, Kwakiutl, Lakota, Lenape, Longhouse, Midewiwin, Native American, Church, Navajo, Nootka, Olmec, Pawnee, Salish, Seneca, Selk'nam,

Smaller religions with real followings: Gnosticism, Mandaeism, Rastafari Movement, Baha'i Faith, Babiism, Scientology, New Age Religions (many), African Traditional Religions, African Diasporic Religions, Zoroastrianism, Eurasian Traditional Religions, Oceania Traditional Religions, Caribbean Religions, Cargo Cults, Satanism, Magic Religions.

And consider occupations. At the time of Independence, the workforce was engaged in only a small number of areas: agriculture was the primary one, but then of course there were the usual basic trades such as carpentry and construction, masonry, blacksmithing and metallurgy, mining, mercantile and retail, transport, medicine, law, printing, shoemaking and more. These were all basic occupations that served the needs of the people in a town, or region. Exports were mainly tobacco, hemp, animal pelts and a few other commodities not found in Europe that largely originated from large plantations and wealthy landholders. Much of the population was engaged in self-subsistence on small farms.

Today, the Department of Labor lists 867 occupations, many of which have sub-specialties. I list them below to give a flavor of the variety of skill sets in our economy. Such amazing diversity in the American labor pool. Blue collar, white collar, skilled trades, skilled professions. Some are predominately urban occupations, others rural; some are represented throughout the U.S. We need all of them, and all of them deserve respect. It doesn't take a great deal of imagination to see the complex interactions each employment category has with other categories and to sense that seemingly small changes in economic sectors can ripple across a large number of workers. Each occupation has its own character and inevitably those employed in one sector will think differently on some things that workers in another sector. The differences might be minute or profound. But there will be differences that will have an impact on the way they think about politics. Take a glance and try to decide which we do not need, which do not deserve consideration, which you and the country can survive without. Not many if you really look at it. We are all interdependent.

Able Seamen	Land Surveyor
Account Collector	Landscape Architect
Accounting Specialist	Landscape Contractor
Adjustment Clerk	Lathe Operator
Administrative Assistant	Law Clerks
Administrative Law Judge	Law Professor
Administrative Service Manager	Legal Assistant
Admiralty Lawyer	Legal Secretary
Adult Literacy and Remedial Education Teachers	Legislative Assistant
	Library Assistant
Advertising Account Executive	Library Consultant
Advertising Agency Coordinator	Library Science Professor
Aeronautical & Aerospace Engineer	Library Technician
Aerospace Engineering Technician	License Clerk
Agricultural Crop Farm Manager	Licensed Practical Nurse (LPN)
Agricultural Engineer	Livestock Commission Agent
Agricultural Equipment Operator	Loan Counselor
Agricultural Inspector	Loan Interviewers and Clerks
Agricultural Product Sorter	Loan Officer
Agricultural Sciences Professor	Locomotive Engineers
Agricultural Technician	Log Graders and Scalers
Air Crew Member	Logging Tractor Operator
Air Crew Officer	Logging Worker Supervisor
Air Traffic Controller	Machine Feeders and Offbearers
Aircraft Assembler	Mail Clerk
Aircraft Body and Bonded Structure Repairer	Mail Machine Operators
Aircraft Cargo Handling Supervisor	Maintenance Supervisor
Aircraft Examiner	Makeup Artists - Theatrical
Aircraft Launch and Recovery Officer	Management Consultant (Analyst)
Aircraft Launch and Recovery Specialist	Manicurists and Pedicurists
Aircraft Mechanic	Manual Arts Therapist
Airfield Operations Specialist	Mapping Technician
Airline Flight Attendant	Marina Boat Charter Administrator
Airline Flight Control Administrator	Marine and Aquatic Biologist
Airline Flight Operations Administrator	Marine Architect
Airline Flight Reservations Administrator	Marine Cargo Surveyor
Airport Administrator	Marine Drafter
Airport Design Engineer	Marine Engineer
Alcohol & Drug Abuse Assistance Coordinator	Marine Surveyor
Alumni Relations Coordinator	Marine/Port Engineer
Ambulance Drivers	Market Research Analyst
Amusement Park & Recreation Attendants	Marketing Managers
Anesthesiologist (MD)	Marking Clerk
Animal Breeder	Marriage and Family Therapists
Animal Control Worker	Massage Therapist
Animal Husbandry Worker Supervisor	Materials Engineer
Animal Keepers and Groomers	Materials Inspector
Animal Kennel Supervisor	Materials Scientist
Animal Scientist	Math Professor

Animal Trainer
Animation Cartoonist
Answering Service Operator
Anthropology and Archeology Professor
Anti-Terrorism Intelligence Agent
Appeals Referee
Aquaculturist (Fish Farmer)
Aquarium Curator
Architecture Professor
Area, Ethnic, and Cultural Studies Professor
Armored Assault Vehicle Crew Member
Armored Assault Vehicle Officer
Art Appraiser
Art Director
Art Restorer
Art Therapist
Art, Drama, and Music Professor
Artillery and Missile Crew Member
Artillery and Missile Officer
Artists Agent (Manager)
Athletes' Business Manager
Athletic Coach
Athletic Director
Athletic Trainer
ATM Machine Servicer
Atmospheric and Space Scientist
Audio-Visual Collections Specialist
Audiovisual Production Specialist
Automobile Mechanic
Automotive Body Repairer
Automotive Engineer
Automotive Glass Installer
Avionics Technician
Baggage Porters and Bellhops
Baker (Commercial)
Ballistics Expert
Bank and Branch Managers
Bank Examiner
Bank Teller
Benefits Manager
Bicycle Mechanic
Billing Specialist
Bindery Machine Set-Up Operators
Bindery Machine Tender
Biological Technician
Biology Professor
Biomedical Engineer
Biomedical Equipment Technician
Boat Builder
Book Editor
Border Patrol Agent
Brattice Builder
Bridge and Lock Tenders
Broadcast News Analyst
Broadcast Technician
Broker's Floor Representative
Brokerage Clerk

Mathematical Technician
Meat Packers
Meat, Poultry, and Fish Trimmers
Mechanical Drafter
Mechanical Engineer
Mechanical Engineering Technician
Mechanical Inspector
Medical Administrative Assistant
Medical and Public Health Social Workers
Medical and Scientific Illustrator
Medical Appliance Technician
Medical Assistant
Medical Equipment Preparer
Medical Examiner/Coroner
Medical Insurance Claims Analyst
Medical Laboratory Technician
Medical Photographer
Medical Records Administrator
Medical Records Technician
Medical Secretary
Medical Technologist
Medical Transcriptionist
Mental Health Counselor
Mentally Retarded Students Teacher
Merchandise Displayer
Metal Casting Machine Operator
Metal Fabricator
Meter Mechanic
Middle School Administrator
Middle School Guidance Counselor
Middle School Teacher
Military Analyst
Military Officer
Military-Enlisted Personnel
Mill Worker
Mine Cutting Machine Operator
Mine Inspector
Mining Engineer
Mining Machine Operator
Mining Shovel Machine Operator
Missing Person Investigator
Missionary Worker (Foreign Country)
Model Maker
Model Makers, Metal and Plastic
Motion Picture Director
Motion Picture Projectionist
Motor Vehicle Inspector
Motorboat Mechanic
Motorcycle Mechanic
Municipal Fire Fighting Supervisor
Museum Curator
Museum Technicians and Conservators
Music Arrangers and Orchestrators
Music Director
Music Teacher
Music Therapist
Musical Instrument Tuner

Budget Accountant
Budget Analyst
Building Inspector
Building Maintenance Mechanic
Bulldozer / Grader Operator
Bus and Truck Mechanics
Bus Boy / Bus Girl
Bus Driver (School)
Bus Driver (Transit)
Business Professor
Business Service Specialist
Cabinet Maker
Camp Director
Caption Writer
Cardiologist (MD)
Cardiopulmonary Technologist
Career Counselor
Cargo and Freight Agents
Carpenter's Assistant
Carpet Installer
Cartographer (Map Scientist)
Cartographic Technician
Cartoonist (Publications)
Casino Cage Worker
Casino Cashier
Casino Dealer
Casino Floor Person
Casino Manager
Casino Pit Boss
Casino Slot Machine Mechanic
Casino Surveillance Officer
Casting Director
Catering Administrator
Ceiling Tile Installer
Cement Mason
Ceramic Engineer
Certified Public Accountant (CPA)
Chaplain (Prison, Military, Hospital)
Chemical Engineer
Chemical Equipment Operator
Chemical Plant Operator
Chemical Technicians
Chemistry Professor
Chief Financial Officer
Child Care Center Administrator
Child Care Worker
Child Life Specialist
Child Support Investigator
Child Support Services Worker
City Planning Aide
Civil Drafter
Civil Engineer
Civil Engineering Technician
Clergy Member (Religious Leader)
Clinical Dietitian
Clinical Psychologist
Clinical Sociologist

Narcotics Investigator (Government)
New Accounts Clerk (Banking)
Newspaper Editor
Newspaper/Magazines Writer
Non-Retail Sales Supervisor
Nuclear Engineer
Nuclear Equipment Operation Technician
Nuclear Fuels Research Engineer
Nuclear Medicine Technologist
Nuclear Monitoring Technician
Nuclear Power Reactor Operator
Nuclear Technicians
Numerical Tool Programmer
Nurse Practitioner
Nurse's Aide
Nursery Workers
Nursing Professor
Obstetrician (MD)
Occupational Analyst
Occupational Physician (MD)
Occupational Safety & Health Inspector
Occupational Therapist
Occupational Therapy Assistant
Oceanographic Assistant
Office Clerk
Office Machine Mechanic
Office Supervisor
Offset Press Operators
Operating Engineers
Operations Management Analyst
Ophthalmic Laboratory Technician
Ophthalmologist (MD)
Oral and Maxillofacial Surgeons
Order Clerk
Order Fillers, Wholesale and Retail Sales
Ordinary Seamen
Ornamental-Metalwork Designer
Orthodontic Assistant
Orthodontic Laboratory Technician
Orthodontist (MD)
Outdoor Education Teacher
Overhead Door Installer
Package Designer
Packaging Machine Operator
Packers and Packagers, Hand
Painter (Industrial)
Painters, Construction and Maintenance
Painters, Transportation Equipment
Park Naturalist
Parking Enforcement Officer
Parking Lot Attendant
Parole Officer
Parts Salesperson
Paste-Up Worker (Graphic Arts)
Patent Agent
Patent Lawyer
Pathologist (MD)

Coatroom and Dressing Room Attendants
College/University Professor
Commercial Designer
Commercial Diver
Commercial Fisherman
Communication Equipment Mechanic
Communications Professor
Community Health Nurse
Community Organization Worker
Community Welfare Worker
Compensation Administrator
Compensation Specialist
Compliance Officer
Computer Aided Design (CAD) Technician
Computer and Information Scientists, Research
Computer and Information Systems Managers
Computer Applications Engineer
Computer Controlled Machine Tool Operators
Computer Customer Support Specialist
Computer Hardware Technician
Computer Operators
Computer Programmer
Computer Science Professor
Computer Security Specialist
Computer Software Engineers
Computer Software Technician
Computer Systems Engineer
Congressional Aide
Conservation Scientist
Construction Driller
Construction Laborer
Construction Manager
Construction Trades Supervisor
Contract Administrator
Contract Specialist
Control Center Specialist (Military)
Controller (Finance)
Cook (Cafeteria)
Cook (Fast Food)
Cook (Private Household)
Cook (Restaurant)
Cook (Short Order)
Copy Writer
Corporation Lawyer
Correction Officer
Correspondence Clerk
Cosmetologist (Hair Stylist)
Cost Accountant
Cost Analysis Engineer
Cost Estimator
Costume Attendant
Counseling Psychologist
Counter and Rental Clerks
County or City Auditor
Couriers and Messengers
Court Administrator
Court Clerk

Payroll and Timekeeping Clerks
PBX Installer and Repairer
Peace Corps Worker (Volunteer)
Pediatric Dentist
Pediatrician (MD)
Personal Service Supervisor
Personnel Administrator
Personnel Assistant
Personnel Recruiter
Pest Control Workers
Pesticide Handlers
Petroleum Engineer
Petroleum Geologist
Petroleum Laboratory Assistant
Petroleum Refinery Operator
Petroleum Technician
Pharmacy Aides
Pharmacy Technician
Philosophy and Religion Professor
Photo-Optics Technician
Photoengravers (Graphic Arts)
Photogrammetric Engineer
Photographic Equipment Mechanic
Photographic Process Workers
Physical Education Instructor
Physical Therapist
Physical Therapist Aides
Physical Therapy Assistant
Physician's Assistant (PA)
Physician's Office Nurse
Physics Professor
Pilot (Commercial Airlines)
Plant Breeder
Plant Manager (Manufacturing)
Plasterers and Stucco Masons
Plastic Surgeon
Platemakers (Graphic Arts)
Plumber (Plumbing Contractor)
Poets and Lyricists
Police and Detectives Supervisor
Police Artist
Police Identification and Records Officers
Police Officer
Political Science Professor
Political Scientist
Postal Service Clerks
Postal Service Mail Carriers
Postal Service Mail Sorter
Postmasters and Mail Superintendents
Power Plant Operators
Power-Line Installer and Mechanic
Precision Devices Inspectors and Testers
Preschool Administrator
Preschool Teacher
Pressing Machine Operator
Pressure Vessel Inspectors
Printing/Graphic Arts Reproduction Technician

Court Reporter
Craft Artist
Crane Operator
Credit Adjuster
Credit Analyst
Credit Reporter
Criminal Investigator (Detective)
Criminal Justice Professor
Criminal Lawyer
Crop Workers Supervisor
Crossing Guard
Custom Tailor
Customer Service Representative (Utilities)
Customer Service Supervisor
Customs Inspector
Cutting Machine Operators
Dairy Technologist
Database Administrator
Deaf Students Teacher
Delivery Driver
Demonstrators and Product Promoters
Dental / Orthodontic Office Administrator
Dental Assistant
Dental Hygienist
Dental Laboratory Technician
Dentist (MD)
Dermatologist (MD)
Desktop Publishing Specialist
Developmental Psychologist
Die Cutter Operator
Dietetic Technician
Dietitian and Nutritionist
Directory Assistance Operator
Disabled Students Teacher
Disk Jockey
Dispatcher (Safety Vehicles)
Door To Door Salesmen
Dry Wall Installer
Economics Professor
Editorial Writer, Newspapers & Magazines
Education and Training Administrator
Education Professor
Educational Administrator
Educational Psychologist
Educational Resource Coordinator
Educational Therapist
EEG Technician/Technologist
Electric Meter Installer
Electric Motor Mechanic
Electrical and Electronic Inspector
Electrical Drafter
Electrical Engineers
Electrical Parts Reconditioner
Electrical Technician
Electro-Mechanical Technicians
Electromechanical Equipment Assembler
Electronic Drafter

Printmaker (Artist)
Private Detectives and Investigators
Private Nurse
Private Sector Executives
Probate Lawyer
Probation Officer
Procurement Clerks
Product Planner
Product Safety Engineer
Production Planner
Production, Planning, and Expediting Clerks
Professional Sports Scout
Proofreaders and Copy Markers
Property Accountant
Property Assessor
Property Managers
Props and Lighting Technicians
Prosthetic Technician
Psychiatric Aide
Psychiatric Technician
Psychiatrist (MD)
Psychology Professor
Public Health Service Officer
Public Relations Manager
Public Relations Specialist
Public Transportation Inspector
Publications Editor
Purchasing Agent
Purchasing Manager
Quality Control Coordinator
Quality Control Engineer
Quality Control Inspector
Quality Control Technician
Quarry Worker
Radar and Sonar Technicians
Radiation Protection Engineer
Radiation Therapists
Radio & TV Announcer
Radio & TV News Commentator
Radio & TV Newscaster
Radio & TV Producer
Radio & TV Program Director
Radio & TV Sports Announcer
Radio & TV Station Administrator
Radio & TV Talk Show Host
Radio Mechanics
Radio Operators
Radiologic Technicians
Radiologic Technologist
Radiologist (MD)
Rail Yard Engineers
Railroad Conductors and Yardmasters
Railroad Engineer
Railroad Inspector
Range Manager
Real Estate Appraiser
Real Estate Assessor

Electronics Engineer
Electronics Technician
Elementary School Administrator
Elementary School Teacher
Elevator Mechanic
Emergency Management Specialist
Emergency Medical Technician
Employee Benefits Analyst
Employee Training Instructor
Employment Administrator
Employment and Placement Specialist
Employment Interviewer
Engine and Machine Assemblers
Engineering Managers
Engineering Professor
English Language and Literature Professor
Environmental Compliance Inspector
Environmental Disease Analyst
Environmental Engineer
Environmental Planner
Environmental Research Analyst
Environmental Science Technician
Environmental Science Professsor
Environmental Technician
Equal Opportunity Representative
Etchers and Engravers
Excavating Machine Operator
Excavating Supervisor
Executive Secretary
Exercise Physiologist
Exhibit Artist
Exhibit Designer
Experimental Psychologist
Explosives Worker
Export Agent
Fabric and Apparel Patternmakers
Facilities Planner
Factory Layout Engineer
Family Caseworker
Family Practitioner (MD)
Farm Equipment Mechanic
Farm Hand
Farm Labor Contractor
Farm Manager
Farm Products Purchasing Agent
Farmers and Ranchers
Fashion Artist
Fashion Coordinator
Fashion Designer
Fashion Model
Fence Installer
Field Contractor
Field Health Officer
File Clerk
Film Editor
Film Laboratory Technician
Finance Manager

Real Estate Broker
Real Estate Lawyer
Real Estate Sales Agents
Recreation Leader
Recreational Protective Service Worker
Recreational Therapist
Recreational Vehicle Mechanic
Referee / Umpire
Refuse and Recyclable Material Collectors
Registrar Administrator
Reliability Engineer
Religious Institution Education Coordinator
Reservation Ticket Agent
Residence Counselor
Resource Recovery Engineer
Resource Teacher
Respiratory Care Technician
Respiratory Therapist
Respiratory Therapy Technicians
Restaurant Food Coordinator
Restaurant Manager
Retail Buyer
Retail Customer Service Representative
Retail Inventory Control Analyst
Retail Sales Department Supervisor
Retail Salespersons
Retail Store Manager
Revenue Agent (Government)
Safety Inspector
Sales Engineers
Sales Floor Stock Clerk
Sales Managers
Sales Promoter
Sales Representative (Aircraft)
Sales Representative (Chemicals & Drugs)
Sales Representative (Computers)
Sales Representative (Graphic Arts)
Sales Representative (Hotel Furnishings)
Sales Representative (Medical Equipment)
Sales Representative (Printed Advertising)
Sales Representative (Radio & TV Time)
Sales Representative (Telecommunications)
Sales Representative (Teleconferencing)
Sales Representative (Education Programs)
Sales Representatives (Agricultural Products)
Sales Representatives (Instruments)
Sales Representatives (Mechanical Equipment)
Sales Representative (Psychological Tests)
Sanitary Engineer
Sawing Machine Operator
Scanner Operators
School Nurse
School Plant Consultant
School Psychologist
Scientific Linguist
Scientific Photographer
Screen Printing Machine Operators

Financial Aid Counselor
Financial Analyst
Financial Examiner
Financial Planner
Financial Services Sales Agent
Fine Artist
Fire Inspector
Fire Investigator
Fire Prevention Engineer
Fire Protection Engineer
Fire Protection Engineering Technician
Fish & Game Warden
Fish Hatchery Specialist
Fishery Worker Supervisor
Fitness Trainer
Flight Engineers
Floral Designer
Food & Drug Inspector
Food Batchmaker
Food Preparation Worker
Food Science Technicians
Food Technologist
Foreign Exchange Trader
Foreign Language Interpreter
Foreign Language Teacher
Foreign Language Translator
Foreign Service Officer
Foreign Service Peacekeeping Specialist
Foreign Student Adviser
Forensic Science Technicians
Forensics Psychologist
Forest and Conservation Technician
Forest Engineer
Forest Fire Prevention Supervisor
Forest Fire Inspector
Forestry and Conservation Professor
Forging Machine Operator
Forklift and Industrial Truck Operators
Fraud Investigator
Freight and Stock Handler
Fund Raiser
Funds Development Administrator
Funeral Attendant
Funeral Director
Furniture Designer
Furniture Finishers
Game Runner
Gas Plant Operator
General and Operations Managers
General Farmworkers
General Internists (MD)
Geography Professor
Geological Data Technicians
Geological Technician (Drafter)
Glass Blower
Gluing Machine Operators
Golf Course Superintendent

Screen Writer
Script Editor
Securities Broker
Security and Fire Alarm Systems Installers
Security Guard
Self-Enrichment Education Teachers
Septic Tank and Sewer Servicers
Service Station Attendants
Set Designer
Set Illustrator
Sewing Machine Operators
Sheet Metal Workers
Ship Carpenters and Joiners
Ship Engineers
Ship Master
Ship Mate
Ship Pilot
Shipping, Receiving, and Traffic Clerks
Shoe Machine Operators
Signal Switch Repairers
Skin Care Specialists
Small Engine Mechanics
Social and Community Service Managers
Social and Human Service Assistants
Social Psychologist
Social Science Research Assistants
Social Service Volunteer
Social Welfare Administrator
Social Work Professor
Social Worker
Sociology Professor
Soil Conservation Technician
Soil Conservationist
Soil Engineer
Soil Scientist
Solar Energy Systems Designer
Solid Waste Disposal Administrator
Sound Engineering Technicians
Special Education Administrator
Special Forces
Special Forces Officers
Speech Pathologist
Speech Writer
Sport Psychologist
Sport's/Entertainment Agent (Manager)
Sports Agent
Sports Events Business Manager
Sports Physician (Orthopedist)
Sportswriter (Journalist)
Stained Glass Artist
Standards Engineer
Statement Clerks
Stationary Engineers
Statistical Assistants
Steel Workers
Storage and Distribution Manager
Stress Analyst Engineer

Government Budget Analyst
Government Property Inspectors
Government Service Executives
Graduate Teaching Assistant
Graphic Designer
Greenhouse and Nursery Manager
Gynecologist (MD)
Hand and Portable Tool Mechanic
Hand Sewer
Harbor Master
Harbor, Lake & Waterways Police
Hardwood Floor Finisher
Hazardous Materials Removal Worker
Hazardous Waste Management Analyst
Health Care Facilities Inspector
Health Case Manager
Health Educators
Health Psychologist
Hearing Officer
Heating, A/C, Refrigeration Technician
Heavy Equipment Mechanic
High School Administrator
High School Guidance Counselor
High School Teacher
Highway Maintenance Worker
Highway Patrol Pilot
Historic Site Administrator
Historical Archivist
History Professor
Home Appliance Installer
Home Appliance Repairer
Home Economics Teacher
Home Economist
Home Entertainment System Installer
Home Health Aide
Home Health Technician
Horticultural Worker Supervisor
Horticulture Therapist
Horticulturist (Vineyard)
Hospital Administrator
Hospital Nurse
Hosts and Hostesses
Hotel and Motel Desk Clerks
Hotel Convention/Events Coordinator
Hotel Manager
Housekeeping Supervisors
Human Factors Psychologist
Human Resources Management Advisor
Human Resources Management Consultant
Hydraulic Engineer
Immigration Inspector
Industrial Air Pollution Analyst
Industrial Arts Teacher
Industrial Designer
Industrial Engineer
Industrial Engineering Technician
Industrial Health Engineer

Structural Drafter
Structural Engineer
Student Admissions Administrator
Student Affairs Administrator
Student Financial Aid Administrator
Substance Abuse Counselor
Subway and Streetcar Conductor
Surgeons (MD)
Surgical Technician/Technologist
Survey Researchers
Surveying Technicians
Switchboard Operator
Systems Accountant
Systems Analyst, Data Processing
Tax Accountant
Tax Auditor
Tax Collector
Tax Examiner
Tax Lawyer
Tax Preparer
Taxi Drivers and Chauffeurs
Teacher of the Blind
Teacher's Aide
Team Assemblers
Technical & Scientific Publications Editor
Technical Directors/Managers
Technical Illustrator
Technical Publications Writer
Technological Espionage Intelligence Agent
Telecommunications Line Installers and
Repairers
Telecommunications Maintenance Worker
Telecommunications Technician
Telephone Station Installers
Textile Bleaching and Dyeing Machine
Operators
Textile Cutting Machine Operators
Textile Designer
Tile and Marble Setters
Title Examiner
Title Searchers
Tool & Machine Designer
Tool and Die Makers
Tool Grinders, Filers, and Sharpeners
Tour Guide
Town Clerk
Traffic Administrator (Freight & Passenger)
Traffic Agent
Traffic Technicians
Transit and Railroad Police
Transportation Attendants
Transportation Systems Design Engineer
Travel Agent
Travel Clerks
Travel Counselor
Travel Writer (Journalist)
Treasurer (Corporate)

Industrial Hygienist	Treatment Plant Operators
Industrial Machinery Mechanics	Tree Trimmers and Pruners
Industrial Relations Analyst	Truck Driver, Light Duty
Industrial Relations Specialist	Truck Driver, Long Distance
Industrial Therapist	Ultrasound Technologist
Industrial Waste Inspector	Unemployment Inspector
Industrial-Organizational Psychologist	Urban and Regional Planner
Infantry Officers	Ushers and Lobby Attendants
Instructional Coordinators	Utility Meter Reader
Instructor, Police-Canine Services	Vending Machine Mechanic
Instrument Technician	Veterinarian (VMD)
Insulation Installer	Veterinarian Technician
Insurance Adjuster	Veterinary Assistant
Insurance Agent	Video Engineer
Insurance Appraiser (Auto Damage)	Vocational Education Instructors College
Insurance Claim Examiner	Vocational Education Teachers, High School
Insurance Claims Adjuster	Vocational Education Teachers, Middle School
Insurance Claims Clerks	Vocational Rehabilitation Counselor
Insurance Estate Planner	Voice Pathologist
Insurance Lawyer	Waiters and Waitresses
Insurance Policy Processing Clerk	Warehouse Stock Clerk
Insurance Underwriter	Watch Repairers
Intelligence Specialist (Government)	Water Pollution Control Inspector
Interior Designer	Weather Observer
Internal Auditor	Web Art Director
Interpreter for the Hearing Impaired	Weighers and Measurers
Irradiated-Fuel Handlers	Welder (Gas, Arc, Plasma, Laser)
Irrigation Engineer	Welfare Eligibility Workers and Interviewers
IT Administrator (Information Technology)	Wholesale Buyers
Janitorial Supervisors	Wildlife Biologist
Job Analyst	Wildlife Control Agent
Job Development Specialist	Windows - Draperies Treatment Specialist
Job Printer (Graphic Arts)	Woodworking Machine Operators
Kindergarten Teacher	Word Processing Specialist
Labor Relations Advisor	Writer /Author
Laboratory Tester	Zoo Veterinarian
	Zoologist

Again, we are very divided in terms of ethnic and national origins, religion, occupation, regions we live in, gender, age and on and on. We cannot expect unified thinking on everything. We must reduce to bare bones the slate of issues we agree are essential to our national, state and local wellbeing as a nation. Then seek common ground, negotiation, and consensus on how best as a people to address the most important issues.

Fortuitously, a wise group of people over 200 years ago provided us a framework which has proven solid for the entire history of our nation – the Constitution. We need to return to the basics, clear the muddy waters, and seek unity on the structures and issues which are common to us all as citizens of the United States of America. A centrist political philosophy is, it seems to me, the only practical, viable direction we can take. And to achieve this we need at least one middle-of-the road political party to represent the wishes of what I believe are the majority of the American people.

Rural vs. Urban

It should be very clear from the preceding that we Americans are deeply, but naturally, divided in so many ways. This is not a bad thing as this diversity adds tremendously to the richness of our culture and enables the individual talents and skills to contribute to a greater whole. We must strive continuously to seek a more perfect Union, but to achieve this goal we must greatly reduce the animosities that fester within the diversity.

Probably the simplest, but most significant division we now face as a country is between the rural and urban communities. One government statistic shows that over 80% of our population is now urban, living in towns and cities. Another statistic, coming out of the 2010 census is that we have now crossed a line where two or three percent more of the population now live in large cities or their suburbs, rather than in rural areas or small-town America. I think this last figure is the most significant as small-town America identifies much more with its rural surroundings and roots than with a big city outlook.

The by-county map of the results of the Presidential 2016 election on the back cover clearly shows the impact of how Americans vote depending on where they live. The Republicans dominated the geographical area of the entire rural/small town United States. The Democrats took virtually all of the big cities, but very little of the actual surface area of the country. Clinton won the popular vote by three million or so. Given that about 137 million people voted, this popular vote win seems to quite accurately reflect the two to three percent dominance in numbers of the urban vs. rural populations.

This phenomenon, if true and I think it is, is the best argument against going to a popular vote for president as many Democrats and city dwellers want. A popular vote would mean the votes of rural and small-town America no longer count. The political direction of the United States would be dominated by city populations for perpetuity. This was the reason that the drafters of the Constitution arrived at the mechanism of the Electoral College. To allow States with small populations to maintain their sovereignty in the national political fabric, and avoid total domination by the most populous States, who even then contained the largest urban communities. That said, the Electoral College as it stands now is somewhat obsolete, and I believe there are interesting propositions out there in which to engage in electoral reform. I will get to that later, but for now I do want to delve deeper into what the rural vs. urban divide represents.

Most significant is how each group perceives, or attempts to paint, the other in a negative way. Animosity and contempt are fueled by Democrats and Republicans, single-issue factions, and partisan media from both sides.

How do city folk through their media portray those in rural areas? As uneducated, ignorant, blue collar, unskilled or semi-skilled, bigoted, racist, bible-thumping, gun-toting, slack-jawed yokels. Republicans, in the city mindset, feed on this class of serfs, constantly "throwing red meat to their base", as it is described by the left-wing press.

And how do those in rural areas view city folk, again as disseminated by their partisan media? As one of our less than illustrious Vice-Presidents said: "effete snobs in their ivory towers". As Airy-Fairy tree huggers, elitists. But also as atheists, illegal immigrants, welfare recipients, gangs, criminals and people with deviant gender identities and sexual preferences. The rural view is that the Democrats galvanize their base by throwing them sushi and quiche, to accompany their glass of chilled Chardonnay.

Those of us with a more centrist and realistic view know that none of this hyperbole is accurate, fair, nice, or constructive. Unfortunately, our current two-party system exacerbates the rural/urban divide and it is unlikely to improve without a third party representing the moderate, and majority segment of the population. While I strongly believe that the rural/urban divide is the foundation of our differences, it is by no means an absolute. Even in a conservative district like mine, Democrats receive about 34% of the vote to the Republican 66%. And in our most liberal communities, Washington D.C. for example, in which Republicans received 4.1% of the vote to the Democrat's 92.8%, there is still intermingling of supporters of both parties. The point is that at local levels people are able to get along despite sharp political differences, but that when issues are raised to a national level, it appears that there can be no meeting of minds. This is why I so strongly advocate that we seek consensus only on issues that pertain to everyone directly affected at a particular political level – national, state or local.

Freedom of Movement

Thankfully, we Americans have a vast country; we are free to live virtually wherever we want. The truth of the matter is that as varied as we are, most people prefer to be among those people, and those environments in which they feel comfortable, prosperous, meaningful. People congregate with their "own kind". That is human nature and we should not disparage it, lamenting that the American "melting pot" is really more like an Irish Stew. Absent the animosities that too often materialize between our many divisions, our diversity in its broadest definition is a very beautiful thing. The United States would be so monochrome, so characterless without the richness of our different cultures, whether they be ethnic or philosophical or occupational. We should take great pride in being the most varied and inclusive society in the world, in human history.

There are many serious problems today in our country related to Americans not getting along with other Americans. We should not stick our heads in the sand and pretend otherwise. We should work to improve the atmosphere but not be overly sanguine in expecting rifts to be healed in short order. The bottom line is that if any of us find our current situation, locality, community too adverse to ourselves we can always move somewhere else. We can change jobs; we can move to another city or State; we can find a new community where we do feel safe, comfortable, purposeful. Realistically, we may not be able to transform our own environment to one more closely modeling our own personal ideal. So, the best decision might be to change our environment.

Let me just use some relatively benign examples here; you can read between the lines and easily come up where more toxic divisions apply. Artistic people – painters, sculptors, writers, musicians and others – very often are most inspired and happiest living and working in a community that has a sizable representation of other artistic people and where the pervasive atmosphere is not only a love of the arts but also a commonality of political, philosophical and social views. There is no shame in someone with an artistic bent moving from a virtual cultural desert such as my rural community to another community where there is a vibrant artistic culture. People who love the activity of city life should move to the city; those who don't should move to the country. Immigrants from certain regions of the world often collect together in communities which have that dominant cultural flavor. All of that is good – just fine with me.

Each of us should be content and happy where we live. If not, for whatever reason, we do have the freedom to move to a community or environment where we can meet those needs. All of us have the right and the great fortune to be somewhere we like among those we like. We need to respect that others very different from ourselves have that same right.

That said, there are some situations which are so contrary to American values that they are intolerable. The next section is about one such area where we should give no quarter.

Racism, Religious Intolerance, Xenophobia, Bigotry, Misogyny, Misandry and Discrimination

After having spent half my life outside the United States – in Europe, the Middle East, Africa, Asia and the Southern Americas – I find it deeply troubling to have this unsettled personal feeling that our country is perhaps the most racist and intolerant country I have lived in. I can explain this as due to our being the most racially/ethnically/religiously diverse country on the planet; so, it is perhaps understandable that we have more divisions within our population that translate into nonacceptance of those not within our own groups. But, I cannot excuse or justify such bigotry that discriminates against our citizens because of their skin color, beliefs, national origin or any other factor that in no way is a reflection of their intelligence, good character, talents or basic humanity.

I have a zero-tolerance policy on any form of bigotry and believe any third party that would appeal to me must also have an immutable stand against any form of such perversions. As there are many forms of intolerance, here I will first address most fully the one that I feel is the most egregious – racism.

Racism is alive and well in the United States in 2018. I clearly remember in the early 1960's returning from overseas as a child and seeing restrooms and water fountains with signs that said, "Whites Only" or "Coloreds Only". I clearly remember an event after the 1964 Civil Rights Act was signed into law when on a road trip in the south. A young black family with three children, about the ages of my brother and me, came into a restaurant where we'd stopped for lunch. They were well dressed, polite, ordinary. I was about nine and had just come back from North Africa. This family started to sit down, but then was told by the owner or manager that they had to leave. I asked my father why, loud enough I guess to get stares from the manager and other customers and the black family. My father told me "hush, I'll tell you later". The black family left quietly without a word, but I was unsettled. My father, who was about as non-racist as one can get, did explain to me later the problem, as well as how volatile the environment was then on race. Through the years, I always hoped that racism would disappear in the United

States but was always disappointed to see the persistent and clear signs that it remained – maybe more covert than overt, but deeply rooted nonetheless. I travel frequently in the South, so my experience is current. In restaurants, institutions, hospitals, retirement homes, country clubs, businesses, the kitchen, housekeeping, manual labor staff will be almost all black, while the customers and clientele and managerial staff will be white. Residential neighborhoods will be clearly divided between black and white areas. If you are driving on the highway with a speed limit of 55 and come up upon a car going 50, invariably the driver will be a middle-aged black. If you see a car pulled over by police, there is a better than 50/50 chance the person stopped will be black. Prison inmates are disproportionally black, students disproportionally white. Median household incomes for blacks are much lower than for whites. Quality of life indicators such as life expectancy, access to healthcare, home ownership, education levels among many societal pointers are much lower for blacks. This should not be happening in the United States.

What is the solution? In my view, we do not need more top-down legislation. We already have plenty of laws against discrimination. We do not need another three decades of Affirmative Action, which if the truth be told was designed and implemented to help white women first, blacks a far second, Hispanics a more distant third and other ethnicities as just token fig leaves. We need "grassroots" activism to address social problems at the local level – problems with the justice system, law enforcement, education, the economy.

We also need to be very careful on what we label racism. Not every word or action by a person, politician, or group is racist just because it does not subscribe to the thinking of a particular group. Too often we see the major political parties and pundits, the media, and particular activist groups fling out the term "racist" injudiciously and liberally no matter what a particularly unpopular public figure does or says. This only serves to exacerbate tensions and cause people or groups to dig in their heels rather than seek mitigation or compromise. Similarly, not every situation is racist and again we need to be very careful bandying the term around as it can be very unhelpful. For example, some African-American groups have been calling our National Anthem, the Star-Spangled Banner racist, demanding that it be retired as the Anthem. Yes, the last two verses use the words hireling, slave and

40

freemen. None of us, including historians can say exactly what Francis Scott Key, the composer, intended by those words. To many, including me, they referred to components of British forces in the War of 1812, including involuntarily conscripted whites as well as freed slaves fighting for the British – not to American blacks held in slavery. Another example: under the Obama administration, changes were approved in the design of our U.S. paper currency, which has been a steady symbol, our "greenback", for as long as we have remembered for generations. Obama's Secretary of the Treasury wanted black and white women added (no black men interestingly enough), replacing Alexander Hamilton and Andrew Jackson: reducing the Lincoln Memorial on one bill to a backdrop for a black singer. How are any efforts or actions like with the Anthem or our money helpful? How do they reduce, not aggravate racial divides? The last two verses of the Anthem are never sung at sporting events and most people probably cannot remember the words anyway. Our paper money is part of history. If we want to honor other notable American figures why not just make a new 15 or $25 bill? The point is we should all try to calm the waters, make things better by concentrating on important issues, not fan the flames with petty distractions.

A moderate centrist party, composed of Americans who do not subscribe to the fringe extremes of either major party can be of great service in being the party of conscience, of fair play, of freedom and justice for all. Why do I include the Democratic Party in my condemnation? The religious right of the Republican Party, the rural and southern party would seem to be the most likely villains. But remember it was President Bill Clinton, who in his eight-year term undertook the biggest prison building project in U.S. history – at a cost of 30 billion – and during his term expanded the incarceration of blacks, mostly young men, by 250,000 so that nationwide, by the end of his term, over 50% of prison inmates were black. In 2018, 37.9% of the prison population is black – an improvement, but look at this: In the United States, the black population has been fairly steady for decades – around 15% - a glaring anomaly in comparison with the black percentage in the prison population. Neither the Republican or Democratic party have done much of anything for blacks or other minorities, a fact that unfortunately these groups do not realize.

Blacks are by no means the only victims of racism, bigotry and xenophobia. People of any skin tone may be, and are, targets of animosity for other groups.

Even whites. All of this is bad, and very sad. My hope is that with a different party based on true Constitutional ideals and ethics, progress will be possible sooner rather than later.

I think it's fascinating, amazing, that with the human genome project of recent years we can each identify some of our own individual makeup. Possibly, if everyone took the plunge and sent in their own test they would find unusual facts in their heritage that might make them look more kindly on others who they think are so different, but who might well share some of the same genetic makeup. Here in the United States, all descendants of immigrants from so many regions of the world, there are bound to be surprises. Whites believing they come from pure European stock might well have a drop or two of Native American or Middle Eastern blood. Many Blacks most certainly have a good deal of white heritage; we should all know that just from history. None of us are pure in anything.

And there are so many other narrow-minded forms of dislike of others:

Arabs that hate Jews. Jews who hate Arabs. Christians who hate Muslims and vice versa. Men who discriminate against women and women who have an intense dislike of men. And I could go on and on. The point I want to make here is that such people are just a minority among Americans at large. Most Americans are broad-minded, kind, considerate and intelligent. That is the majority who I believe will gravitate to a centrist third party; those who are fed up with the extremist factions who are poisoning the political atmosphere; those who are tired of the tail wagging the dog.

I will use some strong words now.

If you are a racist, a bigot, a xenophobe, misogynist or misandrist you are not a Christian, Muslim, Hindu, Buddhist or honest follower of any true religion or of any non-theist humanist philosophy. You are a fraud, and godless, because you have violated the highest precepts of human thought and decency as well as torn at the very foundations of the American nation.

If you are a racist, bigot or xenophobe you are not a Patriot. You are not an American. Go somewhere else and live with your own kind. There are many other countries where intolerance reigns and possibly you would be better off there. America – love it or leave it.

A Democracy vs. a Republic

...in a democracy the people meet and exercise government in person; in a republic they assemble and administer it by their representatives and agents. A democracy, consequently, must be confined to a small spot. A republic may be extended over a large region.

Federalist Papers No. 14 (Madison)

I cringe every time I hear media or politicians refer to "our democracy". We are not a democracy, we are a constitutional, representative Republic. The issue of whether to place power all or more with the people, versus all or more weighted to the federal government was a critical debate before ratification of the Constitution and this debate continues today. A pure democracy would be one in which all citizens could gather together in one place to discuss and vote on all matters of importance. Action on all matters would only be taken when approved by the voters. A pure democracy can only really be practiced in a very small collective such as very small town where everyone can be physically present together and vote on matters that concern that town only. For early America, in which it could take weeks to travel from the farthest reaches of a State to a central point such as the then capital of Philadelphia, gathering together all two and half million citizens would have been impossible – nonsensical. Such a gathering now even if taking advantage of the speed of light information highway of today – is equally impossible. There is no way all 327 million Americans can be brought online simultaneously to debate and vote on the thousands of issues which face the country today!

So, the Founders developed a sensible framework in which the "best and the brightest" from each State and congressional district – "enlightened statesmen" holding the confidence and trust of their constituents – would reside in Washington and conduct the business of the nation. A constitutional, representative Republic. Makes sense to me. This foundation of our Union ain't broke so I wish people would stop trying to fix it. We just need to work on ensuring that the very best minds and only American patriots are elected as our representatives to do our business. A centrist third party can have a positive influence in this direction.

A new centrist party can, however, in this digital age with the phenomenal recent advances in information technology, be the trendsetter in "democratizing" its own party structure, its platform, its choice of candidates, and its agenda. In this day and age, it is entirely possible for each individual in the "grassroots" base of this party to have a vote on the most important elements embodied in the party. This party can truly be "of the people".

Big Government vs. Small Government

"Government's view of the economy could be summed up in a few short phrases: If it moves, tax it. If it keeps moving, regulate it. And if it stops moving, subsidize it."

Ronald Reagan

"Government exists to protect us from each other. Where government has gone beyond its limits is in deciding to protect us from ourselves."

Ronald Reagan

This has been a controversial issue since the founding of our Republic, one that only grew worse as our territory expanded and our population grew. The underlying question is how much do we as citizens need to be governed? Some believe little or not at all, ignoring the great complexity of our immense society. Others, at the opposite extreme, believe we need to be intensively governed – controlled, regulated and legislated in almost every aspect of our individual lives. A centrist party, by inference, should take a practical approach to this question, adopting a posture that we only need a level of governance that serves to protect our national, social and cultural character as a nation. In other words, what level of governance is required to preserve our liberties from internal and external threats; ensure maximum internal order and peace; accord our population the fullest opportunity to pursue a decent quality of life.

My vote is for a lean and trim government apparatus at all levels that serves the people but does not intrude into their freedoms and individual private lives. I think the pendulum has swung too far and that we are now overly regulated, over controlled and that government has intruded too far into our daily lives. Look at this fact: taking into account federal, state and local governments there are now about one government employee for every 14.7 citizens. Viewed from a different perspective this means you and I, during a 40-hour work week are each governed for 2.7 hours. Contrast this with another fact: there are 1.8 government jobs for every one industrial sector job. We govern more than we produce. There is only one way to reverse this dynamic and that is to reduce the scope of what our governments are permitted to perform. We need to reduce government control and regulation in those areas which are least necessary. This reform needs to start at the top – with the federal government, and then continue down the levels to the most basic local government structure.

We cannot expect existing governmental entities to take it upon themselves to reduce or eliminate themselves. It is the nature of all organizations and their members to increase their footprint, their reach, their budget. Change must be driven by the citizenry, who elect new representatives to the various levels of government who themselves are committed to viable reductions and will pursue these changes in office. Such reductions should not be taken precipitously, without study, thought and a measured approach to bring changes over time to avoid unnecessary disruptions and ill-considered decisions. For example, a well-devised tax reform plan that simplifies tax law down to the most basic parameters and procedures would mean less federal, State and local officials will be needed to administer collection of revenue. Similar examples pertain to virtually every federal government department. Do we really need a massive Department of Education at the federal level – 4,400 employees with a $68 billion-dollar budget – when we have State boards of education and local school boards who are closer to their education issues and in many instances are performing work duplicative to that of the federal department. Every single federal department should be scrutinized – expertly and in a non-partisan fashion – to seek ways to reduce costs, reduce duplication, and transfer as many authorities and programs to the States to administer.

At the federal level, under the Executive, these are the cabinet level departments and the separate agencies covering specific areas of the national agenda.

Cabinet Departments	2009 Budget Expenditures	2009 Staff Levels
State	16.39b	18,900
Treasury	19.56b	115,897
Justice	46.20b	113,543
Interior	90.00b	71,436

Agriculture	134.12b	109,832
Commerce	15.77b	43,880
Labor	137.97b	17,347
Defense	651.16b	3,000,000
Health and Human Services	879.20b	67,000
Housing and urban Development	40.53b	10,600
Transportation	93.20b	58,622
Energy	24.10b	109,094
Education	45.40b	4,487
Veterans Administration	97.70b	235,000
Homeland Security	40.00b	240,000
Totals:	2,311,300,000	4,214,652

That's a lot of people and a lot of money! Now look at a list of the major independent agencies under the Executive. I am not including budget or staffing figures because frankly I don't want to take the time to individually research them and in the case of the intelligence agencies those figures are secret anyway. I think we can safely assume that all these agencies together would significantly add to the totals above.

Independent Agencies

Central Intelligence Agency
Commodity Futures Trading Commission
Consumer Financial Protection Bureau
Environmental Protection Agency
Federal Communications Commission
Federal Elections Commission
Federal Energy Regulatory Commission
Federal Reserve Board of Governors
Federal Maritime Commission
Federal Retirement Thrift Investment Board
Federal Trade Commission
General Service Administration
International Trade Commission
National Archives and Records Administration
National Aeronautic and Space Administration
National Labor Relations Board
National Transportation Safety Board
National Reconnaissance Office
Nuclear Regulatory Commission
National Science Foundation

National Security Agency
Postal Regulatory Commission
Security and Exchange Commission
Selective Service System
Small Business Administration
Smithsonian Institution
Social Security Administration
Surface Transportation Board
United States Agency for International Development
United States Postal Service

A centrist third party can be the catalyst for constructive reductions in the federal government footprint. Slimming down the size of the federal government and thus the budget will appeal to a great many voters. Neither of the two major parties are likely to go down this road. However, a new centrist party must avoid arbitrary slashes in budgets and personnel. This process should not be precipitous, but based on careful study and analysis, with a strong emphasis on long-term planning. Any actions should have the support of personnel in the agencies under scrutiny as well as that of outside experts; and of the White House and Congress; and of the States who may pick up some of the responsibilities. This should not be a political ploy to attract votes; it should be inclusive and nonpartisan.

Secularism vs. A One Religion State

"Congress shall make no law respecting an establishment of religion, or prohibiting the free exercise thereof;...."

First Amendment to the Constitution

Previously, I listed the religions and denominations present in the United States today. It should be very clear that we will never agree on the issue of religion. Religion is probably one of the most divisive and contentious issues between groups of people. Wars have been fought throughout human history over religion. Our founders recognized this early on and very wisely stipulated in the Constitution that the United States must, by necessity, be a secular nation.

The current political climate just over the issue of religion has become increasingly poisonous over the past several decades. Throughout the history of the United States, Christianity has been the dominant religion. At the time of Independence, Americans were almost 100% Christian. Today, about 70% of Americans self-identify as Christian of whom about 46% are Protestant and 21% Catholic, and the rest tied to other Christian denominations. Thirty percent of our population are not Christian, almost 100 million people.

There has been a rise in Christian fundamentalism in recent times, playing out with the election of many, too many in my view, members of Congress who openly espouse their religion in national political fora. I was quite shocked when I heard our current Vice-President Mike Pence, in his acceptance speech to be then candidate Trump's running mate, say unequivocally that most important to him was first, his faith in Jesus Christ, second his love for his family, and third the Constitution of the United States. The crowd at the Republican convention broke into cheers. I couldn't help but ask myself, why was he running for the second highest office in the land if this was his order of importance. Why not become a preacher, then just be a voter along with the rest of us? I couldn't help but think that Mr. Pence,

49

like so many on the religious right, believe that we should be a one-religion, Christian nation. I couldn't help but think of our military personnel who placed their country and their oath to protect the Constitution first, leaving their families behind to fight in lands far away.

Religious fundamentalism from any source makes me very nervous as a U.S. citizen. I fail to see how political Christian fundamentalism is any different than political Muslim, Jewish, Hindu or other political religious fundamentalism. All are dangerous to the unity of a nation. But our political leaders seem to have forgotten this. In an effort to capture votes on the fringes, both parties have been pandering to the religious communities – most egregiously on the Republican right, but also the Democrats have used religion as a tool to capture the African-American vote. Almost every political candidate these days, right of left, feels the need to constantly speak of their "faith" as if it is an obligatory box to tick in their campaigns for elected office. Candidates from non-Christian faiths never seem to speak of their own religions during political campaigns. A wise decision, or they would certainly lose votes.

I believe one of the hallmarks of a strong, centrist third-party should be a strict adherence and insistence on secularism in U.S. government at all levels. Third-party members should be self-disciplined enough to keep personal religious views out of their public discourse and be vocal in chastising members of other parties who cross the line and attempt to impose their religious preferences on others. This does not mean we should be anti-religion by any means. We should support and protect the right of all Americans to believe and practice in whatever religious faith they choose, or none at all if that is their wish. The higher religious principles of all religions should serve as guides to their followers in the exercise of their civil and political functions, but not dominate governance. This is a subtle but important difference, in which religion quietly informs only individuals on ethical considerations in issues of national concern but does not direct their decisions. The majority of Americans, if they really think about it, do not want a one-religion nation. We do not want to be a Christian example of Muslim Saudi Arabia and Iran or Jewish Israel or atheist China.

Conservation, Environmentalism, Ecology, Global Warming and Climate Change

These issues, all somewhat different in scope but pertaining to the health of our habitat the Earth, have become unnecessarily contentious. And they do not need to be if pragmatism and realism control the dialogue and two-party politics is muted. A third party, again centrist and strong enough to have weight at State and national levels, can serve as the "adult leadership" in legislatures to arrive at measured, reasonable actions that will improve the quality of life across the nation and, over time, globally as well. This is literally a "clean up our own backyards" category and I'll give three examples of why trying to clean up the backyards of others can be very damaging.

In December 2017, a "good old boy" neighbor knocked on my door and told me there was a Bald Eagle in my field, on the ground walking but not flying – either injured or sick. We decided to capture it and see what we could do. It was a big bird, its head thigh-high to me and weighing about 20 pounds. While the bird could not fly it could run, and we chased it around the woods until we could put a blanket over it and secure it safely in a horse trailer. The next day, a Sunday, three volunteers, from a wildlife hospital two hours away, came and took the bird for examination and treatment. The veterinarian found that the Bald Eagle had lead poisoning and began chelation treatment, but sadly the bird died just after completing the treatment. Its heart was too badly damaged by the lead. What I did not realize is that eagles, owls, hawks and vultures are now primarily carrion eaters, as they have been largely forced out of their once primary habitats along rivers, bays and lakes. Most hunters use shotgun or rifle ammunition that primarily is made of lead. If they kill but can't find an animal they shoot or choose to leave it as with farm pests such as skunk, possum and rats, or if they field dress a deer leaving the unwanted part of the carcass behind, the remains are available for these big birds to eat. They then also consume the lead pellets or bullet fragments and the lead can reach toxic levels, as it did with "my" Bald Eagle, the 55th one to have been brought to the wildlife hospital in 2017.

So, what's the answer to lead poisoning in wildlife. The city folk, tree huggers will of course say "ban all lead ammunition", right? According to the wildlife hospital I was dealing with, this approach was attempted in 2010, over the strong objections of this hospital and other conservation groups. The two wildlife activist groups, northern and city-based, launched a well-funded national campaign to ban all lead-based ammunition. Perhaps they had their hearts in the right place, but they were ignorant on both the issue and the hunting/pro-gun environment. There was a massive outcry from the National Rifle Association and other pro-gun and hunting groups. Why? Don't all Americans love our national bird and other beautiful big birds? Of course they do, frankly much more than city people who never see them. The issue was that banning all lead-based ammunition essentially meant or was perceived as a backdoor attempt to ban all firearms. At that time, virtually all ammunition was lead-based – for hunting, target shooting, self-defense, law enforcement, and the military. These ignorant activists essentially killed the issue by trying to clean up the backyards of others – they set back solutions to this problem by a decade or more. It didn't have to be like that. In 1991, the federal government banned the use of lead shotgun shot for hunting waterfowl. This program was phased in over four years prior, and only after years of debate and education, following clear evidence that about four million waterfowl yearly were dying from ingested lead shot. Time was given to educate waterfowl hunters and for manufacturers to produce steel bird shot. This measured and instructive pace proved successful. However, the issue of lead ammunition being used for upland hunting was not pursued unfortunately, largely because the problems lead presented to raptors and other large birds was not known until just a decade ago. This is an area where "grassroots" activism arising from and directing activities within a locale, in other words home-based, could be very successful. The solution, and policy of my wildlife hospital, very simple, is use non-lead ammunition if it is available, but if not then carry out or bury your kill. Most hunters would support this if the outreach and education came from their own kind. But they do not want to be lectured, controlled, legislated by city folk, many of whom really do want to ban all hunting and take away all guns.

My second example on conservation is also in my backyard. A bill was introduced in the Virginia Assembly to require an annual inspection of all farm property to ensure the owners were complying with best practices regarding storage and disposal of manure from livestock and other raised animals; to ensure that runoff of fertilizers, herbicides, and pesticides as well as soil from erosion areas was not entering creeks, rivers and streams and thus the Chesapeake Bay watershed. The inspections were to be at the cost of the farm owners as well as any steps to meet compliance. There were to be penalties including fines and stoppages on operations for noncompliance. Again, this bill originated from urban activists with no role in or real knowledge of farms, agriculture or animal husbandry. Fortunately, the bill failed to pass but it once again did serve to widen the divide between the rural population and the urban would-be regulators.

What the urban population fails to realize, in large part, is that owners of rural properties are the best protectors and stewards of their land. Their land is integrally connected with their livelihood, their heritage and their hearts. They love their land and will do all possible to protect it, care for it, improve it. Now sometimes they do not do all they can, usually because they cannot afford to or because they are not aware of steps that can be taken in certain areas. But, I know first-hand that my neighbors will enthusiastically pursue new technologies or methods to improve their properties and mitigate possible impact elsewhere on other properties or on nature in general – when they learn about it and if they can afford it. Once again, "grassroots" benevolent and helpful activism from any source can be effective. More costly rules and regulations imposed from the top down will be very unhelpful.

The third example is of an even larger scale, the 2010 BP oil spill in the Gulf of Mexico. This was one of the worst ecological disasters in the history of the United States, if not the worst. However, President Obama's response with a six-month moratorium on offshore drilling in the Gulf was an economic disaster for the Gulf States whose impact is still being felt in this area. There was a huge ripple effect in local economies from this moratorium because so many hundreds of thousands of households depended directly or indirectly on the petroleum industry. I personally know people who lost jobs, lost homes, had to move in with families, had to take their children out of college; and have still not recovered financially eight years later. For all the national outrage over the spill, undeniably deserved, the moratorium was a bad move because it was imposed by leaders who did not have a stake hold in the region and whether they cared or did not care about the impact on the people in the region, it certainly was perceived in the Gulf States as a blatant disregard for their welfare. This sense of disenfranchisement hardened voters' distaste for both Democrats and traditional Republicans and translated at the ballot box to massive support for Trump, who called for deregulation of environmental controls.

These are just three examples among countless others of what I see as widely disparate viewpoints represented by the two major parties. Viewpoints that translate into radical and counterproductive actions by whichever party happens to be in power. A third party can offer moderation and constructive compromise, a buffer between the extremisms that most Americans find disturbing.

To be effective in its approach to the broad and varying issues that are encompassed by the heading to this section, a third party will first have to identify in which areas it can be the most effective and constructive, and in which it can mold multi-partisan support. The first step should be to recognize that in some areas it will not be possible to find this support, and the areas of global warming and climate change are clearly ones where the gap is too wide to bridge. This is not to say that those areas are not significant. It is clear to me that the climate is changing in my immediate home area, in other parts of the country, and globally. Winters are shorter here where I live and when once several heavy snowfalls were guaranteed we have now had about five years with little to no snow. We have longer periods of drought in the summer, but also in the other three seasons. There are clear anomalies in what vegetation is most prominent and which is struggling. There are considerable variations between now and before of what insects and wildlife is present. What I cannot say, and what I do not see experts convincingly present, is whether these changes are cyclical or permanent and which of the changes are attributable to human activities and what is due to natural events beyond human control. It is clear at the national level, when one views the pictures from space of our country lit up like a Christmas tree particularly around our megalopolises, that the impact of humans is immense in terms of energy consumption. But what should we do? Call for brown-outs or institute electricity free hours during each day? Unrealistic, unlikely to happen, and hypocritical of me to suggest such things for people in the city to do, when I live in the country! I think it is unrealistic and unproductive for us as a country to make global warming and climate change national issues that require legislation and pervasive controls, when in effect we can accomplish so little with top down policies. Particularly when we really do not know what we are talking about.

Conservation, ecology and environmentalism are different stories and in sum work in these areas will have a positive effect on the more nebulous areas of global warming and climate change. We can make differences but, again and I stress this, the most gains we can make will come from the local and personal efforts of citizens on their own home ground. We need action at the bottom more than actions imposed on us from the top. If we discipline ourselves to buy fuel efficient cars, and millions of others throughout the country do so as well, the car manufacturers will see this and respond accordingly by producing more fuel-saving cars. If we use efficient LED light bulbs rather than ones that consume more energy we will help with our power bills and lower the consumption of fossil fuels. If, at a local level, we call for and support more mass transit, and others elsewhere do so as well, either government entities or private entrepreneurial capitalist will find ways to satisfy the demand. If, at a local level, we participate actively in town, city and county meetings and voice concerns over environmentally damaging actions, or support positive programs and initiatives, there will be results locally that if also pursued elsewhere will have a cumulative effect nationwide. It will be a slow-go, and we will probably not see results soon. But we will know there will be results at some time down the road. And be satisfied we did our best.

So much positive can be done personally or locally that it is difficult to see where one would find the time to take steps through the State or national levels. And we really do not want or need higher levels, removed from us both physically and philosophically, deciding what is best for us locally. However, State and national ethics that are supportive of "grassroots" efforts would be helpful, and here again a third party can be the voice of reason.

Globalism vs. Isolationism vs. Protectionism

One of the scarier divides, in my view, between the Democratic and Republican parties is on the issue of globalism versus isolationism. In the extreme, some factions of the Democratic party lean heavily towards the mindset that the United States should move to being just one member of many countries under a global world government. Some Republican extremists believe the United States should totally isolate itself from the rest of the world, be completely self-sufficient, and take no responsibility for what happens in the world outside our country. Again, these are extreme views but to some extent those views have permeated throughout the party ideologies.

A centrist party needs to take a very centrist view on these issues. The planet is not and never will be a "global village" as Hillary Clinton termed it. The image of a 'global village" is attractive, idyllic. Happy people sitting on logs under palm trees, eating bananas plucked for free from the pristine jungle. Everyone singing and dancing. This is a pipe dream. From my experience, village life in most areas of the world is not so lovely – poverty, disease, hunger, ignorance, violence, abuse of power, the strong preying on the weak. We Americans do not want to live like that. I guarantee you. But shouldn't we seek to raise the quality of life in less privileged areas of the world to the American level the standard of living? That would be wonderful, and not impossible, but it is entirely unrealistic without a concerted effort by the developed world to make this happen over a very long period. Shouldn't we be willing to lower our standard of living so that we can bring up that of the less fortunate – spread the wealth in other words? A significant number of Democrats as well as "independents" and members of minor parties lean in the direction of shared wealth, global government, global equality in terms of opportunity and quality of life. The ideals in and of themselves are utopian – a perfect world in which everyone is happy. But, sadly, this will never take place. The reality is that the per capita Gross Domestic Product (GDP) in the U.S. is $59,000 which produces for Americans a median household income of $54,000. The world per capita GDP is $10,200, and the world median household income is $9,700. People in the poorest countries such as Zambia, with the lowest per capita annual income of $270, would be ecstatic if they were to reach the current global median of $9,700. Citizens in developed countries like ours would not be so happy.

A centrist party needs to make national sovereignty a cornerstone of its philosophy and program. We need to protect our own country, the lives of our own people first. We should not subordinate ourselves to governance and oversight by other countries, even in a collective such as the United Nations. We should not allow our military to be under the command of foreign powers. But we should be very active and supportive of a viable United Nations, which it is not now, that can achieve consensus among members and take action on matters of global concern.

On the Republican side, to which I would add the minor conservative parties, there is generally a tilt towards the side of isolationism. Only a few conservatives would really support total or virtual isolation from the rest of the world, however there is certainly a flavor among most conservatives that America must be dominant in the world – financially, materially, militarily, politically – and that if the rest of the world is negatively affected by our actions or suffers because of their own actions, so be it. It's not our concern. Such a stance is as unrealistic and potentially as harmful to U.S. interests as the "progressive" posture on globalism.

A centrist party should take the practical viewpoint that the United States should be moderately "global" and moderately "isolationist". We need to interact constructively with other countries in a great number of areas – commerce, mutual defense, combatting evils such as abuses by dictators of their people and so many others. But we do need, as a country, to take care of ourselves. We need to be as self-sufficient as possible in terms of providing for our own material needs, and thus protect and improve our own economy. I believe in a degree of protectionism for our industrial and other production sectors. I do not believe unbridled free trade is in the best interests of the country. As it stands now, all I am seeing is that some other countries are unrestricted in trading with us, and can buy our companies and property, while preventing us from doing the same in their countries. We need to understand that national security does not mean just national defense with a strong military. That it also includes a wide range of sectors that directly impact on our prosperity as a nation.

Immigration

The immigration issue is one that has bitterly divided the country into two factions – the extreme pro and anti-groups of the Democratic and Republican parties respectively. The far left and right groups of these parties have pushed the agendas of these parties very much away from the center, which is where I believe the majority of the American population reside politically on this issue. There are reasonable, practical and logical solutions to immigration. First some facts.

The population of the United States when I was born in 1955 was at 165 million. Today in 2018 our population has almost doubled to 327 million. The world population in 1955 was 2.8 billion. Today it is at 7.6 billion. Almost tripled in my lifetime.

Over-population used to be widely discussed decades ago, but it is rare to hear the subject raised now. Some 40 years ago, we would hear a lot of talk about achieving zero population growth but hear little about it now. Some developed countries have reached a zero-growth level, others like the United States, now at about a 1.88/2 persons pace, are actually below the natural birth per person replacement rate. But our population continues to grow, partially because as our longevity has increased the birth rate is double the death rate; and because we increase our population further through immigration. Immigrants also have higher birth rates than the one to one replacement level necessary for zero population growth; so over time it is credible that the overall U.S. rate will surpass the current 1.88/2 level. Approximately one million new American citizens are naturalized each year, and the pipeline of new immigrants continues at about the same rate. The Census Bureau estimates in 2050 the U.S. population will be 390 million and the world population is estimated to reach 9.6 billion. By 2100, the US will have 447 million people and the world population will be over 11 billion. Much of the increase in world population is, and will be, in underdeveloped countries, where people suffer from poverty, famine, water shortages, disease, war and other ills. It is perfectly understandable that people in the world who are suffering in these conditions want to go elsewhere so their quality of life will be improved. Understandably, emigrating to the United States is a dream for many and those who come here, legally or illegally, regard our country as their salvation.

This is a major dilemma. We Americans, including African-Americans, mostly come from immigrant roots. The only group who can legitimately say they are not descended from immigrants are Native Americans, as with them we would be talking about immigration from thousands of years ago. The great majority of Americans are compassionate people, who feel deeply for those suffering under terrible conditions in foreign countries. We want to help. But, how large a population should we have in the U.S.? Cities grow larger, rural areas become more developed. Green space and farming areas shrink. A larger population demands more roads, housing, food, commodities, jobs. I don't see much long-term planning going on to address how we can accommodate more people and ensure they, and the already resident population, can maintain a standard of living that befits our American culture. Until we have a viable plan, we need to slow growth. We cannot arrest growth because, again, the birth rate outstrips the death rate by a factor of two. Sadly, the only component of our population increase we can control to some extent is in admitting new immigrants. I do not like that, it frankly makes me feel bad, but I cannot think of any other short to medium term solution. Over-population globally, particularly in the poorest countries, will put enormous stresses on the most vulnerable, and these persons will be desperate to go elsewhere. The United States and other developed countries will be under considerable pressure to accept more legal immigrants. Efforts to enter the U.S. illegally will also increase. Possibly in the long term we can build both up and down, like in the science fiction stories, with thousand-story habitats and still preserve the agricultural land and natural wilderness. We should think and plan for that eventuality.

But, for now we need to factor immigration to the growth rate, as predicated on the birth to death rates. As outlined above, this cannot be an absolute. Otherwise, we would have to stop immigration entirely as our population continues to grow even without immigration. But we can establish and meet certain levels for legal immigration, and control illegal immigration. Historically, many illegal immigrants eventually are legalized in some fashion. Once a critical level of illegal immigrants reaches the public awareness, one program or another - amnesties and special acts such as the DACA bill before Congress now - will wash the slate clean, ostensibly to have a fresh start. Illegal immigration is an explosive issue that brings out some really ugly characteristics in our divided political camps. On one side there are the xenophobic reactions of some factions of the Republican party, calling for bans on Muslims, vilifying minority groups and calling for a wall to be built across the entire southern border. On the Democratic side, entire cities – "sanctuary cities" - have chosen to ignore federal immigration law, essentially defying the constitutionally assigned authority of the national government. Neither camp is correct, both contribute to the ugliness. My hope is that a third party, one that is centrist and composed of responsible, intelligent people, can set the country on a path with a pragmatic and humane immigration policy. We want immigrants. We need immigrants. But, we need to resist overpopulation if we hope to sustain a reasonable quality of American life.

A pragmatic third party should be cautious, not precipitously spew out promises in the hopes of capturing votes of a certain faction or another. There is nothing wrong with saying that we do not have all the answers. We can say that through working together and harnessing the collective wisdom and talents of our citizens, we can arrive at the best possible solutions. Reaching solutions, for the short, medium and long terms should be the aim of a third party.

Patriotism

The previous commentaries all present nice segues into this simple but extremely crucial discussion. The last section on immigration is almost an introduction to the concept of patriotism, a word which is bandied about frequently but too often means too many different things to Americans. First and foremost, as we enter into a period in which a strong, centrist, positive thinking third party may emerge, with you and I contributing to the process we need to reflect on what patriotism means to us individually and collectively. Subsequent calculations on the best ways forward should develop from this foundation.

The history of my grandmother plays an important part in my views of what it means to be an American. She was born in Poland on a five-acre subsistence farm in a region governed by a feudal lord, a count. At this time the count had total authority to approve or deny marriages. A pretty and intelligent girl, she was to be married off at sixteen to a much older wealthy man. The count's adjutant and she were in love, but neither had the right to oppose the arranged marriage and get married to each other. The adjutant arranged and paid for her to be smuggled out of Poland to the United States, sixteen and alone. This was 1910. They never saw each other again. My grandmother worked for a number of years as a Harvey Girl, at a number of the railroad depot restaurants in the Southwest. She later travelled for several years by horseback throughout Texas, New Mexico and Arizona. This was still very much the frontier Far West. She eventually ended up marrying and raising a family in Michigan, weathering the Great Depression doing whatever she and the family could do in the Mid-Atlantic states. For the last ten years of her life, in San Antonio, Texas, she was bedridden with rheumatoid arthritis and cared for by a daughter. Here's the point: for the 13 years I knew her before she died she had an unwavering routine. She listened to one radio station that began its broadcast at six AM and ended for the day at 8 PM. She started her day with the station's opening broadcast which began with the Pledge of Allegiance. She ended her day when the station tuned out with the Star-Spangled Banner. This extraordinary woman, an immigrant, was a patriot. She had an unwavering belief in the goodness of America.

Patriotism within the immigrant community is somewhat of a mixed bag today – stronger possibly among those who came here to escape poverty and war than those who migrated for just economic reasons. But it does exist, though in different manifestations than listening to the National Anthem daily as my grandmother did or reciting the Pledge of Allegiance daily in elementary school as I did. Patriotism in some form is still there as this example illustrates. I am quite close to a West African immigrant community in Philadelphia. Some of these people are now citizens, some legal permanent residents, some illegals. But during the last Super Bowl, they were all rabid Eagles fans – taking to the streets with team tee-shirts and hats before the game, glued to the TV during the game, and ecstatic when the Eagles won; taking to the streets again in the mass public celebration that followed. This group of people escaped warfare and poverty. They had not known what American football was back in Africa, soccer being the sport over there, but here they are every bit as American as you and I, rooting for their home team.

Among native-born Americans patriotism is also a mixed bag. Some display their belief in America visibly – those who serve in the military or government, those who celebrate the Fourth of July, Veterans Day, Thanksgiving and other national holidays with parades and special events and fervor. Others are quieter, but still firm in their convictions that the United States is special and their personal actions show their belief in many ways. Some Americans tinge their self-professed patriotism with nastiness – xenophobia and bigotry – and this group I cannot call patriots. Other Americans, maybe those who are disenfranchised, who possibly have not achieved the American dream, just don't seem to care anymore.

One of the many roles which a third party can assume is that of inspiring the great bulk of Americans to believe more passionately in the United States. Not via the slogans such as "Make America Great Again" or the anti-immigrant, anti-Muslim, anti-this, anti-that stupidities. But through inclusion of most Americans in an agenda that encompasses commonly held beliefs, that is pragmatic, that is compassionate, and that is ultimately effective in moving America forward.

Here is an example of how I would like a centrist leader to act, as opposed to how a partisan politician acts. Last year, Vice President Mike Pence flew to a major football game – on Air Force Two, with full entourage – ostensibly to cheer on his home team. However, when the National Anthem was played the majority of the football players "took a knee", a symbolic protest against violence and discrimination directed against African-Americans. This protest was expected and had been many times repeated at previous football games, so the Vice President knew it was coming. He stood and held his hand to his heart during the Anthem, then when it ended left the game in protest at what many on the right view as disrespect to the Flag. Then flew back to Washington, a big polemical show at great taxpayer expense.

Now how about if the scenario went like this? Vice President Pence arrives early at the game and has a private consultation with the team captains proposing the following. He, the VP, would come out to the field with the two teams. They all would stand with their hands on their hearts for the duration of the Anthem. Then he and the teams would "take the knee" together for a moment of silence to recognize their shared concerns over the inequities present in our country. This could have been a unifying moment of considerable import nationally. I hope that some senior leaders around the country will read this and set an example by doing what I just suggested above. It's football season now. If you take such an initiative, it will be a victory for everyone.

A Cold Civil War

Carl Bernstein, of Watergate fame, recently coined the phrase "cold civil war" in reference to the considerable divide in attitudes between those in the South and those in the North. One hundred and fifty years after the end of the Civil War, many of us native to the South are suspicious and distrustful when it appears Northerners, or a coalition of Northerners, are attempting to impose their views on us via government mechanisms. People in the North do not realize that there remains a deeply rooted affection and pride in our Southern heritage, history and values. Too often people in the North lump all Southern attitudes under an overall umbrella of racism and atavism, ignorance and religious fanaticism. This is far from fair. Let me illustrate why with a few examples.

In 2008, while campaigning for the Presidency, then candidate Barack Obama spoke to a crowd in his "hometown" of Chicago. He referred to people in the South, most of whom traditionally voted Republican, as "clinging to their Bibles and their guns". For Southerners who were devout Christians and for Southerners who take gun ownership seriously, this comment was dismissive and insulting. Southerners like myself who are not church-goers and do not own guns, and supported Obama, also found the comment offensive. In many ways, those words summed up for us what we had always felt - that the South is still dominated by a more politically and economically powerful North. Most people do not remember that post-Civil War reconstruction policies, designed in many ways to keep the South from reemerging as a threat to the Union did not really end until 100 years later. The South was kept poor and politically impotent until there was an economic resurgence in the 1960's and thereafter. Poverty, a lack of education, low standings on quality of life markers such as health, longevity, infant mortality all persisted until recent times. In fact, in some ways the South has still not fully recovered from its defeat in the War between the States.

Another example. Three of my grandparents were born in Poland and emigrated to the U.S. in the early 1900's. My remaining 25% ancestry was centered in the New York, Connecticut, Massachusetts region. There was no association with slavery or the Civil War. But, I was born in Richmond,

Virginia and my middle-name is "Lee". I still remember the awe I felt as a young child walking down Monument Avenue in Richmond, looking at the massive statues of Confederate heroes Robert E. Lee, J.E.B Stuart, Thomas "Stonewall" Jackson, Jefferson Davis, and Matthew Fontaine Maury.

I've found it very disturbing that such statues have been removed or destroyed throughout the Deep South – actions taken, it seems, in cities which had been "captured" by a Democratic political majority. I can understand African-American aversion to these Civil War symbols. Slavery, and the racism that continues today, are ugly stains on our nation. However, these statues do represent an important period in our American history and are symbols of much more than just slavery. They represent honor, courage, dignity, chivalry, and liberty as well – to many of us. The tragic events in Charlottesville, Virginia last year do represent the continuing North/South divide. Democrats, "progressives", and Northerners have fixated on this event having been caused solely by white supremacists/Neo Nazis who they obliquely suggest are a significant portion of the Southern population. They ignore the fact that those idiots mostly came from elsewhere than Virginia. They ignore the fact that the alt-left people, the nationally well-organized group called AntiFa, came from outside Virginia with riot helmets and shields and baseball bats and attacked the Neo Nazis. This same AntiFa group, one August 5, 2018, dressed in black paramilitary dress and black masks, ransacked the U.S, Marine Corps Recruiting Office in Berkeley, California. And this is the group the left-leaning press promoted at the time of Charlottesville as the good guys?

Actually, the Charlottesville protest began with a separate small group of peaceful local protesters who objected only to the removal of the statue of Robert E. Lee which had been in place since 1924. There was also a fourth group of peaceful local protesters who came to protest the Neo-Nazis, one of whom was tragically killed by a Nazi assailant. These two groups were peaceful and well within their rights to protest on different sides. The other two groups were actually "bad guys" and both deserved reprobation.

Meanwhile, drunken and corrupt Ulysses S. Grant, the Civil War victor and later President, has a national monument, Grant's Tomb, in his honor and statues and paintings throughout the North. He and his family were slave owners themselves up to a year before the War. General William Tecumseh Sherman, who burned and pillaged a swath from Atlanta to

Savannah, destroying those cities and everything in the path, is honored in Washington D.C. by a huge equestrian statue. Sherman later advocated "total war" against the American Indians and commanded the U.S. forces that waged it. In my early years in the South, Sherman was seen as the arch villain of the Civil War. Meanwhile today, there is a very active effort to raise a statue in Washington D.C. to former mayor Marion Barry. Look at his history and see if you think the majority of Americans will have the same level of respect as do his ardent supporters. To the victor goes the spoils it is said, but people in the North should better understand that Southern feelings about the Civil War and its aftermath do not match Northern views. Removing or destroying Confederate statues is a very stupid and unproductive way to socially "re-engineer" Southern attitudes on race and "progressive" ideologies. There is only one solution here – everyone is entitled to their own statues, monuments and heroes. You keep yours, and I will keep mine. After all what are they really but magnificent art objects of bronze and stone; and the persons represented are just history now.

Bernstein's phrase about a "cold civil war" is apt, but something both the North and South should strive to avoid becoming a reality. Both South and North are becoming entrenched in increasingly extreme positions, largely centered on Republican vs. Democrat ideologies. This is not healthy for the Union. A strong, centrist party can bridge this gap by centering its platform and agenda on issues that all Americans can support, rather than on divisive and unproductive issues such as removing Confederate statues. This third-party, to be successful and relevant, needs to reach deep into the populations of North and South, so that each group can take "ownership" in their own States. It would be a mistake for a third-party to arise in the North and attempt to "convert" the South to Northern views – or vice versa.

Fake News

"I am a firm believer in the people. If given the truth, they can be depended upon to meet any national crisis. The great point is to bring them the real facts.

Abraham Lincoln

Donald Trump coined the term "fake news" to counter left-leaning national media's perceived bias against him and for Hillary Clinton. Understandably, he favored the right-leaning media which praised him and vilified Clinton. We tout our First Amendment rights to a free press as one of our most treasured liberties as a republic and rightfully so. A free press enables us to keep watch on ourselves and our leaders. A free press keeps us honest and educates we the voters on the issues pertinent to the preservation of our Union.

Sadly, in recent decades, the media has deviated from the journalistic principles upheld for most of our history, and now seeks to influence the viewing audience as much as report facts and events. Mainstream media is owned by large corporations, that for whatever reason have political biases which by design are assumed and transmitted by the journalists and reporters beholden to their employers. Slant and spin are all part and parcel of media to convince the public in a certain political direction. Left or right, to me this is "fake news".

This last national campaign has brought out the worst in the journalistic profession, in my opinion. Television news, online news, and radio are all egregious, again both left and right. I have friends and family who are ardent followers of one camp or the other. Unfortunately, they are so attuned to just one political camp that they do not even try to understand the total picture by watching the other side's "news". The bottom line is that much of what we watch or follow is not news but editorializing, passing off opinions as news.

Even though I have checked out Fox News, and Breitbart and the alt-right talk radio, I am most familiar with CNN, the media arm of the alt-left. CNN has a global reach, is well financed, and has superb journalists on its payroll. But, CNN provides very little actual news from around the country and around the world. It will focus on one subject for days at a time, repeat the same story time after time throughout the day, and real news stories fall through the cracks. Basically, the American viewing audience remains ignorant of other national or world news, which is too bad because in many cases these news items are important to having an educated voter population. Our news reporters have dumbed down the content and as a result we have a pretty dumb population – on both the left and the right.

Some years ago, I discovered that the most comprehensive and even-handed international news was found on Al-Jazeera, an Arab station! Now that station has been removed from my TV network. How can the American electorate be educated on foreign affairs issues and the rest of the world when there is no domestic coverage of those issues?

The current CNN news menu is almost exclusively directed at the goings on in the White House – tweet by tweet coverage, scandal by scandal coverage and the bias is palpable. Some of the CNN news anchors are quite balanced, others are so slanted they might as well be wearing "Hillary! Hillary! 2020" tee-shirts. The CNN spin and slant and bias is so obvious. Now, everything that can be seen as negative to the Trump White House, not just the very real issues that should concern us all, is blown up out of proportion: slant is so prevalent at times, crude and ham-handed. CNN viewers soak it in. They are hearing what they want to hear, and they become increasingly frenzied over every issue.

Fox News viewers are no different. Fox can say anything on the air negative about the Democratic camp and the viewers swallow it, true or false.

There are no even-handed, nonbiased television or radio news sources in the country. Online sources are often questionable. Print media is perhaps quite better but even here the bias is apparent. Most major newspaper seem to tilt to the Democratic side. The absence of balanced, factual news is a real shame, because an educated electorate is necessary if our best representatives are to be elected for the important work of government.

Privacy

"Love your neighbor; yet don't pull down your hedge."

Benjamin Franklin in Poor Richard's Almanack

One of the hallmark American qualities has been a love of personal independence. To be able to strike out on one's own, conquer a "wilderness" whatever that might be, and be free from intrusion or control by government or other people. This was easy to obtain when there actually was a wilderness and an American had few neighbors and government reach was minimal. Much harder to do now in this digital age. For all its stupendous achievements and value to our society, information technology has resulted in both government and the private sector having a powerful tool to peer into our personal lives and not only snoop, but to also manipulate our personal lives.

It used to be that an individual had to sign a release to a lender or other entity, even government, for that institution to process a credit check on an individual. The individual could refuse, but then the institution could refuse the person a loan or a job or whatever was offered. Now, any institution, private or public, or even any individual can run a full credit check on an individual.

It used to be that criminal records or civil court records were retained in law enforcement or court systems, only releasable to the public under limited circumstances and only after certain strict procedures were followed. Now anyone can pay a private company $9.99 per month and have unlimited access to anyone's recorded interactions with the law whether found guilty or not guilty.

Just these two examples of invasion of privacy can have significant implications for an individual in terms of employment as well as personal reputation in a community. This open book policy makes it hard for someone convicted of a crime to start a new life after having paid the "debt to society". It makes it possible for the commercial sector to target specific individuals for specific services via unsolicited email, internet and phone outreaches.

Honestly, who is not deluged with junk mail, junk email, soliciting and "robo" telephone calls?

With all the current fascination with social media, are people conscious of how much their lives have become open to the world? When your physical location is tracked wherever you go; when your purchases are tracked; when advertisements are tailored to your interests and habits; when your email addresses, telephone numbers, mailing addresses are open to everyone then where is the privacy?

Take it a step further. There have been calls in past years for a central national medical data system to be created. On the surface this sounds like a good thing. All of your medical providers will have current data on your health. That makes sense. But, if all of our court-related information, financial information, contact information, social media accounts are already penetrated and open to everyone does anyone expect that our medical information will remain confidential? Does anyone really want any governmental office, commercial entity or individual citizen to have access to their medical records? I am very suspicious of the unrelenting efforts to break down our personal "hedges". I have absolutely no idea how we can put a stop to this, but I sure wish we could maintain a modicum of privacy in our private lives.

And yet another step. Be confident that our government, at varying degrees at different levels, has the capability to monitor our private lives in ways not even dreamt of at the time of the founding of the United States. And this capability is being exercised to some degree, we just do not know to what extent and for what purposes. We have seen how following recent mass killings law enforcement has been able to fully access social media accounts, email correspondence and telephone records of suspects and persons close to them – releasing information to the public within hours of the event. Clearly law enforcement is able to rapidly receive authorization from the courts and the carriers – Facebook, Twitter, Microsoft etc. – or they already have blanket authorization to use backdoor protocols to enter private accounts. In cases such as the mass killings and other violence where public security is at risk I think most of us would welcome government entities having the authority and tools to prevent more violence. We should be very distrustful, however, of unconstrained authorities and mass efforts to gather and compile information on law-abiding citizens in an effort to profile and ferret out a small minority who might be potential risks.

As mentioned above, capabilities for electronic monitoring, tracking, storage and analysis of data are incredibly sophisticated today. Without drawing out my concerns too long, here's just a hypothetical example of how things could go very wrong if government is not under any constraints as to collection of information on citizens. Law enforcement at some levels currently does filter electronic media – social, email, internet browsing selections – for keywords that are used by individuals repeatedly. Words related to terrorism, bombs, explosives, killing, suspect groups like Isis, right wing militias, threats against our leaders etc. All well and good, we do want to catch the really bad guys.

But look how blanket monitoring could go very sour. Say an individual is disgruntled with a particular national leader and expresses this on social media; then this person communicates by email and telephone with a group, left or right it doesn't matter, that is vehemently opposed to that leader, then information from that person's medical records passes automatically into the government database that the person has just spoken to a doctor about feeling depressed. No intentions were ever expressed to commit a violent act in any of these situations. Then the person decides to buy a firearm legally, filling out the forms for the background check. At the government database center, a red alarm goes off. Too many bits and pieces when put together indicating that there MAY be a problem here. The law enforcement machine, something that once rolling is difficult to turn off, moves forward. The person is interviewed, family, friends, employers, doctors, local police and associates are questioned. The person undergoes considerable stress; his/her reputation is damaged. And no crime was committed and there was no intention of the person to commit a crime.

We need to be very, very careful that we do not allow government or private information gathering and intrusion that undermines our individual freedoms and liberty, sacrosanct American values. A centrist party can be key in developing pragmatic, realistic solutions to this issue, one of which should be a bolder engagement by the Supreme Court on the problem.

NATIONAL ISSUES

The Economy

When it really comes down to it, the state of Americans' personal wellbeing outweighs every other issue in the political arena. For some reason, the two major parties have not seemed to grasp this fact, nor the majority of the political leadership that the parties present to the voters. Sure, they all pay lip service to the economy – all promising to produce "jobs", raise wages, rectify trade imbalances, improve benefits such as health care, preserve or expand Social Security and Medicare, balance the budget, eliminate the national debt etc. But where is the substance, the "meat", the plan? What have they achieved to date?

Again, "bread and butter" issues are at the forefront of individual American concerns – particularly for the majority of Americans whose incomes hover at a fragile middle-middle-class level or lower. It is difficult for anyone to be content when worried about how they will make house and car payments, pay medical bills, send their kids to college. A strong and stable full-fledged middle-class situation is what the majority of Americans strive for. They are not greedy. They just do not want to worry about providing the basic necessities for themselves and their families.

A new centrist party should take the lead in developing and implementing a comprehensive and workable economic plan that will ensure all Americans can enjoy a decent and average standard of living.

Economics is complex, and not an exact science. Our economy is intricate, everchanging, and very difficult to package into a neat, guaranteed plan of action. Nevertheless, we must try. We must do better than those currently "manning the ship". As with all my short commentaries, the economy deserves a full collaborative effort by our best economists – in academia, government and the private sector – to present credible steps that can be adopted by all players regardless of party to stabilize the economy so that Americans can achieve the average level of prosperity they expect.

The American economy is dependent on a partnership between individual citizens, their immediate communities, State and regional economic entities, and our vast and varied national forces. For most of our history there has been a national mindset that we all have the opportunity to achieve an acceptable standard of living with hard work and perseverance. I do not think we have lost that drive and dedication and hope, just maybe become overly distracted and overwhelmed by the complexity of our modern world.

The Poor and the Rich

"But the most common and durable source of factions has been the various and unequal distribution of property."

Federalist Papers No. 10 (Madison)

The above quote speaks of a divide that is so basic to human society that one would think by now we would have come up with a solution to the problem. At least in America. A few years ago, there was a worldwide protest movement that became known as the "Occupy" movement with a theme of "We are the 99 Percent". This lengthy and extensive protest centered on an objection to the disproportionate wealth concentrated in one percent of our population. The protests eventually disappeared with only a whimper, largely because there was no substance behind them – no solutions offered, just an expression of discontent.

In the whole history of human civilization there have always been wealthy people and poor ones, in societies a step up or more from stone age and hunting and gathering cultures that is. Protesting against the rich is futile. However, working to eliminate poverty is a worthy goal, and an attainable one, in the United States of America. Ensuring all Americans can be members of a real and stable middle-class is also achievable. If all of our population were at a middle-class standard of living I can just about guarantee that today's bitter resentment against the wealthy would subside if not almost disappear. Possibly the majority of the "99 percent" would realize that for whatever reasons the "one percent" were propelled to affluence, they were and are exceptional engines of growth and prosperity in the economy. They create employment, whether directly through businesses they create or through an elevated level of personal consumption of goods and services. They can also afford to be more generous than the average American in philanthropic areas. Many wealthy Americans have been devoted public servants. So, let's leave the rich alone and concentrate our attention on those who are less fortunate.

The Individual

"The way to wealth is as plain as the way to market. It depends chiefly on two words, industry and frugality: that is, waste neither time nor money, but make the best use of both. Without industry and frugality nothing will do, and with them everything."

Benjamin Franklin

The individual is the foundation, the nucleus of the economy. I by no means intend to be patronizing or condescending in stating the obvious, just to refresh us on the basic fact that each and every one of us is to a large degree the maker of our own destiny. We seem to have entered an era, however, in which so many Americans blame "them" – the rich or the poor, the Republicans or Democrats, "Wall Street" or the Marxist-Socialists, the men or the women, and of course "Washington".

Almost every individual has the capability to be successful, to live the American Dream if they apply their talents, energy, time and personal resources towards that goal. There will always be obstacles, impediments, forces beyond our control that will slow or stall our efforts but with 'industry and frugality" as Benjamin Franklin wrote, and a touch of patience, we will always move forward.

What would be helpful is if today's Americans would take the concept of "frugality" more to heart. We have become a credit rather than cash dominated economy and the credit industry is a powerful one, highly influential in business as well as political circles. We cannot expect either of the latter to be helpful in turning back the clock, to the days when the only credit Americans usually took out was for a home mortgage, or possibly for a car or a one-time furniture installment for their home for a lifetime. Today, virtually everything can be bought on credit, and most Americans obligate themselves to purchases that in their totality represent amounts far beyond their means. Many citizens get themselves into deep trouble with credit and their inability to extricate themselves from their debt burden is a personal, self-inflicted hardship that must also have unhealthy effects on the economy at large. We cannot expect great degrees of entrepreneurial activity and self-reliance from large groups of people whose extra disposable income is locked up in credit payments and the attending interest. In essence, Americans have been giving up their own financial independence, turning over their personal "profits" to financial institutions which do not have individuals at heart, just their own organizations and stockholders.

I would like to see the "engine" of the American economy once more be based on the individual – not on the spending of the individual but on the energy and production of that individual.

Local Economies

The inexorable movement of the American population from rural to urban concentrations has fractured what was once one of our great strengths – self-sufficiency within relatively small geographical areas. At one time, an individual county might have been composed of many small family-operated farms that produced enough food for themselves, and excess products sufficient for the needs of others in the county. There would have been small active townships with sole-proprietorship businesses that provided the goods and services required for the county population: mercantile, medical, and the full range of needs for the community. There would often have been larger businesses – light industrial, heavy industrial and manufacturing – which provided steady employment for local wage-earners, served the needs of the local economy, and possibly "exported" their production regionally or even nationwide.

Small-town and rural America were once the bastion of core American values, such as strong communities, stable families; judicial, law enforcement and local government institutions that were valued and respected; a belief in education, hard work, frugality and helping one another. These communities were overwhelmingly patriotic and held their higher governmental institutions – State and federal – in high esteem.

Sadly, in my view, a great deal of the self-sufficiency of local communities has dissolved: small family farms are a thing of the past and food is transported in from faraway places, even overseas; small local businesses and industries have closed, and people have either moved to urban areas or commute long distances to them; the majority of goods and materials once produced locally are now imported in by large corporate entities which put small local concerns out of business. Families are no longer as stable as they once were; the local education standards are lower than they could be; the courts and local law enforcement not as respected and valued as in the past.

Many people today believe that small-town and rural America is a thing of the past and that it is futile to work to restore it; but, I disagree. The clock cannot be turned back, but we can restore a good deal of the economic independence and stability of local communities. The impetus for this must, however, come from within the communities themselves. There is little the federal government can do to assist in this area, except for one major initiative that would be earth-shaking in its impact – restrict the importation of foreign goods – agricultural and manufactured – that have made it impossible for local family farms and businesses to compete. If local communities strongly support the production and services of their local farms, businesses and industries – make "Buy Local" and support "Made in America" a philosophical stance put into practice - it is quite possible in-roads can be made.

A local chapter of a centrist party can be helpful in changing the local mindset – now often one of discouragement and helplessness in the face of what seems like inexorable forces poised against them such as unsympathetic big government, mega-corporations, the flood of cheap foreign products. So how to change the mindset? Local members of this party, being members of a community, can seek ways that local government can remove or reduce impediments to local farmers and businesses – through tax incentives, exemptions from overly restrictive regulations, through formation of cooperatives and collectives that can share costs of expanded farmers markets and locally owned and run supermarkets, hardware stores, shops that carry local products, the sharing of now abandoned industrial facilities by multiple smaller manufacturers. This can be done, with effort, imagination and the American 'can do" attitude.

For urban communities the dynamic is different but at the same time not so dissimilar. Cities once had distinct neighborhoods with stable communities and small businesses. Today, "Mom and Pop" grocery stores have virtually disappeared; sole-proprietorship shops selling supplies and merchandise have sold out; light and heavy manufacturing is almost non-existent. This can be at least partially turned around if people in city neighborhoods really want it to and private and governmental entities are supportive. For example, fresh local produce – fresher and tastier than that found in supermarket chains - can be purchased from small farms not all that far away and sold in neighborhood grocery stores. Hardware stores can be supportive of local city, or nearby rural manufacturers by selling their American-made products and excluding cheaper foreign-made products of the same type from their shelves. Local tailors and seamstresses can band together to acquire a common workplace and marketplace for their individual clothing production. There is a market for American-made, high-quality products – but only if we have the people making them and selling them.

Local communities and economies, whether urban or rural, are the backbone of our national economy; but they are threatened by large corporate monopolies and foreign products that have the advantage of economy of scale as with any corporation, or of low wages and inferior quality in the case of foreign imports. This can only be turned around by local communities themselves, supporting their local producers and voluntarily, not by regulation, withdrawing as consumers from supporting non-local "invaders" of their local economy.

State and Interstate Commerce

At the foundation of our Republic, States were virtually self-sufficient in their economies, containing the wide variety of goods and services necessary for their own citizens. This has eroded over time as transportation and technology have made products and services throughout the country accessible to any other region. From one perspective this is a good thing — increasing the availability of a greater diversity of products throughout the country. From another perspective, this has also concentrated the production and sale of these commodities into a relatively small number of "hands", i.e. large corporations that dominate a particular industry and/or retail empire. Individuals and small businesses have a great deal of difficulty competing against huge enterprises which are able to undersell any smaller competitor. Monopolies are not good for our economy as they stifle entrepreneurship and growth at the local and State levels. That said, large corporations are now so important to our economy that it is unrealistic to think that their reach even into small communities will diminish.

I am very much opposed to overregulation and adding to the overabundance of laws. However, in the interest of stimulating State and Intrastate economies I think it would be well worth looking at ways in which States and collections of States can both stimulate local producers and manufacturers without discouraging the larger corporate interests from participating in those economies. For example, there are several very large national chains that sell lumber, building supplies and related products. I have seen firsthand that once these concerns come to a smaller community the independent lumber/supply businesses close shop. They cannot compete. Small businesses that once supplied these retailers also close down because they no longer have a sales outlet, plus they cannot compete against the lower cost products, often foreign made, that the national chains put on their shelves.

Possibly corporate, State and local government, and community partnerships are possible to stimulate local production. For example, State and local tax relief could be given to corporations which encouraged local products, e.g. under agreements that corporate retail establishments would stock a certain percentage of products, supplies, produce or commodities in return for tax incentives. The best solutions would be ones that came voluntarily, that are win-win for all concerned.

States need once again to be empowered to serve their own constituencies. Once again, too much power has become entrenched in the federal government and, for some reason State and local governments, like citizens at large focus on Washington as both the cause and solution to economic concerns. Under the Constitution, States have been given great power to administer their own territories. They need to pick up the reins and be proactive in stimulating and maintaining a vibrant commercial and agricultural climate within their own States and regionally with their neighboring States.

Our Domestic Economy

I remember when some thirty years ago political and economic theorists put a lot of weight into the concept that the United States has entered into the post-industrial age, the information age in which essentially, we Americans would do the thinking and communicating while the rest of the world, still stuck in the industrial or pre-industrial tiers, respectively, would do the manufacturing or supply the raw materials. In other words, we were to be the brains and "they" would be the brawn. The premise was fallacious in my view. We do have great minds in all fields who with the aid of advanced information technology can make great advances in these fields. Nevertheless, we cannot eat an "app", drive a computer-aided design, open a can with a bit or byte. We want or need "things" and a large percentage of our citizens are happiest "doing" rather than "thinking". I by no means intend that to be pejorative. Quite the opposite. I applaud all those people with varied talents and interests, many or most of which I am not as good at. We need to harness and value the abilities of everyone, and the only way to really do this is by having a robust economy that utilizes what everyone has to offer. Our domestic economy is so vast that I believe this can be done, but only if government protects our economy, our people, our workers.

In my view, the conclusion of the theorists mentioned above – that the United States would reside in the top tier of the post-industrial/information world and all the other countries remain below – was a pipe dream. Other people around the world also have great minds, talented people who are just as capable as our own "best of the best". Other countries also have capable, energetic people engaged in the work-a-day world who are just as productive as our own "ordinary" citizens. The hazard in terms of our domestic economy is that we will be putting all of our eggs in one or just several baskets, losing the diversity within our economy. If we are no longer independent as a country in terms of our own economy, it stands to reason that we will become dependent on other countries.

I know this is not a popular position, but I think a certain degree of protectionism is in order. Reasonable, well thought out protectionism – not knee-jerk actions that hurt our closest allies and do nothing to help our citizens. We need to give serious thought to which American industries and occupations we want/need to protect or restore or revive. We then need to decide on the best steps to take and on what timetable. The point is that the more diversified our economy is the more independent we become and are in a much stronger position the economically weather whatever problems — economic, political, or defense-related — are present elsewhere in the world.

The U.S. in a Global Economy

Basically, we Americans are a caring people who cherish our country, its heritage and its astounding successes in forging a nation based on freedom, individual liberty, and prosperity for all. We would like the rest of the world to share in these successes, but the simple fact is that we do not want to sink to some common denominator level for the sake of global equality. If others rise to our level, hats off to them as long as it is not at our expense. From an alternate perspective we do not want to prosper at the expense of others either. We were never a colonial power which conquered then exploited underdeveloped countries to enrich ourselves. However, we, like other powers have used our powerful industrial, commercial and financial resources to dominate important sectors of the world economy such as in natural resource extraction and agricultural commodities. We were once an important player as well in the world market with certain industrial and manufacturing products; "Made in America" was once the hallmark of quality; consumers around the world knew it and responded with their pocketbook. Not so any more and it is difficult to pin down what actually our role is now in the global economy.

We remain the wealthiest and most potent economy in the world, but our share hold in the global economy is sliding. We once had the strongest steel industry in the world, for domestic consumption and export. Our steel industry collapsed, and we now export iron ore to Asia, then import the steel or finished product from them. We used to export vehicles of all kinds, from passenger cars to trucks and heavy machinery. We now import them or assemble them here with a great deal of foreign parts, under foreign corporate ownership. We once had the largest furniture manufacturing industry in the world. We now export our raw timber to Asia where it is made into furniture and sold back to us. We allow foreign individuals or corporate entities to purchase U.S land and businesses, when in many cases we cannot do the same in their countries. Foreign entities own a significant portion of our agricultural industry. Foreigners are heavily invested in our media and entertainment industries. There is no longer an American electronics industry; think of that - we basically invented that sector and its gone. For

85

many countries in the world today which have become strong industrial leaders it was originally American inventions, technology and processes, such as development of mass production, that were responsible for their success. We invented, they reverse-engineered our developments skipping our earlier struggles, and they kept progressing. We stalled and regressed.

Do I sound xenophobic? I certainly do not mean to; in fact, I have a great deal of admiration for the foreigners who learned all we could teach them about industry, manufacturing, agriculture, commerce, and finance then excelled at putting this knowledge to use. Hats off to them, they beat us at our own game!

But, for the sake of our own country we must turn this around. We must be producers once more, and attempt to reenter the world export market, not as a dominating power but as a constructive and fair partner with other countries which hold the same business ethic. It'll be a hard slog, but I know we can do it.

Free Trade

For some reason, "free trade" has been the mantra of every successive U.S. administration since the Ronald Reagan era, one shared by Republicans and Democrats alike. "Free trade" is somewhat of an oxymoron in my view; there is nothing free in trade unless one party is willing to lose its shirt. For thousands of years, since the earliest recorded history, trade has been based on the principle that one trading partner has a product that the other does not produce, but wants, and vice versa. Why else would the Venetians have sent ships and caravans to Asia on trips that took years round trip to trade for silk, spices and other commodities if they could have produced them in Venice. And of course, China and others in Asia would have had to want something the Venetians could offer in return.

With the world market as it stands today, there is really no need for the U.S. to attempt selling U.S. cars or electronics or household merchandise to Asia when their own exports to us in these sectors are of equal or better quality and cheaper than our own. The only answer I can see is for us to invent/develop superior products and reenter the world market from the top end. Here are a few examples. "Jeep", along with the British Land Rover were once the preferred off-road, four-wheel drive vehicles in many underdeveloped regions in the world. Now, unfortunately, the Jeep and other American made off-road vehicles cannot stand up to the rugged conditions in these countries. Nissan and Toyota became the preferred makes over 30 years ago; and in the past few years Land Rover has had a comeback. We could have a comeback too if our automotive designers wished to penetrate this significant market. Steel – the U.S. the UK and Germany once had the dominant and highest quality steel industries in the world. We certainly don't anymore and what we are importing from China as finished products are inferior. The Chinese will use our grading system for stainless steel products, for example, but they are fake. The stainless steel is not of the grade purported and it will rust in short order. We could regenerate our steel industry and restore our reputation as making only the finest quality products in this sector.

I wonder sometimes why we do not see more products available in the U.S. from South and Central America which one would think, along with Canada, should be our closest logical trading partners. Yes, we do import fresh fruits and vegetables and yes Mexico manufactures a significant amount of parts for the American auto industry, but I think we have barely scratched the surface in terms of trading possibilities. NAFTA was an attempt, but not one that favored the U.S. As with any treaty we enter into all parties should benefit – including the U.S., especially the U.S. A third, centrist party should seek to foster foreign trade, but not at the expense of the U.S. economy. Absolute free trade will not work for us. We need to refine our national perspective on this issue and seek balance, an even playing field.

Balanced Budgets and Elimination of the National Debt

The United States has not had a balanced budget submission submitted by the President and approved by Congress, our "keepers of the purse", in I don't know how long. For many years, probably decades, Congress debates and then votes on an annual budget, then throughout the year on many different spending bills, ones directed to specific sectors of the government or short-term needs, but there has been no true budget per se, much less a balanced one. I think Americans have a right to know how much of their taxpayer money is going to what areas, and that they have a right to expect that revenue matches expenditures; that the ledger sheet zeroes out at the bottom. Years ago, there was significant public demand for a balanced budget, and this demand from the "grassroots" was echoed by their representatives in Congress. Recently there has been silence on this issue, both from the political parties and the public. This needs to change if our national financial health is to be preserved. The 2018 government budget is just over $4 trillion. Over the next ten years it will add at least $6 trillion to the deficit. The deficit is estimated to reach $22 trillion in 2027. Just paying the interest on the U.S. debt each year amounts to about five percent of the U.S. revenue from taxes and other sources, and we are not paying off the debt rather we are increasing it!

In addition, The United States is trapped budget-wise into paying about two-thirds of revenue into "entitlements", mandatory spending on Social Security, Medicare, government and military pensions etc., leaving only about one-third of the budget for discretionary spending such as operations of all Executive departments and agencies, including defense, and for infrastructure improvements, disasters, and the unforeseen. Very hard choices are necessary. Cuts are necessary. This will not happen under our current two-party system, with the two sides bitterly opposed to compromise. The Democratic Party has been long called the "tax and spend party", calling for higher taxes and more spending, particularly on social programs. The Republican Party has consistently called for lower taxes and reduced spending, particularly on social programs among which are Social Security,

Medicare and welfare payments. Basically, there is stagnation in Congress and in the Executive, with no efforts to resolve our budget problems via compromise and intelligent and pragmatic long-term planning.

A third party needs to be at the forefront of the national debate on a balanced budget and elimination of the national debt. From the beginning, the party needs to have within its party ranks expert economists, not bound to party lines, who can arrive at viable solutions, present them to voters during campaigns, and provide credible apolitical support to elected representatives at all levels whether of this third party or not. I believe the American public would strongly support such a nonpartisan effort to bring about a healthy national financial plan. Here are some of my thoughts on areas that must be addressed. I know all of them will be unpopular in one camp or another, thus unlikely to be publicly expressed by our current set of national leaders.

1. A balanced national budget, in which revenues and expenditures are matched to arrive at a zero-balance bottom line.
2. Mandatory inclusion within the budget of a reasonable percentage earmarked to reduce the national debt over a predetermined number of years.
3. A reformed tax plan, as described in another section, which provides the revenue needed to operate our federal government.
4. Significant reduction in expenditures for "mandatory entitlements" in the federal budget, now two-thirds of the budget and seemingly untouchable. Americans need to face the music: as important as Social Security has been since enacted in 1935, this is a different world in 2018 and the program is not affordable. That said, citizens who have contributed deserve their money back. I am recommending a gradual withdrawal by stages, with contributions by working citizens continuing until the program ends. The stages I see are: those currently on Social Security would continue receiving payments uninterrupted or reduced. Those below Social Security age but close to it – say age 50 and over would continue to contribute while working but when 62, now the earliest age to receive benefits, would receive monthly payments that would reimburse them over the course of ten years for the amounts they had contributed over their lifetime in present day dollars. No interest, but with adjustments made for

inflation since they entered the workforce. Those under 50 would continue contributing for 15 years, then receive monthly reimbursements for ten years, again at present day dollar rates. A program such as this would enable us to disengage entirely from Social Security over a 25-year period. There would no longer be this safety net for the elderly who are truly in need, however other needs-based programs could provide help at the State level. Frankly, many seniors receive Social Security who do not really need it. But everyone who has contributed deserves back what they put in. Medicare is similar in that many people do not need it; they have their own resources. However, health care is a sensitive subject and we cannot withdraw support from those who have no other coverage. I will address health care elsewhere in this book. Welfare is also a difficult subject – there are people who need it and we Americans need to take care of our own. However, the federal government should not be involved – this is State and county business.

5. Reduction in military expenditures, currently our largest single budget category, without hurting our ability to address external threats.

6. Eliminate all "pork" in the federal budget. The federal government should not be directly funding State projects. "Pork" encumbers so many spending bills, tacked onto legitimate legislation as bargaining chips to get members of Congress to vote in favor. As outlined elsewhere, if a significant percentage of federal revenues from taxation are re-distributed back to the States, earmarked for broad areas such as infrastructure improvement but not specific projects, this will eliminate the nonsensical jockeying in Congress that delays enactment of good bills and results in "bridges to nowhere". A centrist third party should be known as the "no pork" party.

Energy

The production, supply and utilization of energy is one of the key components of our economy and the American quality of life. We should have a long-term energy policy – one that looks forward at least 20 years not one that pertains to a four-year presidential term. This is an issue that impacts on Republican, Democrat, centrist, independent and all Americans alike. Short term, knee-jerk policy making on energy serves only to raise concerns and divisions, not serve the needs of the country.

As on so many other issues, a third, centrist party can serve as the long-term planning party, developing plans and strategies based on hard data and attracting multi-partisan support throughout the country for cogent policies that will be maintained by whatever political party is in power over the short term. To develop a realistic policy, it is essential that experts be assembled in all the energy sub-sectors to reach consensus on what will work and over what stretch of time. We do not need precipitous, rash actions that will fail. We need smooth transitional steps to reach our goals, ensuring that no sectors of our population are hurt in the process, particularly those in energy industries such as those sourced in fossil fuels. Corporations and workers in the petroleum, coal and gas industries need to be fully engaged and have a sense of "ownership" in any policies and strategies developed. We can also hope that the companies currently operating in the energy sector will take the lead in transitioning to alternative energy sources, realizing that it is in their own long-term interest to do so. We should not expect government to be the financier of alternative energy programs – we need to reduce government budgets not increase them, plus government is unlikely to do as good a job in energy as the experts who know the field.

Any long-term energy plan needs to seriously consider all energy sources – solar, wind, geothermal, hydro, ocean wave power, and yes nuclear. Nuclear energy has been anathema in public and governmental discussions on energy. Following the nuclear disasters at Three Mile Island, Chernobyl, and Fukushima there has been considerable public fear that nuclear energy is too great a risk for the country to reconsider. Yes, the risks given current nuclear technology are real; however, how can we diminish risks if we are not engaged in the development of more modern and improved technologies? My understanding is that very few people decide to study nuclear energy technology today – because there are few jobs available. Who can blame young people for going elsewhere; this is pretty much a dead career field. But that is a shame – nuclear energy has the potential to be a virtually unlimited power source, one that with enough brainpower behind it can be made as safe as any other. Nuclear has enormous potential in transportation – we have already proven that with our naval vessels which can go as long as ten years without refueling, and in space travel where most of our satellites and long-distance probes are nuclear fueled. Just think if we could do the same with our cars, planes, trains and commercial ships. We would be short-sighted and negligent to not include nuclear in our long-term planning.

Whatever the details, let's develop an intelligent, comprehensive and workable energy plan that has the American people fully in support.

Transportation

At the time of the drafting of the Constitution, the term "navigation" was used to generally apply to transportation, given that there were few roads and the majority of movement of people and products was by waterway – river, lake and sea. The Founders all recognized that commerce depended on the ability to travel between areas already developed – cities and rural areas – and expanding into what was then "wilderness", not under control of the new nation. There was a general acceptance among Americans in those days that the federal government had a vital role to play in assuring that a viable transportation system was developed. Today, we are just as dependent, and possibly more dependent, on our transportation systems than ever before. Commerce at all levels – local, interstate, national and foreign depends on the movement of goods and products by land, sea and air. People rely on some form of transportation – car, rail, plane or boat – for business and personal needs.

To be frank, all of our transportation systems are overloaded and outdated. Upgrades that will meet the needs of today as well as the future are sorely needed. We have too many cars, clogging up too many roads. Our rail system is woefully outdated. Our airports and skies are almost overwhelmed. And our merchant marine, our commercial shipping capabilities are next to none; despite us once having had the largest fleet of commercial ships on the oceans of the world.

I mention in several different sections of this book that a new centrist party needs to be a planning party. No other political party offers plans for the future, beyond presenting ideas and promises for the next term in office. This is not helpful in regard to transportation as any initiatives and development of our capabilities will require the support of first the voters, and then that of their elected representatives. Improvements in our transportation capabilities will be costly and long-term programs. That is not a valid reason for us to "kick the can down the road".

Americans love their cars – a practical symbol of American independence; we can go anywhere whenever we want. However, I think most Americans realize they do not have to go by car everywhere all the time. Most Americans, I believe would welcome the freedom to choose an alternative mode of conveyance, if it was easily accessible, less costly than a car, and acceptably time-efficient.

We need state-of-the art mass transit systems, particularly in metropolitan areas which today are, in fact, huge areas that encompass not only city centers and their suburbs but large stretches of rural areas from which people commute. Current roadways in and to metropolitan areas are overwhelmed by cars, often carrying just the one driver, and commutes to work often require an hour or two at each end of a work day to travel a relatively short distance. We need new types of conveyance on new travel grids exploiting new technologies to the fullest. Planning, design, and implementation of new strategies is something we as a country should fully support.

We once had the most extensive and efficient rail system in the world. This was one of the most important factors in our opening up the full extent of the country. However, rather than modernizing and improving our railways, we abandoned a great many of our tracks, let others remain in operation without improvement, and generally let rail travel, particularly passenger travel fall into obsolescence. This could be turned around with highspeed trains on new tracks and routes designed to accommodate them. However, this would be essentially a new rail system, starting virtually from scratch. It will be high-cost, and a lengthy multi-decade long effort, but one that we should begin now and support through its completion. This is a project that will need support from all levels of government and partnership with the private business community, but also this will need strong support from our citizens. A third centrist party can be instrumental in exciting public support for this project, and also press for the solidarity of other political parties with us in this national effort.

The demand for air travel will continue to expand, maybe even explode, for the foreseeable future. This will place considerable demands on the current capacity of our airports as well as air routes, air traffic control, and the related supporting services. Government at all levels – particularly in cities where our largest airports are located – and the private sector absolutely must evaluate where we are now, and where we need to be in the future. I am not calling for another "study" which at the end of a high-cost and lengthy interlude is published in a thick book which then just gathers dust on a lot of shelves. What we need is a proactive, constructive and practical plan which contains serious steps to be taken over given time periods – steps that have the broad acceptance of all concerned.

The United States is now just a minor player in the global shipping industry and in ship building. This is curious, as shipping is an important part of international commerce and our fleet was once the largest in the world. Similarly, we have lost much of our shipbuilding capability while China, Japan and Korea have excelled in this area. Shipping is a huge and vital industry. Why have we lost our part in sea transportation and why are there no efforts to bring it back? I find it curious that some of our newest Navy ships, the littoral combat ship and the expeditionary fast transport ship are being built by an Australian company in Mobile, AL. This is a five-billion-dollar contract. The company took over an existing shipyard, converted and improved it to include building a full-size jet-capable airstrip, and is completing the contract on-time, within budget and with an outstanding product. Australians are our staunch allies and good friends, so I may sound a bit ungrateful and peevish here, but why can't we build our own Navy ships? Why have most of our shipyards closed shop or are barely hanging on, but other countries can be successful, overseas and even here?

I am a staunch supporter of the U.S. continuing to be at the forefront of space travel. For one, it is an adventure, an exploration of a new "wilderness", a challenge to open up new frontiers. Space travel and exploration is also valuable to us, and the human race as well, as it pays enormous dividends through the discovery and development of new technologies that roll over into many sectors of our economy. There are a significant number of Americans, however, who think taxpayer money should not be "wasted" on space but diverted into social welfare programs. I hope a new centrist party will disagree and seek a national consensus that our space programs are of considerable importance.

Taxation

"The genius of the people will ill brook the inquisitive and peremptory spirit of excise laws. The pockets of the farmers, on the other hand, will reluctantly yield but scanty supplies in the unwelcome shape of impositions on their houses and lands; and personal property is too precarious and invisible a fund to be laid hold of in any other way than by the imperceptible agency of taxes on consumption."

Federalist Paper No. 12 (Hamilton)

The Founders of the United States recognized that the Union could not prevail without revenue to support the activities of government. However, they recognized as well that taxation was almost ubiquitously unpopular, and that certain forms of taxation were more unpopular than others. They chose at the time of the writing of the Constitution to rely most heavily on "imposts" – duties on goods imported from foreign countries. There was no income tax at that time, largely because there was little "income" available from an agrarian, mostly subsistence economy, but also because the structures necessary to collect income taxes would necessarily require a complex structure that made no sense at the time. The country relied on imposts for over 100 years, but revenue proved insufficient to maintain government functions in a rapidly growing country.

In 1913, the 16th Amendment to the Constitution was ratified, permanently legalizing an income tax. With the addition of a payroll tax (Social Security and Medicare, today) and excise taxes (alcohol, tobacco, tires, gasoline, diesel fuel, coal, firearms, telephone service, air transportation, unregistered bonds, and many other goods and services), revenue collections soared from less than three % of Gross Domestic Product (GDP) to over twenty% in 1940, a level which is maintained today. The Federal Government also collects estate and gift taxes. Individuals and corporations must pay capital gains taxes, and business entities are taxed on their income, as separate from what is disbursed to shareholders.

States and local governments also collect a variety of taxes. These vary by state and locality, but may include, income, property, sales, and other taxes. Plus, fees for certain services, as does the federal government.

The total tax burden for individuals, including all federal, state and local taxes varies by income group from about 17% to over 30%. However, the great majority of the population pay between 25 and 30% of their income in taxes. As much as Americans dislike paying taxes and feel that at every turn there is a new tax or fee imposed by the government, we actually pay less as citizens than citizens of the majority of other developed countries. Taxes are a source of considerable discontent among the general population, and divisiveness among the income groups. The rich (the 1% most affluent) protest that they pay much higher percentages on income than those less fortunate, and some groups pay little or no federal taxes, forgetting that these groups do pay local taxes, as well as excise taxes and fees from all levels of government. The poor, who may pay no federal income tax, and the middle-class, who may pay the lowest rate of 20%, protest that their tax burden is too heavy and that the rich should pay their "fair share" meaning even higher rates than the maximum assessment of 39.6% that exists today.

In my view, there is nothing "fair" about different tax rates for different classes of people. I fully understand that taxes impact most on citizens who are struggling, barely keeping their heads above water financially; while the rich may very well not even notice the reduction in disposable income. However, the tax issue is one of the most divisive dilemmas in our current political climate. The bottom line is that the only methodology that can be fair is a flat tax system, that eliminates the complexity of the current tax code, which few understand, and which is widely perceived as taking from the poor and giving to the rich.

The Constitution, and arguments expressed in the Federalist Papers, make it clear that the Founders of our Union understood that government at all levels – federal, state and local – needed reliable sources of revenue to be able to adequately serve the needs of citizens. A view, strongly expressed at that time, was that while the federal government needed the power to collect revenue for needs at that level, states needed to retain full rights to assess their needs and collect the revenue necessary for the varying needs of their localities. In other words, there was not, and is not, a practical, constitutional means to establish a tax policy that will equalize the total tax burden imposed by federal, state, and local governments for all Americans. So, in the following skeleton of a tax plan, I will address only the taxes and revenues collected by the federal government.

First, let me outline the current economic classes as I see them.

Destitute: those who are unable to provide adequately for their food, lodging and other essential needs for survival. These persons would be those with no income – wage or otherwise earned. These persons would not be taxed.

The poor: those who can barely provide for their essential needs month to month. In other words, those people whose quality of life, as a factor of financial stability, live under the threshold of what we as a nation envision as a minimum American standard. Absent a scientific study of what income level represents "poor", I will use as placeholders the figures $20,000 for an individual and $40,000 for a family, regardless of size. These persons would pay tax at the same flat-tax rate as everyone else. I know this is a radical suggestion, one that social "progressives" will say is unjust. However, take into consideration that if every American citizen – poor, middle class, rich - pays the same rate no one class of citizens will be legitimately be able to cry foul. Each American who enters the voting booth will be able to claim on a firm foundation that he/she is on equal standing with all others, paying a fair share of our shared national expenses. And the poor, along with the destitute will certainly be the beneficiaries of needs-based public assistance that will amount to far more than the federal tax they pay. But they will be taxpayers at exactly the same rate as any other American.

Middle-class, upper middle-class, and wealthy. All would be taxed on all income – from one dollar to a billion or more.

I propose a universal federal tax rate of 25% that would apply to all gross incomes – individual salaried, self-employed, sole proprietors, small businesses, corporations, capital gains.

I propose elimination of all deductions from gross income for individuals, all of them: mortgage, individual and family credits, state and local taxes, medical, charity, child care etc. All of them.

This may sound harsh, but look how "fair" it will be, and sensible. I will only address the mortgage deduction, understanding that each other deduction under the current tax system has its ardent supporters. But the principle behind eliminating the other deductions remains the same as this. A lower middle-class person/family buying a home will be less likely to buy one out of their reach, projecting on the "savings" they will get on a mortgage deduction. In other words, they will budget properly and live within their means without the deduction "carrot" dangled out so frequently by real estate agents and financial institutions. Moreover, they will have a firm income figure to plan on. If a family makes $50,000, they will know that they will pay $12,500 in federal income tax based on 25% of their total income. Most salaried employees would never see that deducted tax or have to file more than a simple return that reports income from other sources. Private business people will just have to be honest – and most will be, if the philosophy behind the U.S. tax system is seen as necessary to our national interests, and fair to all.

At the other end of the scale, the rich would not be able to deduct the mortgage on a house worth millions, or a second house worth millions, or a luxury car, plane or boat ostensibly used for "business". They too, the wealthy, would pay a flat 25% of their gross income.

On the business and corporate side, a similar reduction in eligible deductions would take place. For example: cars, boats, planes, houses for already wealthy executives would no longer be deductible as "business" expenses. Salaries for employees would be valid business expenses, but only up to a certain threshold. How does $500,000 sound? Are there many Americans out there who do not believe someone can live on that amount? Of course not. This does not mean that a corporation cannot pay its CEO $25 million. It's just that the corporation cannot reduce its gross reportable income by that amount. A 25% corporate tax would match the 25% tax on individuals – a symbolic "fairness" and one not that far from the level set in the recent tax reform bill passed in Congress. In addition, American companies that have "out-sourced" their operations to foreign countries should be treated as foreign entities for taxation and tariff purposes. Plus, salaries to foreign workers, in American-owned but foreign based businesses should not be deducted as business expenses.

Interest, dividends, and capital gains should all be taxed at 25%. Again, simplicity and fairness are key.

I would eliminate estate and gift taxes. These are not fair. Citizens that save their money, worked hard to build an estate to pass on to their descendants should be congratulated, not penalized. Caring citizens who choose to give family, friends or others a monetary gift should also not be penalized. These taxes are double taxes – the funds or property passed on had already been taxed before. Many, particularly those concerned by the wide disparities in wealth in the country, think that estate and gift taxes are a way to redistribute the wealth, to tax the rich and give to the poor. But, is this fair? Is this an American concept? I believe most Americans believe all Americans have a basic right to accumulate property and wealth, whether it be by hard work alone, good luck, or because one's parents or ancestors worked hard or were lucky. Great divisions in wealth are unhealthy for the national psyche, but mostly when ordinary, hardworking Americans feel that they cannot themselves, or their offspring cannot also achieve, higher levels of financial achievement too if they work hard. And as to estate taxes, these do not affect the rich alone. Those people who inherit land and property, but are not rich, very often must sell them off because they do not have the cash to pay the taxes. Such a shame to see family properties, held often for generations, sold off to developers or the wealthy because the inheritors could not pay the tax. Plus, inheritance taxes are double taxation like gift taxes. The funds or properties have been taxed before.

I would eliminate all federal excise taxes – on alcohol, tobacco, gasoline and all other commodities that are currently taxed. Also, federal fees related to commodities, such as distributorships and permits for these commodities, should also be eliminated. The federal government should not be in "business". There is too much room in this area for corruption, abuse, and restrictions on competition.

I would significantly increase the application of tariffs on imported foreign commodities from countries that undercut our own production base. I will get into this more later, but I do believe significant revenue can be collected from these sources, which will also serve to restore our economy and skilled labor force. We have the capability to produce the great majority of our country's needs. But we cannot do so and maintain a respectable American quality of life for our workforce without protecting our industries and production capabilities.

Finally, I believe that taking the above steps would bring on essentially the same revenues as the federal government now collects. Our national needs would be met. We can pay off the deficit in a measured period of time.

But I would add one more step – return 10% of all revenues collected as federal taxes to the States, on a per capita basis, for use at their discretion in specific areas identified as of national interest: defense, infrastructure, transportation, energy, commerce, conservation, health, social assistance and other key concerns that may change over time. This would enable the federal government to transfer a significant amount of authority and administration from Washington back to the States, which as the implementers and beneficiaries of a good number of federal programs are best positioned to make the best decisions on those programs. This move would reduce the federal workforce and the federal budget, by eliminating duplication between federal and state levels. It would also greatly reduce efforts by members of Congress to add state-specific "pork" to each and every national bill, a bad habit which significantly adds to the time taken to develop good legislation and adds to the political acrimony between party camps. This return of revenues to the States could also conceivably allow them to reduce and simplify their own tax systems.

Again, this is the skeleton of what I believe is a fair plan. Beyond adequately funding our national government, the aim is to change perceptions and to lessen the tension and hostility so palpable between the economic classes, which is caused by the perception among each that they are being unfairly treated. Possibly, and this is a hope, such a revamped system will restore a bit of American pride and sense of sharing equally in American opportunities, while also sharing equally in the responsibility to keep the Union funded. Does anyone remember from not that long ago when paying one's taxes, on time and honestly was a source of pride for many Americans? A solemn responsibility for adult citizens, for voters? A simple system of taxation, with fair and equal treatment for all could go a long way to reduce some of the bitterness so visible today between the classes.

Jobs vs. Careers

When a significant portion of the electorate is not enjoying the prosperity of the "American Dream" this should be of considerable concern to the whole nation. And it should be a major focus of our government representatives at all levels. Throughout human political history, when a large segment of the population of a country, kingdom, or empire is under-supplied with the basic needs of existence – food, shelter, clothing – there has been dissension and even revolt. Kingdoms and empires have fallen.

Those of some wealth, those who are financially comfortable, might think that I am being overly dramatic here; forecasting doom when the situation does not seem so dire, from their vantage point anyway. Most of our political leadership class, comfortable themselves, do not recognize the groundswell of discontent permeating the lower economic classes. Essentially, I would define households whose incomes are less than $50,000 per year as lower class; between 50 and $75,000 as lower middle-class; between 75 and $125,000 as middle-class; between 125 and $250,000 as upper-middle class; and above $250,000 as wealthy.

You might think my figures are too high, that Americans at the bottom classes can survive well enough on much less. True, they can survive. But do they feel prosperous, financially stable, content? No, they don't, and this is not because of greed. They do not feel like they are participating in the "American Dream" which to most of us means working hard throughout a lifetime and in return having the financial stability to not worry how to meet a reasonable standard of basic needs for a family, pay bills at the end of the month, and help our children achieve this same level of financial stability.

The national median household income in the U.S. is about $54,000. So, half our population is in a household making less than that. The poverty line in 2017 was considered to be at $24,300 for a household. 15% or 46 million people live at or below this level. That is a lot of people! But does adding ten, twenty, thirty more thousand to income for these people then make them feel financially secure? Unfortunately not, and again this is not because of greed. To feel secure most Americans, again, want to be able to live modestly, work hard and not worry about providing the basic needs for their household, save regularly, and retire in dignity. Most Americans are happy with and seek a middle-class quality of life. They do not resent or envy the wealthy – often they rather admire those who succeed far beyond what "regular" people can achieve. But, most Americans do want to feel secure. Too many people feel very insecure, and this is not good for the health of the nation.

In the last several national elections the buzzword over and over was "jobs". Every politician, Democrat and Republican, put "jobs" at the forefront of their campaigns. They didn't say how they would bring in new "jobs". They didn't define what a "job" was. They didn't even take the next step and say "good jobs". Over and over it was just "jobs, jobs, jobs"!

Most Americans now, just as throughout our history, do not want a "job". They want a career. They want a solid occupation that places them in the middle-class bracket. They are content to start at the bottom when young, work hard throughout their life, build skills and experience, get promotions, increase their income gradually over the years until they reach a respectable level of seniority within that field. And then most people want to retire with a decent pension or level of savings to carry them through to the end of their lives.

What is a career? Anything can be a career – blue collar, white collar, trade, profession, craft – any field of endeavor that involves income in return for work. But the difference between a "job" and a career is that a career represents an occupation that someone wants to do, is satisfied with in terms of it meeting the person's needs, and in which the person can feel a certain amount of pride. After all, our work represents a major portion of our waking hours and our lives. We should all feel a certain level of pride and satisfaction in our work, in our life-long career. If working for an organization or company, we should like that company, be proud of its product, feel loyalty towards it and feel the company is loyal to us.

What then is a "job"? A job is something we must do for some reason. We work at a job because we need the income but might rather be working elsewhere in another field – a career that is unavailable or otherwise out of reach. A job may have low pay, inadequate hours, poor benefits, bad working conditions, uncaring supervisors, and insecurity as to how long it will last. A "job", as it provides income, is not a bad thing – it's better than being unemployed - but we can't call it a good thing either.

Employment Levels vs. Productivity

I am going to really go out on a limb here with this conjecture. I expect it will incense many people. I think it quite possible that we have a labor glut due to the push to have almost total and equivalent employment for both men and women. This has been a major item on the feminist agenda since the 1960's.

Let me make it clear that I believe all men and women who want a career deserve to have one, and deserve equal pay for equal work. I just question whether we have enough work in the traditional labor market to fully employ all American adults. In other words, is the productivity, the output for each employee optimized. Or is the current situation one in which two adults each do half a person's work for half a person's pay. Here's how I see it.

An American household has the same basic needs that it did 50 years ago, when generally men worked for a salary and women took care of the home and the children and were involved intimately with the community. The family, then and today, needed one lodging, the same amount of food, the same amount of clothes, the same amount of furniture, appliances, education, vacations, savings etc. One person entered the workforce and provided for those needs. Somehow, one wage earner provided an American middle-class lifestyle. Today it takes two wage-earners in a family to maybe provide a lifestyle that is a bit less than the lifestyle of 50 years ago. Why?

The foundation of our economy is that we provide for our basic needs. It's no different really than at the time of Independence. Most people at that time were farmers and grew most of their own food and raised animals for personal consumption. The input of men, women and often children was essential to the household. Excesses were sold to those who did not produce those commodities but provided goods and services that the farming household did not produce. There was an approximate equilibrium in supply and demand. Some households produced more of a good or service and thus increased their prosperity a bit more, but for the most part productivity and work were balanced to the needs of individuals, communities and regions.

The United States has lost a great deal of its industrial base – heavy or light, large corporate or small sole proprietorship. Much of the loss has been out-sourced to foreign countries. They produce, we retail and consume the products. This is not a healthy situation for an economy. An economy is essentially a complex barter system in which individual productivity is traded for another individuals' productivity. Consumption is not productivity. What does the consumer exchange for the product? Money yes, but conceptually what productivity unit backs up that money? Perhaps if we still had a vibrant industrial sector that not only produced the needs of our population but also exported heavily to other countries, we would still have the demand for additional labor to provide for the demands greater than those internal to the United States. And then with a higher need for labor, employers would value that labor accordingly. Wages would be higher, benefits better, employment security improved.

I do not see much hope for the American economy unless we can fully harness the exceptional energies of the American worker. I think this requires we return to producing the goods we need here at home, plus regain some of that good ol' American ingenuity and apply it to other sectors and areas that we have let lapse or not yet explored. New products, new solutions, new frontiers. We did this throughout our history and can do it again. We do not need to be trapped into obsolete and stagnant economic systems that hold no hope for the future. We do not need to feel there is no other option than salaried employment – at half wages - with large corporations. Opportunities are limitless, if we can recapture some of the drive and commitment Americans were once famous for.

One perception that in the past few years constantly gets under my skin is the mostly urban and white-collar conviction that our "blue-collar" workforce needs to give up any hopes of returning to the days of semi-skilled and skilled labor on factory assembly lines, in fossil fuel mining, in agriculture, in making and fixing "things". Their frequent refrain is that people in these occupations need to "re-train in IT", information technology. Hillary Clinton said this to coal miners in West Virginia. She didn't get their votes I can assure you. This viewpoint is very myopic and demonstrates again the rural vs. urban divide.

First of all, while IT continues to be a strong growth field, it is not by any means the sole or even primary solution for America in a post-industrial age.

107

For one, it is a service sector that is only useful if applied to other sectors, whether industrial, governmental, retail, social (as in media). Second, the rest of the world has become almost equally strong in IT as we are. Try to find a computer that is not manufactured in China. IT professionals in India and elsewhere are very good, in fact our IT companies in the U.S. seek them out bring them here; or out-source many functions to them.

Third, most of our rural population, and not just those with skill sets in mineral extraction, agricultural, ranching, do not want to move to the city, put on dockers and a tie, and sit in a call-center cubicle at a keyboard. They like what they do, have generational roots in their communities and land, and believe their quality of life is better than city life. They like the great outdoors. They like to fish and hunt and boat and have dogs. So, the urban elite will say they just have to suck it up, just as Clinton in essence said to the West Virginia miners. But no, they most certainly don't have to suck it up. There are many exciting new opportunities that would fit in well with rural lifestyles and skill sets. They need to pursue those, and there is no reason we as a nation should not encourage replacement of obsolete occupations with new ones.

For example, I was travelling in a rural area of North Carolina recently and met a good old boy who was getting ready to retire after 40 years of work as a heavy industrial electrician at a chemical plant. He had great experience and seniority. But, he told me with some wistfulness that he really wished he knew more about solar energy. Time and again, I've heard similar comments throughout the South from people involved in the petroleum and other energy-related fields. They are excited by the new technologies, see that alternative energies such as solar, wind, thermal are the wave of the future, and want to be part of it. This is very important. The urban intelligentsia have been trying to brand workers in these and other fields as ignorant and recalcitrant. This is very far from the truth. Considering that the skills needed for fossil fuel extraction, electrical energy production, construction, maintenance are so similar to those needed in the alternative energy fields, the prudent direction for our national leadership to take would be to utilize those citizens in the new technologies. Rather than tell coal miners or petroleum workers they need to pack it up and go re-train in IT, we should be able to find ways to put solar and wind fields right in those same mining or oil production areas; use their skills to move forward and avoid creating unnecessary economic and social stress on these large communities.

American Production for American Consumption

When I was growing up, the label "Made in America" stood for quality and pride at the time in the unique qualities of American ingenuity, hard work and entrepreneurship. It is very difficult to find that "Made in America" label now. Our national automobile manufacturers – Ford/Lincoln, Chrysler/Dodge/Jeep, Chevrolet/GMC/Pontiac/Cadillac/Oldsmobile – are too a large extent foreign-owned; and the vehicles are assembled in the majority of cases from components manufactured in foreign countries – Japan, China, Mexico, Italy, Korea being some of the primary sources. Our ordinary consumer needs – clothing, housewares, tools etc. – again come mostly from foreign sources. Even our food is often imported – Mexico and South America being major sources. Here is a personal example I found baffling. Once, at our local grocery store, the only fresh asparagus we could find was "organic", grown and packaged in China! This made no sense! Are American farmers unable to grow asparagus profitably while China can grow and ship it by air to us for a profit? How credible is it that China, with a terrible environmental protection record, can produce "organic" asparagus, while our farmers must meet stringent Food and Drug Administration (FDA) regulations to label a food product organic; and thus, must charge double for the product vice a non-organic product. Does anyone really believe that our FDA inspects the Chinese farms, or the imported products, for compliance with our organic regulations?

Today, about 12 million Americans work in the manufacturing sector. In 1941, prior to World War II, we had more people working in industry than now, despite having less than half today's population. In 1941, over 32 million people worked in agriculture, ranching, forestry and fishing. Today, less than two and half million are employed in these sectors. Following World War II, United States trade policy tilted dramatically from one of protectionism, in which tariffs on imported goods played a significant role in protecting U.S. industry, to free trade policies that reduced tariffs to almost nil. The reason was that following World War II much of the industrial capacity in Europe and Asia had been decimated and the U.S. saw an opportunity to increase our industrial and other exports. Over the next 30 years, however, the industrial capabilities of other countries rose and during the 1970's we saw the beginning of the decline in U.S. industrial production and an influx of cheaper foreign goods. Nonetheless, the free trade mantra continued without check up to the present, although for some reason our elected leadership, from both parties, continues to beat the drum that free trade is good for our economy. I disagree. There is no way our American products can compete with products from countries like China where workers' wages are one-tenth those of American workers. So, without policy changes it is doubtful we can reestablish our manufacturing base. And, as mentioned elsewhere, a consumer economy is not a healthy one.

Our founders, and subsequent leaders up until 1913 when the income tax was instituted, strongly believed that American industry and products needed to be protected and that foreign trade needed to be managed under a tariff system, with rates set appropriate to individual situations with our trading partners. I favor an intelligent, measured protectionist policy, with tariffs, so that we can revitalize the manufacturing sector in this country. Over time, I believe this will be to our great benefit. Here's why.

I'll use the basic vegetable peeler as an example, since I know this product first hand as a continuous source of irritation to me. We used to be able to buy an inexpensive, American-made, high quality stainless steel peeler that would last maybe ten years. These are no longer made here, rather all we can find is low quality Chinese made peelers that might last six months. Yes, these peelers are cheap, maybe four dollars. However, over a ten-year period the cost to the consumer might be $40. There is no way an American company can produce even an inferior grade peeler for even twice as much as the Chinese can. However, I believe an enterprising American could produce, at a profit, a superior quality peeler for maybe $10. But how would the American consumer react? With a $10 peeler on the rack next to the four-dollar one, the likelihood is that the consumer would go for the cheaper one, not taking into account the quality. However, if a 150% tariff had been placed on the Chinese peeler, it would be necessary for it to be marketed at $10 just like the American one. In this case, it is quite likely the consumer would buy the American, higher quality one, knowing that it would last ten years while the Chinese one would have to be replaced twenty times at a total cost of $200 over the same ten-year period!

Obviously, this is an extreme and possibly exaggerated example, but I do think it illustrates that American products can compete in our marketplace if the quality of the product is worth the price, and if we protect our manufacturers and workers from competition by countries whose workers earn a small fraction of what American workers need to have an American standard of living.

Why are so many large, once branded American companies, now foreign owned? It baffles me that Chrysler/Dodge/Jeep, once one of the iconic "Big Three" American car companies, is now fully owned by Italian Fiat. And its cars and trucks are manufactured, or shall we say assembled in the United States with American workers, profitably. Up to 60% of components, depending on model, come from other countries such as Italy, Mexico and Korea, but nonetheless somehow the Italians can profitably run a company, once American, in the United States. While we cannot. So can the Germans, Koreans, Japanese, Chinese and others. This does not make sense to me. The only viable solution I can see for returning the U.S. to the domestic manufacturing marketplace is to reinstate a new, intelligent, calculated system of tariffs. A knee-jerk reaction, such as the current administration appears to be undertaking can only be harmful. And we do not need to return to the system of the past that listed thousands of different products and affixed separate tariff rates to them. We do not need to alienate our closest allies and trading partners. However, some degree of protection for our industries, those serving our domestic market and employing our workers, is warranted. All that we would really need to do is undertake a professional "shopping basket" survey of goods imported from a specific country, factor in American labor costs in comparison to that for the exporting company, then use this as a baseline for a global tariff rate for that country. In the early days of this Republic, tariff rates were negotiated with foreign countries and this can be resumed. For example, we might find that industrialized countries with a comparable standard of living as ours would not be set much of a tariff rate at all, if any; while countries like China would be charged much higher rates. The point is not to stop foreign trade, but to protect our industries and protect our workers. In addition, revenue from tariffs could substantially reduce and simplify direct and indirect taxation of citizens by the federal government.

I know this position will not be popular. "Free trade" has been the mantra since the Reagan days – among Republicans and Democrats alike. However, what has unbridled "free trade" really done for the American economy? We have lost a significant portion of our industries, skilled employment opportunities have been outsourced, and the diversity of our economy in terms of occupational range has been severely restricted. Again, we seem to have become a country of consumers and retailers, which is not a very firm foundation for an economy. Yes, the products we buy now are cheaper than if American wages were tacked onto the sticker price. But what happens when the countries who currently have lower wage rates improve their standard of living, reach wage rates approximating ours, and sell their products to us at prices which would be viable to us if we were the manufacturers? Would we be able to rebound and resume our industries? I think it would take a very long time. It's a better bet to start now. We need to produce the majority of what we consume to have an economy with a strong, vibrant foundation.

American Ingenuity – Where are the Better Mousetraps Today?

"Let both sides seek to invoke the wonders of science instead of its terrors. Together let us explore the stars, conquer the deserts, eradicate disease, tap the ocean depths, and encourage the arts and commerce."

John F. Kennedy

Since the days of the first explorers to the North American continent, there has been a special quality to Americans that has distinguished our people from among almost all others in the history of human exploration, migration, and settlement. This quality is hard to define in just one word, but many words help give a sense of the uniqueness of the American character – adventurous, determined, courageous, intrepid, perseverant, hardworking, creative, inventive are some descriptions of the human qualities that brought our country into being and made our country what it is today.

Americans as a people were never complacent, however there is a risk now that we could become so. When settlers in the 17 and 1800's set off west and south to make new lives for themselves, very often they went out with basically nothing, on foot or with a wagon pulled by oxen; bringing with them a few shovels, saws, axes and nails and bags of seeds. And somehow in a relatively short period of time they build shelter, cleared land, grew crops, established towns and became part of a viable national economy that by the 1970's was the far dominant world economy.

American's have always been creative and inventive. If our ancestors only had a few tools, or not the right ones, they made new ones to fit the task. "Necessity was the mother of invention". They built grain mills, foundries, ship yards, machinery to harvest crops, ships and barges etc. etc. etc. all in a period of history which was pre-industrial, pre-electrical, pre-fossil fuel, pre-mass communications. What they needed they invented and then built, then improved upon. So what happened? The rest of the world saw what the United States had accomplished and sought to imitate us. Fair enough, but the question are we now being left behind by more industrious and motivated cultures? Will we become, technologically and economically, a second-tier country, say in 50 or 100 years? I'm certain most Americans would hope not, but unfortunately, I do not believe many people really think that far ahead and our political and economic leadership appear to be most focused on two, four or six-year terms in office rather than America's future.

Sadly, the incentives that once sparked the American imagination, focused the unique drive of the American spirit are much less obvious today. Necessity is not on the front-burner. We are consumers, not inventors, not producers. Can better mousetraps still be invented and produced? Of course, this world is replete with challenges of all sorts. But aren't we letting others – the Chinese, Japanese, Koreans and other now industrialized countries - assume a role in which we were once firmly situated?

The long-term ramifications are quite unsettling. We often hear that American children are regressing in terms of education levels of past eras, surpassed by children in countries that we once considered far behind us. But why just complain – this is a logical result of being an importer of goods rather than a producer? Why should American children be inspired to pursue advanced fields such as engineering, alternative energy, new technologies in transportation or construction and so many other disciplines if at the end of their studies they will have little choice but to work in positions related to our retail economy. Science and technology remain virtually limitless fields in which our people can apply themselves.

National attention should be drawn to our need to be competitive, if not superior, in the realm of science, technology, and production – from the most basic needs to the far advanced needs of the future. Our current political leadership is just not stepping up to the plate. A new, centrist party can be instrumental in stimulating the people of this great country towards conquering new "wildernesses".

Justice

"There is one transcendent advantage belonging to the province of the State governments, which alone suffices to place the matter in a clear and satisfactory light – I mean the ordinary administration of criminal and civil justice. This, of all others, is the most powerful, most universal, and most attractive source of popular obedience and attachment."

Federalist Paper No. 17 (Hamilton)

The Supreme Court

"The judicial Power of the United States, shall be vested in one supreme Court, and in such inferior Courts as the Congress may from time to time ordain and establish."

Constitution of the United States
Article III, Section 1

"In all Cases affecting Ambassadors, other public Ministers and Consuls, and those in which a State shall be a Party, the supreme Court shall have original jurisdiction. In all the other Cases before mentioned, the supreme Court shall have appellate jurisdiction, both as to Law and Fact, with such Exceptions, and under such Regulations as the Congress shall make."

Constitution of the United States
Article III, Section 2.

I think most Americans like myself are a bit perplexed and uneasy about the character and role of the Supreme Court as it pertains to this era. The Constitution clearly intends for there to be a separation of powers between the three branches of government, executive, legislative and judicial. However, the Constitution does not spell out the functions and authorities of the Supreme Court in quite the detail that it does the other two branches. There is no question on appellate authority – the Supreme Court is the court of last appeal in the United States, whether a case originated in a State or federal court.

However, the circumstances under which the Supreme Court has original jurisdiction are a lot mushier. Practically speaking, it does not appear to me that Supreme Court is being proactive in areas where it might actually have the authority to initiate judicial action. In addition, I interpret the Constitution to say that Congress has the authority to legislatively grant the Supreme Court authorities in certain areas in which inferior courts, State or federal, have original jurisdiction. I believe it is time for Congress to undertake a formal discussion on ways to officially delineate authorities under the purview of the Supreme Court, particularly areas in which the Court can proactively engage subjects with Constitutional implications without waiting for decisions then referrals from inferior courts.

There are several recent or current situations which stimulate my thinking that guidelines for the Court need to be updated. One is the 2012 Colorado wedding cake case, in which a bakery owner refused on religious grounds to bake a wedding cake for a same-sex couple. This case was referred and accepted for review by the Supreme Court in 2017 and a decision was reached mid-2018. Five years to work its way through the inferior courts, then almost two years for a ruling in the final court of appeal. Seven years is much too long. With this particular case, at first I thought it frivolous, unworthy of the august station of the Supreme Court. In my mind, the case should have been handled quickly and neatly at the local level – first by whatever city or county office issues business licenses to owners, then if necessary at the local district court. But obviously this case, though seemingly trivial, had national implications on civil rights grounds. If a business owner can deny services to certain segments of the public, such as same-sex couples in this instance, why can't other business owners refuse to serve or work with people of different races/ethnic backgrounds or religions or other characteristics protected under the Constitution? Remember that African-Americans were banned from restaurants, schools, drinking fountains, bathrooms and neighborhoods not so long ago. If a bakery can refuse to serve gays this time on religious grounds it would be very easy for this owner or others to refuse to serve Muslims on religious grounds as well, or Jews, or Hispanics etc. Though seemingly nonsensical, this case is important and possibly the Supreme Court, if permitted by law to be proactive, could have taken this case at a much earlier stage and resolved the legal issue swiftly instead of seven years after the event. The Supreme Court just reached its decision, in favor of the baker – perhaps an unfortunate decision, as I believe, perhaps not. Nonetheless at some point we all should respect that Supreme Court decisions, regardless if the Court is majority or liberal, are the law of the land, as intended by the Framers of the Constitution.

Here is another example of where a proactive, responsive Supreme Court could have a positive effect on public confidence in our judicial system. President Trump is currently under investigation by a Special Prosecutor, who was appointed by the Deputy Attorney General. The White House has continuously issued vague threats that the President would fire the Special Prosecutor and/or the D/AG. The White House has also gone back and forth whether the President would or would not appear for an interview. Questions have been raised on both sides on whether the President can be subpoenaed. The White House has even suggested that the President has the power to pardon himself. Members of Congress, legal experts, the press, the public have been going on and on for well over a year on whether anyone at all has any authority in these matters involving the President! In essence, some are saying a President has ultimate, unrestrained power, which from a constitutional perspective is very far from the truth.

Under the Constitution it is clear Congress can establish "Exceptions" and "Regulations" to allow the Supreme Court original jurisdiction in areas not granted in the original wording of the Constitution. My reading of the excerpts quoted above is that Congress could explicitly state that any senior member of the Executive, i.e. "public Minister" who is engaged in an investigation of members of the Executive, including of the President, is protected from removal from office or other harassment. I believe the Supreme Court also has the power to take a similar position.

In the cake case, as it has national implications, additional wording could be devised granting the Supreme Court authority to engage proactively without referral in cases that have Constitutional implications – in this case civil rights and discrimination.

Just during the 17 months of this administration there have been other instances involving Executive decisions in which the Supreme Court could have/should have made quick rulings such as with the travel ban the White House attempted to impose on several countries. Two federal district courts did rule that the ban was not Constitutional, but the fact of the matter is these were federal district courts which do not have blanket national jurisdiction. The Supreme Court is the only national court and should have been there from the very beginning and made a ruling. I do wonder why the

Department of Justice falls under the Executive rather than the Supreme Court. I can understand that the law enforcement and investigatory components of the DOJ – FBI, ATF, ICE etc. – are most appropriate under the Executive branch; but the prosecutorial and judicial aspects, most specifically the federal courts and interaction with State courts, seems most appropriately aligned with the Supreme Court. This bears consideration.

Here is another example begging for a proactive Supreme Court. Under the Constitution, Congress has the sole authority to declare war while the President is clearly Commander in Chief of our military forces. President after President has put our military units into combat without securing Congressional approval. The War Powers Resolution of 1973 attempted to delineate express Presidential vs, Congressional authorities by giving the Executive authority for limited actions of up to 60 days, after informing Congress, but before requiring Congressional authorization. The last time Congress formally declared war was in World War II. Each of our conflicts since then has been quasi- "declared" via authorizations or spending bills. Many of our conflicts since WW2, have lingered on past the 60 days granted by the Resolution, sometimes without congressional explicit authorization. Our military engagements today – Iraq, Afghanistan, Syria, North Africa among others – are only covered by the very fragile fig leaf of an authorization granted by Congress following the 9/11 Twin Tower for the President to strike at terrorists responsible for the tragedy. A decision and process is required spelling out precisely who has the authority to commit our troops to combat – for how long, under what circumstances and through what process. The Constitution is clear that only Congress can declare war, but in practice the Executive has usurped that authority. Who can we expect to mediate and decide an issue which involves two of the three branches of government? It can only be the Supreme Court. And what entity can or would be motivated to refer that issue to the Court? Only Congress or the President are on equal standing with the Court in our system and neither branch is likely to want to open this can of worms. So that leaves only the Court with sufficient standing to proactively assume this issue, on its own authority, as one of Constitutional and national importance.

The Supreme Court is one of our most outstanding creations as a nation and the only one in the current era that can have an effect on our two other federal branches. The men and women appointed to the Supreme Court for life have been, are, and will be the finest legal minds in our country – regardless of whether as individuals they lean to the conservative or liberal. In terms of a body of Americans who are most able to deliberate on the Nation's affairs, virtual untouchables, these are our grey-bearded gods on Mount Olympus. I do not think the Supreme Court is being utilized to the fullest extent intended by our Founders. I believe it is time for us to call for a strengthening of the powers of the Supreme Court. We need a true balance of powers between our three branches. Only a new centrist party, given the self-serving characters of the two major parties, has the capacity to spark such an effort.

Fair Treatment Under the Law

I will not attempt an analysis of our entire American system of law and justice. The subject is too vast to undertake in its entirety. What needs to be made clear is that under the Constitution the bulk of the responsibility for enforcing laws and administering justice resides with the States, which do so through courts at the local level – county and municipality. Yes, the Supreme Court and federal district courts do have original jurisdiction in particular situations, but in most situations that affect the ordinary citizen directly it is local law enforcement and the local courts where the application of the American justice system is encountered. This is an important distinction. As in so many other situations citizens turn to the federal government to protest perceived inequalities or abuses in the law enforcement and legal systems in their community, when in reality the federal government does not have the authority to intervene, except possibly much later in an appellate role. In other words, protests to Washington are relatively pointless. Correction of injustices at the local level must be taken at the local level – State, county, town/city – so people seeking those corrections should be directing their objections to the local level. Marching and demonstrating in front of the White House or the Capitol might help vent frustrations, but it is unlikely to produce change.

Here is the issue – Blacks, Hispanics, and the poor of any race are more likely than whites of a higher economic class to be arrested, appear before a court, judged guilty and incarcerated. That is just a fact. Why? Here we get onto some shaky ground because there are not just a few perfect, accurate answers. So, let's address just two of the perceptions of the roots to inequity, each of which reflects the views of opposing factions.

1. Among minorities, the poor, and social activists with "progressive" political views, the opinion is that law enforcement disproportionally targets minorities and the poor; that courts are more likely to convict and apply heavier sentences to those of these groups. Statistically, I believe this is entirely correct.

2. From a white, generally middle-class or above perspective, the view is that criminality is higher among non-white and poor communities. I believe this is also statistically correct.

What then is the solution? Obviously, there is no one solution because there is not just one problem. All American citizens need to be confident that our justice system is fair, evenhanded for all. That is not the case in America today and perceptions must improve if the overall impression that America's system of governance is a good one, a functional one, is to be a commonly held conviction among the people as a whole. Again, solutions must be directed at local situations. Not every police force in the country targets minorities. Some apparently do have a record of bias but not every officer within that force should be tarred with the same brush. Some courts appear to have a bias, others don't. At the local level, everyone has a responsibility to bring fairness to the system – this includes judges, prosecutors, defense attorneys, local government and local civil groups.

For the other underlying, generalized problem – poverty or a community of a lower income class being more susceptible to criminality – the only solution is to raise the standard of living of that community.

There is no immediate solution to either situation, only long-term ones requiring sustained efforts by all. These are worthy goals, ones that a centrist party should be part of without taking intractable positions that will call in question the objectivity of the party. We need to be a strong supporter of fairness in our justice system, but also be fair to all sides as well.

As with so many of the issues I am discussing in this book, to arrive at the best solutions to problems we need experts in those fields to be heavily engaged, motivated to clean up their own professional "backyards". Where there are serious problems in local law enforcement and courts the police officers, judges, attorneys and elected government officials should be the most active, publicly visible as active, in resolving deficiencies. In communities which exhibit a high crime rate attributable in some extent to economic conditions, again all those in an official function plus the community itself should devote maximum efforts to improve conditions. Both efforts need to be concurrent, nonpartisan, nonpolemical to the extent possible. Judicial reforms must first occur at the local level, at the level which citizens encounter first-hand. There are issues which must be addressed at State and national levels, however, it is nonsensical to think that top-down, one-size-fits all reforms imposed upon local jurisdictions will be useful without ordinary citizens concurring in those reforms. A centrist party can be an "honest broker" between the two major parties in de-politicizing initiatives to restore confidence in our legal system.

Incarceration

The United States – "land of the free and home of the brave" – has more citizens in in jail and prison than any other country in the world. We have 2.2 million citizens incarcerated in federal and State prisons and county jails. China, our closest competitor with four times our population has 1.7 million of its people behind bars. The United States has 4,575 prisons, excluding county jails. Russia has one-fourth our number of prisons.

Approximately 25 million Americans, now out of prison, are ex-felons. About one in three Americans in their lifetime will be arrested by the police and held in some form of confinement – jail or prison, if only for a few hours. Blacks, who represent 15% of the U.S. populations, comprise 40% of the prison population. Veterans represent 20% of the prison population.

Prisons are big business, at a cost to the taxpayer of about 75 billion annually, which does not include overall court and police costs of an additional 150 billion. There is now a large for-profit component to prisons as well – a good number are operated by for-profit private contractors. There are also ancillary for-profit players in the industry as well – for example, one among many, some businesses run prison and jail commissary monopolies where inmates buy commodities at up to four times the cost on the "outside"; some vendors provide the only telephone service option allowed, paid for by family and friends on the "outside" at a dollar a minute.

About 60 percent of those in prison were convicted of nonviolent crimes, most notably drug possession which quadrupled the U.S. prison population after 1980 when the "War on Drugs" was declared.

These statistics should provoke sobering thoughts in all Americans. Actually, these facts should scare the hell out of us! Are we a police state, a prison state, a despotic state? No, of course not. Most Americans just don't know that this situation exists. If they did know, Americans would be outraged.

A new centrist party can play an important part in turning this dreadful situation around. The two major parties aren't doing anything, our representatives in elected State and federal positions are doing nothing. In fact, few, even in the press from both camps, is saying a word. This must change. This is a must-win issue.

The Death Penalty

Over three thousand persons remain on death row in the United States, in the 31 States that retain the death penalty. Forty-one percent are black, 42 percent white. We are the only country in the Western industrialized world that maintains the death penalty. This must change.

Yes, there are very evil human beings who have committed heinous, unspeakable crimes. There are monsters. We Americans have the very important right to insist that under no circumstance will these individuals ever be allowed out amongst us again. But we should not lose our own humanity, our own inherent goodness as people and as Americans. We do not need to commit a barbaric act to punish barbaric acts. We do not have to execute these worst of the worst examples of human beings. We can lock them away and make sure they never come out again.

There is no reliable evidence that the death penalty deters violent crime. Psychopaths/Sociopaths are not deterred – something is so wrong with them that they will do what they do no matter what. We just need to make sure that life imprisonment with absolutely no chance for parole or escape is the only option in what are now death penalty cases.

I wonder sometimes, but have no facts to back them up, that in death penalty cases juries may be less likely to convict if the death penalty is an option but would be readier to convict if life without parole was the maximum sentence.

The Supreme Court has never ruled on the constitutionality of the death penalty, though it has ruled that the court proceedings of certain States on death penalty cases was unconstitutional. I think it's time to resurrect this old debate and seek for the Court to decide once and for all on whether the death penalty is a "cruel and unusual punishment" as worded in the Constitution, or not. I believe ending the death penalty would send a strong signal to our population and the rest of the world that we Americans are an enlightened people, ones who seek to depart from the savagery of past human eras.

The War on Drugs

The War on Drugs, launched by President Nixon in 1971 and supported by every President thereafter regardless of party, has been a disaster and contributed to the incarceration, disenfranchisement, and alienation of millions of Americans. The War on Drugs has not solved the drug problem, rehabilitated the users, reduced the number of dealers, or cut into the massive profits collected by criminal drug organizations.

A new centrist party can be at the forefront on this issue - calling for an official end to this national "war" and calling for practical, humane policies that can be accepted by the majority of Americans. The major parties are too weak-kneed, too concerned for their votes, to take this effort on.

The first step is to take marijuana almost completely out of the picture. There is no credible evidence that marijuana causes criminality or damages health (any more than do the thousands of other foods, chemicals, lifestyle habits of Americans). Marijuana needs to be legalized. Political and society leaders need to realize this is not an issue restricted to a certain set of "criminals". Marijuana is smoked or consumed by young, old, rich, poor, educated or less educated, black, white, Northerners, Southerners, rednecks and intellectuals. Just by legalizing marijuana there will be an immediate reduction in law enforcement activities, court cases, prison populations, and government expenditures at all levels. And a significant reduction in ruined lives and fragmented family structures.

Yes, there should be age limits on marijuana consumption. And restrictions on its use when driving, operating heavy equipment, or holding responsibility for the lives and safety of others. However, beyond that marijuana is not a dangerous drug. It has few documentable negative effects on health, public safety, or societal structure – much less so in fact than alcohol. Has anyone registered the hypocrisy of government - on one side taking draconian measures against marijuana users, while in essence being the biggest drug dealer of all, i.e., with alcohol? Government at all levels brings in large amounts of revenue taxing consumers of alcohol, licensing at high fees the distributors, licensing and taxing the manufacturers and importers. Government should not be doing business with any commodity, including alcohol and maybe, if legal, marijuana.

Hard drugs – heroin and other opiates, amphetamines, "designer" drugs, hallucinogens and others that are either addictive or produce significant loss of mental and/or physical control in the user are a completely different story. Users need to be treated and rehabilitated. This is where government, the medical establishment and civil society can and should join together to help people, individuals. To incarcerate them and criminalize them for their lifetimes is barbaric and must stop. We cannot continue to produce and perpetuate a sub-class of Americans who have lost most hope of achieving an American dream.

I believe those addicted to hard drugs as listed above should be remanded to a lock-down addiction hospital for a year minimum and helped to conquer their addiction – with no criminal record attached. Sound like a prison situation? Absolutely, because addicts have a very difficult chance of getting "clean" on the outside. But prisons only punish, they do not treat or rehabilitate and the criminal record with which ex-addicts exit will haunt them for the rest of their lives.

A word on prescription opiate addiction. Does anyone wonder where the prescription drugs come from? My experience with doctors is that they are very, sometimes overly cautious in prescribing any addictive drug. So, are we talking about a few rogue physicians feeding what is billed as a national epidemic? Or possibly are the pharmaceutical companies grossly negligent in controlling the distribution of opiates, allowing massive amounts to reach the illegal street market? Or are American citizens illegally producing them? Or are foreign entities illegally smuggling them into the United States? I would think our governments at all levels should pin down who the providers, the "dealers", are and direct legal action against them. Put them away, but treat the addicts in a humane, medically responsible manner.

National Security

Intelligence

For the United States to protect itself against enemies "foreign and domestic" it must first know what the threats are, everything possible that can be known about them, then report this information to the Executive and Legislative branches for action. Both diplomacy and military involvement rely on current, accurate and detailed information on our adversaries and their plans. Our federal government has extensive intelligence resources at its disposal, 16 agencies banded together loosely under the cabinet level Office of the Director of National Intelligence. This group of agencies is often referred to as the "Intelligence Community", and includes the Central Intelligence Agency, Defense Intelligence Agency, Federal Bureau of Investigation, National Geospatial-Intelligence Agency, National Reconnaissance Office, National Security Agency/Central Security Service, Department of Energy, Department of Homeland Security, Department of State, Department of the Treasury, Drug Enforcement Agency, U.S. Air Force, U.S. Army, U.S. Coast Guard, U.S Marine Corps, U.S. Navy. I think it fair to call these agencies the "power group" of the U.S. government, dealing with the most critical security issues and wielding the most authority.

I have worked with most of these agencies in some fashion or another and hold them in high esteem as institutions as well as admire the dedicated men and women who serve in them, their actions and achievements often unknown and unheralded by the American people due to the secrecy that necessarily surrounds them. A new centrist party should openly recognize the importance of the Intelligence Community at large.

That said, this centrist party should also step forward and seek an analysis of how the intelligence function can be improved. I think an evaluation of the 17 agencies, their individual functions, and how they interact and coordinate with each other, plus how the Office of the Director of National Intelligence coordinates and uses the gathered intelligence, is merited. It would be rash to call for elimination or combination of agencies, reductions in personnel or budgets. Without expert evaluation of how these agencies are meeting current needs, we cannot assess what changes, if any, are warranted. However, we would be negligent not to undertake an intensive look at how the entire Intelligence Community performs as a group and as individual parts. A centrist party should openly express unequivocal support for the intelligence agencies, but also demand oversight by the highest levels of government of this function; for one to ensure they provide what we as a country need, but also to ensure they do not overstep their bounds and infringe on freedoms and liberties of the American people. We, as individual citizens, cannot be the overseers due to the secrecy and sensitivities involved. But we should expect our most senior leadership – President, Congress and Supreme Court – to pay close attention to the functions of this group.

Diplomacy

"The supreme art of war is to subdue the enemy without fighting"

Sun Tzu, The Art of War

"Diplomacy is the art of telling people to go to hell in such a way that they ask for directions"

Winston S. Churchill

"When you have them by the balls, their hearts and minds will follow"

President Theodore Roosevelt

At the time of the drafting of the Constitution, diplomacy was considered to be one of the most essential responsibilities of the federal government. Thus, the Department of State was created as the most senior of the Executive departments and throughout our history has drawn in as Secretary some of the most illustrious statesmen of the times country. Diplomatic historians and other experts on American history understandably have varying opinions on which of the 69 Secretaries of State in our history were the most influential. Here I've combined two quite different lists, one ranked by conservatives the other by liberal historians, of Secretaries considered among our top ten best. Several made both lists, so are repeated below in different positions. Two, Henry Kissinger and John Hay, were ranked identically on both lists. All of the Secretaries listed represent some of our finest minds and public servants, ones who shaped our history.

1. George C. Marshall, who served under President Harry Truman from 1947-1949.
   John Quincy Adams, who served under President James Monroe from 1817-1825.

2. Thomas Jefferson, under President George Washington from 1790-1793.
   William H. Seward, under Presidents Abraham Lincoln and Andrew Johnson from 1861-1869.

3. John Quincy Adams, under President James Monroe from 1817-1825.

Hamilton Fish, under President Ulysses S. Grant from 1869-1877.

4. William H. Seward, under President Abraham Lincoln and Andrew Johnson from 1861-1869.
   Charles Evans Hughes, who served Presidents Harding and Coolidge from 1869-1877.

5. James Madison, under Thomas Jefferson from 1801-1809.
   George C. Marshall, serving President Harry Truman from 1947-1949.

6. James Monroe, serving President James Madison from 1811-1817.
   Dean Acheson, under President Harry Truman from 1949-1953.

7. Henry Kissinger, serving Presidents Richard Nixon and Gerald Ford from 1973-1977.

8. James Baker, serving President George H. W. Bush from 1989-1992.
   Daniel Webster, under Presidents William Harrison, John Tyler, 1841-1843, and Millard Fillmore from 1850-1852.

9. George P. Shultz, under President Ronald Reagan 1982-1989.
   Thomas Jefferson, under President George Washington 1790-1793.

10. John Hay, under Presidents William McKinley and Theodore Roosevelt 1898-1905.

What I am trying to illustrate here is that the Department of State, since the early days of the Union, was and still should be considered the most senior department. It is also the 11th smallest of the 17 Departments with 19,000 employees compared to the largest, the Department of Defense with over 600,000 civilians (not including military). What most people do not realize is that the Department of State is comprised of two services – the Civil Service who serve in Washington and are generally subject and area specialists, and the Foreign Service, generalists, who serve overseas at embassies but with periodic assignments to Washington as well. The Foreign Service is a commissioned service, much as the military has its commissioned officers.

The distinction is that Foreign Service Officers (FSOs) are the only true diplomats, commissioned by the President and confirmed by the Senate, while military officers are commissioned by the Secretary of Defense and approved by the President. These distinctions may seem minor, but the point is that the Foreign Service was designed to be an elite group of the most broadly educated public servants, assigned to conduct U.S. foreign affairs abroad as representatives of the President. Only about one percent of the 20,000 candidates who applied I when I did, were able to pass the extensive written and verbal examinations, plus the strict security and medical standards. Only a small number of FSO's reach the senior Foreign Service, the military general/admiral equivalent ranks. Only a small number of the senior diplomats become an Ambassador. Technically, an Ambassador is the personal representative of the President and as such outranks all American officials in his/her country of assignment – including the Vice President though I do believe an Ambassador would not want to push that one too far!

Sadly, the diplomatic role of the Foreign Service has eroded over the past five decades – basically since the Kennedy years. The State Department often comes into direct confrontation with Presidents and White House administrations on foreign policy, and thus there has been a tendency for Presidents to distrust State; thus, the pattern of Presidents appointing a high number of political appointees to the senior positions, both in Washington and overseas as Ambassadors.

Another factor contributing to erosion of State's role in national foreign policy has been the significant augmentation of representatives from other Executive departments serving tours at embassies overseas – Department of Defense, Department of Commerce, FBI, and others particularly at larger embassies. Each of the other Department representatives has its own reporting channels back to their home offices in Washington, and quite often these other Departments, each with its separate reporting channels to the White House, will present viewpoints different from those of the career diplomatic service. One might think that such diversity in opinion on foreign policy is constructive, but again pointing to the exceptional qualifications of career FSO's let me illustrate the problem with an old Foreign Service joke.

An Ambassador and an Admiral were both approaching retirement and discussing what they would like to do afterwards. The Admiral said he was thinking of becoming an Ambassador. The Ambassador said he was thinking of commanding an aircraft carrier. The Admiral protested saying the Ambassador couldn't do that because he wasn't qualified! While funny, this does illustrate the view held by many, including senior officials in the White House, Congress, in other Executive departments, and among the wider American public that the Department of State is just a bunch of cookie pushers wearing striped pants (diplomats did have a uniform up until the early 1900's) or clerks and jerks (a reference to State Department support staff having swelled enormously to handle embassy operations overseas).

Not all so long ago, the major media gave much more credence to the observations of senior diplomats on subjects drawing national attention. Ambassadors and senior Washington-based officials such as Under Secretaries and Assistant Secretaries were regularly interviewed on Foreign Affairs issues on which they had extensive knowledge. Today, the media does not even cover the State daily press briefing, once a staple of reporting on Washington.

To the best of my knowledge no political party, major or small, has included in its platform a strong affirmation of the necessity for a strong Department of State. In other words, diplomacy is not a major interest for these parties. A third party should step into this vacuum and call for a reinvigoration of State as the lead player in Foreign Affairs. The party should call for a close look at embassy operations, possibly trimming down the size of our embassies abroad with a reduction in presence of representatives from other agencies and of State support staff. It should call for virtually eliminating the practice of political appointees filling a high percentage of Ambassadorships and senior Washington positions. The career diplomats should be permitted to perform the function to which they were chosen, managing the Foreign Affairs of the United States. In my experience, the career personnel of the State Department -both Civil and Foreign Service – are the most talented, skilled, intrepid and often brave group of people I know. And they are being overlooked and ignored, to the considerable detriment of our national goals in the international arena.

It is worth noting that senior military officers are some of the strongest supporters of robust diplomacy, and first to lament when it proves lacking. Many in the general public, often mostly those who support a "progressive" i.e. Democratic agenda, think of senior officers, the generals and admirals, as being warmongers, sabre rattlers. Nothing could be further from the truth. These officers have experienced the horrors of war. They have been bloodied themselves. They have lost their Soldiers, Marines, Sailors and Airmen, many who were the age of their children. Many have followed a family tradition in the military and lost a parent, a sibling, a cousin or a child. While members of the military of all ranks believe in what they do and will fight to their own death to preserve the Union, they do not crave war and conflict. They welcome a strong diplomacy to avoid the terrible destruction of war.

Both diplomats and military do realize however that diplomacy can only be strong when backed by a strong military. These two disciplines are so closely intertwined that, as a nation, we should fully back both. Diplomacy is not a genteel sport, it is serious business that demands the best our country can offer.

Our Military Forces

Each of the major parties, and most of the minor ones spout the mantra that the United States must have a strong military to defend the country against external threats. This is a mandatory inclusion in all party platforms, but to a large extent it is a hollow stance, just a box ticked to appeal to voters. No party is able to articulate what a strong defense or strong military actually means. Generally, the Republican party calls for a strong military needing more military personnel, more equipment and more money but cannot credibly explain why expansion is needed. Generally, the Democratic party also calls for a strong military but with fewer personnel, less equipment and less money, but cannot elaborate on how this can be achieved. The Green Party calls for a 50% across-the-board reduction of military expenditures but presents no backup material on how it thinks this could be accomplished.

A third centrist party needs to extensively examine, relying on an expert team of military and civilian experts, how our national policy on defense for 2018 and beyond can be designed and implemented to serve the country best. We need to confront external threats with such overwhelming force that our victory is certain with minimum loss of American lives. We also must avoid becoming a militaristic society, an international aggressor, or the "policemen of the world". We need to ensure, for the overall health of our domestic economy that our defense budget is as trim as possible and still optimum for the achievement of our military victory if we are faced with conflict anywhere and of any scale.

This is an extremely complex issue and a highly charged political one. Any party that seems weak on defense is likely to lose elections, particularly for President. However, a third party with a policy of promoting a strong defense needs to present credible plans, backed by respected experts, to intelligently direct our policies towards current as well as future needs. The military, both active duty personnel and veterans, need to take the lead in formulating the plans and agenda and there must be broad public support, crossing political party lines. Therefore, it is essential that a third, centrist party attract strong support from the most committed and knowledgeable advocates for a strong defense.

I have a few theories that I would like to offer as starting points for discussion. I know many will see these ideas as a radical departure from past and current analysis of our defense needs, and I full admit they would need expert analysis on whether they could be viable. But, I do hope these points will at least be looked at seriously.

We currently have about 1,308,600 military personnel on active duty – Army, Marines, Navy, Air Force and Coast Guard. We have 455,000 personnel in the Reserves of all branches. We have 356,000 Army and Air Force National Guard units, controlled by the States but deployable by the federal government.

Our United States budget for defense is our largest expenditure – 38% of our discretionary spending. For 2018, the total United States budget for the military is 639 billion. We must find ways to reduce this amount, without diminishing our capabilities.

My belief is that we can reduce the active duty strength of our military by one-third, but then triple our reserve levels, without harming our national preparedness. Here's why. The likelihood of the United States launching invasions overseas with massive land forces has diminished over time. The likelihood of us engaging in sea battles on a large scale is also less likely. Similarly, battles in the air on a large scale are also probably of the past. People will question, quite rightly, how I can state this when we are still immersed in wars in Iraq and Afghanistan, which did require significant troops to take and retain territory and over the years put enormous strains on our active and reserve forces. Here's my rationale.

In Afghanistan our strategy and objectives were sorely deficient. Following the tragic assault on U.S. territory on 9/11/2001, we launched a robust counterattack on the Taliban and Al Qaeda in Afghanistan and almost defeated them. We did not finish the job, diverting our attention and resources to Iraq, allowing Al Qaeda and the Taliban to regroup and regain strength, while we installed a corrupt and incompetent civil government that was incapable of fighting our common enemies. We had to come back in and resume our military efforts to retake and hold territory, while attempting to build up Afghani forces in the hope they would establish control – something that still has not happened.

With Iraq, our invasion was a serious mistake. First it was predicated on the lie that our U.S. national security was in jeopardy, while in fact under Saddam Hussein, terrible as he was, the country was not harboring weapons of mass destruction or Al Qaeda elements that could have been a threat to us. We did not need to launch this war, which still continues, and which actually increased the threat to the United States by: allowing ISIS to form under disbanded Saddam-loyal senior military officers: opening Iraq to increased Iranian influence: increasing instability in the Middle East: and damaging our credibility in world opinion.

It is highly unlikely that the United States will ever enter into a ground war with Russia or China. We all recognize that such a war would be cataclysmic for all concerned, plus our long-established protocols revolving around nuclear deterrence virtually ensure that neither we nor they would risk direct conflict.

Today, Iran and North Korea are possibly our only serious threats, but are they the kind of threat that would require us to launch a massive ground attack and then maintain a large force in place for an extended period? I do not believe so. The threat to the United States and "free world" from these countries is largely due to their quest for nuclear weapons capabilities. This is a very real threat, one that we and our allies, plus Russia and China, will work on together to quell through diplomatic and economic means. Of course, all of us will be able to back our efforts up with force, which is something both Iran and North Korea do understand. But the United States does not need a large active standing force to present a deterrence. A more robust and prepared reserve force would be just as potent, as I will elaborate on later.

The United States is most likely to face threats of a smaller scale – local wars, for example in the Middle East or Asia, in which our allies are affected but not us per se. In other words, we will have strategic interests in maintaining stability in certain regions but would not be under direct threat on our own territory. This is an important distinction, one that should always be factored in when our government makes decisions regarding intervention overseas. We do not always need to intervene. A moderate degree of isolationism is warranted. We should expect our allies, such as those in the

Middle East, to address their own regional problems. Why should we spill our blood and spend our money on their security when they will not? In addition, why does the United States have to bear the burden of global security alone? We should expect all the countries of the world to bear a fair share of that burden. This is one of the most important justifications for a strong U.S. diplomacy.

Our active duty forces should be reformulated to address the conflicts that we are most likely to face in the future. In my mind this means relying on light infantry forces that are designed to go into a battle zone quickly, squash the threat, then withdraw. I would maintain the Marine Corps at full strength and also units such as the Army's 82nd Airborne and 101st Air Assault divisions. Potent specialty units like the Army Rangers, Marine Force Recon and Navy Seals would be significantly increased in size. Heavy infantry divisions, tank divisions and other units that are designed for massive land assaults and occupying territory would be reduced in strength as active units but moved over in greater strength to the reserve forces.

The Reserves in turn would be significantly strengthened both in terms of personnel and equipment, but also in terms of experience of personnel. All reserve personnel will have served a full term of service in the active forces prior to being transferred to reserve status. How would this work? Currently, personnel are able to enlist or be commissioned as reservists without serving on active duty, and active duty personnel have the option after their required term is complete, of serving in the active reserves or not. My concept is that whether enlisted or officer, military personnel will first serve active duty - for a two year standard period in peacetime, then be transferred for another four-year term to the active reserves. The minimum term of service would therefore be six years, in whatever combination of active and reserve service is provided by the individual, i.e. a soldier could serve all six years on active duty, or four years active then two reserves. This would be an "up or out" system, in which serving additional years beyond the two-year standard would be based on achieving rank, so of course a full military career would remain an option just as today.

This system is a departure from the current one, however not, I believe, to the detriment of either active or reserve service. It would make career service more elite; and it would bring more concentrated current experience into the reserves. And if reserve units were co-located with the active units, joint training, equipment maintenance, and reserve readiness would be enhanced.

Both the active and reserve forces should rely more heavily on an up or out system to ensure flow through of personnel and ensuring that our military personnel are younger, maintaining their strengths and skills. There should be no assurance that once in service a full career in the military, active or reserve, is assured. Here are several examples to illustrate this point. An eighteen-year-old enlists as an Army private and after two years on active duty has become a private first class (PFC). He/she wants to reenlist and pursue a full career. However, he/she will need to move up, based on merit, to an available corporal position to continue on active duty; if not permitted to continue in active status he/she is transferred to reserve status for the remaining four-year obligation. Here again, if he/she wants to continue on in the reserves after the six-year total service cap, the service would make the decision on whether a slot was available at the next grade and whether the person was the best choice within the pool of eligible applicants. It may sound harsh, possibly denying dedicated military personnel a full career either active or reserve, however military service should be just that – service to the country, something given freely and with pride. There should be no promise of or entitlement to a career.

Reducing the size of the active forces and increasing the size of the reserves should produce cost savings. Reservists currently serve one weekend a month and a full month during the summer. If active duty personnel are reduced by one-third there will be significant decrease in salaries, benefits, pensions and support costs. In addition, there will be a proportional reduction in equipment and maintenance costs. How much cost savings there would be, if any, would require some skilled accountancy, far beyond the scope of this book or my qualifications. This is an area that requires the study and insights of many experts and leaders. It will be vitally important that the military concur with whatever plans are considered.

I would propose that the reserves and the national guard be combined into one, possibly renamed as the militia specific to each State, i.e. the Virginia Militia, California Militia etc. to conform to the terminology used in the Constitution and following constitutional guidelines. This could help augment state pride and instill a bit more patriotism at "grassroots" levels.

National Service

"My fellow Americans, ask not what your country can do for you, ask what you can do for your country."

John F. Kennedy

"Every day, people serve their neighbors and our nation in many different ways, from helping a child learn and easing the loneliness of those without a family to defending our freedom overseas. It is in this spirit of dedication to others and to our country that I believe service should be broadly and deeply encouraged."

John McCain

"Service to others is the rent you pay for your room here on earth."

Muhammad Ali

"I wish to be useful, and every kind of service necessary to the public good becomes honorable by being necessary."

Nathan Hale

"People of different faiths, like yours and mine, sometimes wonder where we can meet in common purpose, when there are so many differences in creed and theology. Surely the answer is that we can meet in service, in shared moral convictions about our nation stemming from a common worldview."

Mitt Romney

"If the great American people will only keep their temper, on both sides of the line, the troubles will come to an end, and the question which now distracts the country will be settled just as surely as all other difficulties of like character which have originated in this government have been adjusted."

Abraham Lincoln

The Active Duty Military

One thing is clear. No greater national service can be performed by American citizens than undertaking military service. We owe those currently serving and those who once served our deepest respect, gratitude and unwavering support. We the people should insist on this basic ethic being a strong component of our national program, one put in action by our representatives at all levels of government. Our military members and veterans should always know that they have their country behind them, be proud to serve. We all should be very proud of them.

The Framers of the Constitution were deeply divided on the issue of whether to permit maintenance of a standing army. On one side were those who feared that a permanent army could either assume power on its own and dominate and repress the people; or that a powerful Executive, as Commander in Chief could use the army to establish a dictatorship. On the other side were those who felt a standing army was essential for preparedness against foreign foes who could threaten the new Republic. Both camps had valid points so thus the Constitution remains vague on this point; neither expressly prohibiting or permitting the maintenance of a permanent military force.

Our history has proven that we have no fears on the first count; our military has always without exception proven its unwavering loyalty to the Constitution and served the United States with distinction and honor. On the second count, those who felt a standing military was essential have been proven correct on numerous occasions when our national security was threatened, and an immediate defense was crucial: the War of 1812, WWI, WW2, the Korean War, and our response in Afghanistan following the 9/11 attack on our soil stand out as examples. Our involvement in other conflicts is more difficult to argue: the Mexican-American War, the Spanish American War and the Iraq War were prosecuted on false pretenses – essentially staged by presidencies with expansionist or political ambitions. The Vietnam War, in retrospect, may actually have been initiated for valid reasons – halting the spread of authoritarian communist states; however, this was a war that deeply divided our country, with so much American blood shed over so many years, that only history will possibly decide on whether it was justified. None of these examples in any way reflect negatively on our military – but in some cases they do bring into question the integrity of their civilian leadership. But, this prelude is not the point.

The question I do want to raise is whether our political and military strategies as relate to our military match our real security requirements for 2018 and beyond. I submit that for one we should not shed American "blood and treasure" on military adventurism in foreign countries. Our military actions should only be directed against real threats to our national security; and while sometimes "the best defense is a good offense" we should be very careful in assessing when we must defend ourselves against a threat. Thus, I strongly support the Constitutional mandate of only the Congress declaring war, with the President pursuing its conduct as Commander in Chief.

It is quite possible that we could re-orient our thinking on the disposition of our military forces, as warranted by current and future external threats. There are three basic components to war; neutralize the capabilities of the enemy, take territory, and hold territory; in that order. We do not necessarily have to proceed through all three steps in every conflict. Possibly in this day and age, given a relatively small set of countries who pose a real threat, we could possibly focus the mission of our active forces differently, re-forming the active forces into lighter, mobile, special operations-type units, while relying on substantially augmented reserve forces for the massive, but ponderous and costly, firepower of heavy divisions – infantry, artillery, armor etc.

I think a fresh look at our defense needs is warranted, both in terms of threats and our capabilities to withstand them. I believe we need to look closely and consider reducing the semi-permanent U.S. military presence overseas in regions such as Europe, Korea, and many other regions where our military have been staged for over half a century, largely as a deterrent to the expansion of communism. The Cold War is over, our defense needs have changed. Does an extensive American military presence around the world really best serve our defense needs today? We need to look at this as well as many other factors regarding how and when our military is deployed.

A centrist third party, with a strong pro-military stance, could perform a real national service in bringing the best analytical minds together to offer the American people real solutions as opposed to the current emotional, venal and sometimes craven hyperbole of the two major parties.

The Reserves

I have previously proposed a reduction of active forces and a significant increase in our reserve strength. I could see a ratio of one to two as a possibility; one million active and two million reserves. This would be workable in terms of intake and outflow if two years were served active and four years in reserve status. As I frequently qualify, any such changes would require extensive study, input and agreement by the military, intelligence, diplomatic, academic and political entities who have a comprehensive understanding of these matters. However, if we were to change our outlook on our actual defense needs and parameters for intervention outside our borders our active forces would be less engaged, but a significantly stronger reserve component would be operationally ready to provide the "overwhelming force" to back up the active military.

I could see combining the reserves and national guard into one, with all active military branches represented; in essence having State "militias", citizen-soldiers who return from active duty to their homes and complete their service within their State. I would emphasize the role of the States in managing the reserves, understanding that the President would still remain Commander in Chief over them. State pride in their reserves should be fostered; I could even see each State calling their reserve units by State names – New York Militia, Virginia Militia etc.; possibly with a shoulder patch carrying that name.

As is the case now, reservists would belong to the "grassroots" and as such be influential at the community level; but with much larger numbers of reservists their visibility and potential for positive influence on the civilian population would be greater. Reservists would, in a way, be "ambassadors" of national service; the point being to increase the sensitivity of our citizens to our common responsibilities in preserving our United States and thus increasing their support.

Civilian Government

It saddens me that so many Americans in the private sector view government employees at local, state or federal levels, as overpaid, underworked, and uncaring. In my own 25-year experience at the federal level, during which I had ample dealings with state and local levels as well, I found that the great majority of government workers, from county clerk to state official to Secretary in the Presidential cabinet, are of the highest caliber – hardworking, dedicated, patriotic and caring deeply about the issues they work and the citizens they serve. So why this general antipathy and even hostility towards government employees? I think there are two principle reasons: (1) there are "bad apples in every barrel", and at whatever level these ones draw the most attention and all the "good apples" are unfairly tainted along with them; (2) the excessive intrusion of government into our personal lives – overregulated, over-legislated, over-lawed, over enforced, over-taxed. These can all be corrected through our electoral process and through increased vigilance and activism by our citizens. Good governance is for the people, but it is a team sport and everyone must participate.

I do not want to get into too much detail here but beg the reader to consider carefully that our career civil servants at all levels of government are an integral part to our national security. Prominent leaders, with their successes or foibles, get our attention, but it is really the rank and file government employees who keep our vast government structures maintained and running day by day, year by year, from one administration to the next. They should be well-paid, supported and respected for their service.

Infrastructure and Emergency Management, a new "WPA"

The Works Progress Administration (WPA; renamed in 1939 as the Work Projects Administration) was the largest and most ambitious American New Deal Agency employing millions of people (mostly unskilled men) to carry out public works projects, including the construction of public buildings and roads. In a much smaller project, Federal Project Number One, the WPA employed musicians, artists, writers, actors and directors in large arts, drama, media, and literacy projects.

Almost every community in the United States had a new park, bridge or school constructed by the agency. The WPA's initial appropriation in 1935 was for $4.9 billion (about 6.7 percent of the 1935 GDP).

The WPA provided jobs and income to the unemployed during the Great Depression. At its peak in 1938, it provided paid jobs for three million unemployed men and women, as well as youth in a separate division, the National Youth Administration. Between 1935 and 1943, when the agency was disbanded, the WPA employed 8.5 million people. Most people who needed a job were eligible for employment in some capacity.

Extracted from Wikipedia

The WPA of the Depression Era was one of the most successful national programs the United States undertook to both provide employment and to build new infrastructure. I think a close look is needed to see if a modified up-to-date WPA-like program could be developed that would be cost effective, replace many welfare programs, develop skills of participants, build or repair infrastructure that is currently needed and stimulate broader awareness and discussion on the national level of our infrastructure needs. It could conceivably also reinvigorate a sense of national service and patriotism, particularly among the young.

I would model a new "WPA" on a military-type structure, minus the combat and fighting components of the military, but including the discipline and teamwork emphasis of a structured environment. There would be shared barracks, "mess halls", group training, group transportation to work sites etc. To include participants who are constrained from physically demanding work there would be administrative functions, facilities maintenance work, childcare operations, food preparation and other essential positions. With childcare facilities, there would be realistic opportunities for single parents to serve as well.

This again would be a national service program – not some sort of Marxist-Leninist "rehabilitation", social re-engineering program. This would be an initiative providing real though modestly paid employment serving real national needs. Welfare programs would be reduced, national costs for infrastructure rebuilding would be reduced, participants would receive training and experience that would have value in the future and have a chance to contribute to their country.

Beyond the immeasurable contribution of our service members in providing for the defense needs of the country, there have been many other positive benefits of military service in a social context. One has been the intermingling of people from different regions of the country, mixing of races, religions, political leanings under the common umbrella of national identity. People in the military have no option but to work as a team with others who are very different. Such a process tends to reduce bias and build commonality. I would strive to create a similar atmosphere in a civilian national service. Participants would most likely not be assigned to their home community but serve outside their State in some other area of the country. This operational philosophy would serve to break down barriers between people, but also focus participants on their national service obligation rather than be still enmeshed in their familiar social and financial structures.

Again, this would not be a leftist/socialist program. It would be a civilian "army" serving real national needs, funded by returns of federal tax collections to the States. Some will say such a program would be too costly. Not if done right. Eligibility for welfare would be tightened up significantly. No longer would able-bodied people be able to receive welfare payments, food stamps, free healthcare coverage so readily. Those in need, if capable, would be offered the choice of entry into the "WPA" program or receive no

151

government assistance. No more "free money". Welfare costs for the federal government and State and local offices, would be reduced if this program is planned and administered properly. Costs for infrastructure rebuilding would also be reduced. Essentially, the participants would be providing unskilled, semi-skilled and skilled labor at pay levels somewhat lower than that of a military private (to recognize the additional risk faced by the military) and without the additional cost of annual pay increases and promotions. State managed programs are one option, but, in addition, private construction firms, who most likely would receive the contracts for State infrastructure projects, would be able to hire "WPA" participants from the state-managed program at a lower cost than commercial salary rates, savings which would reduce the overall cost to the State for the project.

Those on our political left need to realize that those on the right, even moderate conservatives, object to capable people who are able to work, receiving "free money" so readily and making little effort to work for their living. Those on our political right must also be realistic and accept that there are American citizens who are disadvantaged and need help from the greater American community, plus are anxious to work. The aim of national civilian services should be to provide real work, honorable work for national needs.

Participants would receive a basic salary, lodging, healthcare. They would serve a two-year active term of service and four years of active reserve service on the military model. They would be eligible for "GI Bill" type benefits upon completion of their term – four years of university or trade school education at the State rate and 100% government-backed mortgage financing. They would depart with on-the-job training experience, an employment record, and hopefully with a sense of pride in service and the respect of the public.

Conservation, a new "CCC"

The Civilian Conservation Corps (CCC) was a public work relief program that operated from 1933 to 1942 in the United States for unemployed, unmarried men. Originally for young men ages 18–25, it was eventually expanded to ages 17–28. The CCC provided unskilled manual labor jobs related to the conservation and development of rural lands owned by federal, state, and local governments. The CCC was designed to provide jobs for young men and to relieve families who had difficulty finding jobs during the Great Depression. Maximum enrollment at any one time was 300,000. Through the course of its nine years in operation, 3 million young men participated in the CCC, which provided them with shelter, clothing, and food, together with a wage of $30 (about $570 in 2017) per month

The CCC also led to a greater public awareness and appreciation of the outdoors and the nation's natural resources, and the continued need for a carefully planned, comprehensive national program for the protection and development of natural resources.

Enrollees of the CCC planted nearly 3 billion trees to help reforest America; constructed trails, lodges, and related facilities in more than 800 parks nationwide; and upgraded most state parks, updated forest fire fighting methods, and built a network of service buildings and public roadways in remote areas.

Extracted from Wikipedia

Again, in the spirit of national service, I think a look at recreating a "CCC" has a great deal of merit. Many Americans are passionate about conservation and ecology, but opposition comes from many corners of the country, primarily because of economics – fear of losing "jobs" in important employment sectors as well as concerns of increasing the federal budget and deficit.

A new "CCC" could be a partial solution if planned well. It would provide jobs for the young, recent high school or college graduates who often have problems finding employment or are uncertain of what career path to follow. It could also bring significant improvements in areas where our natural environment is being degraded by overdevelopment and overpopulation. Young people would be salaried – at a lower level than a private in the military to reflect the lesser risk, provided food and shelter, and earn "GI Bill" equivalent benefits. They would gain experience translatable to improved employability.

I would operate a new "CCC" on a military-like model – shared lodging, common dining halls, and training all under an atmosphere of discipline and control. Obviously, there would not be military-type training – firearms, fighting skills etc. – but this would not be a country club. Those who signed on would be obligated to fulfill their contract for two years active duty and four years active reserves, just like the military.

As I have suggested for other programs, a new "CCC" would be funded by returns of federal tax revenues to the States. The federal government would not create a huge new agency to administer the program. Hopefully, State governments would be frugal and direct the majority of resources to conservation programs that were of particular concern in the State. This would be a serious program, not just one to employ young people, but one that would actually accomplish objectives in conservation that hopefully would also increase public awareness and attract wider support for initiatives in protecting the environment.

A Medical Service Corps

Healthcare is at present one of the most divisive issues in the United States, as perceived from the respective vantage points of the two major parties. As expressed earlier, extensive reforms are needed to reduce the for-profit element within the current corporate triumvirate of hospitals and other providers, health insurance companies and pharmaceutical manufacturers. Establishing nonprofit systems in these industries would be an important step towards ensuring that all Americans have access to affordable healthcare, but it is likely to be a very slow effort that will require commitment and compromise among all the players, including government. However, steps to provide healthcare to those who are currently under-served due to the cost requires immediate attention on solely ethical grounds. A centrist third party could serve a useful purpose as a mediator in the discussion.

Many people are calling for an expansion of Medicare to cover all those who cannot afford health insurance. Just as many people object to Medicare expansion on the basis that entitlements in the federal government budget already consume an unhealthy percentage of expenditures. My personal view is that we need to devise a long-term plan to extract ourselves from Medicare, but not precipitously. We need to improve healthcare delivery to those who really need it, while freeing up the government budget from Medicare and Medicaid entitlements.

One idea that could serve as a constructive measure, a temporary one initially to gauge its impact and viability, would be to create a Medical Services Corps, in the spirit of national service. Such a Corps would be comprised of newly graduated or credentialed medical personnel in all the specialties who would serve for a four-term providing quality healthcare to those who currently have limited or no access. New, presumably younger, medical personnel would be provided a professional, entry-level salary (civil service equivalent) for their tour of service. At the end of their term, they would also be reimbursed for up to four years of their medical education at state university rates. In addition, they would be eligible for "GI Bill" type benefits such as 100% financed mortgages and possibly, as an additional incentive, low-cost loans for establishing their own practice. They would also gain considerable experience over their four-year terms, experience that should translate into more opportunities for them when they enter private practice.

Young doctors, nurses, technicians and other medical professionals might well find such an idea attractive, given that many exit school with huge student loans and by necessity seek the highest paying positions and specialties in order to get on firmer financial ground.

Such a Corps would be funded by the federal government via return of tax revenues to the States. However, management of the program would be under State and local governments in order to tailor the program to immediate needs of their communities. There is no one-size-fits-all answer to healthcare and the federal government should not be expected to develop one. However, establishing a national entity such as a Medical Service Corps is certainly within the federal purview – just as were creation of the Peace Corps and VISTA. This idea merits further study.

A Legal Service Corps

Another volunteer national service that may have considerable merit is to create a legal service corps that would provide legal services free of charge in certain situations to those Americans financially unable to engage private legal counsel. Again, this would pertain to certain critical situations only, most notably providing legal defense to those accused of crimes. Currently, as derived from the Constitution, every court is required to appoint a Public Defender to represent defendants in criminal cases when the person is unable to afford a private attorney. All private attorneys registered with a court as defense attorneys are required to serve as Public Defenders, at minimum reimbursement by the court. They serve at the discretion of the court, being appointed from a rotating list of attorneys when defendants in need are charged with a crime.

While it is a tribute to the American legal system that we entitle all defendants to legal representation regardless of financial standing, the Public Defender system is imperfect. Public Defenders are first and foremost private attorneys whose livelihood is based on private clients who pay their full fees. While most Public Defenders take their civic responsibility very seriously, it is understandable from the human perspective that they do not always provide non-paying clients as much attention as they would someone who pays. For someone charged with a crime and taking the Public Defender option for defense, the situation may be uncomfortable. Pending trial, whether incarcerated or not, the defendant may not see their Public Defender for days after being charged and may only see him/her several times before the trial. It is problematic whether the Public Defender would go the extra mile for a nonpaying client in terms of research, providing witnesses supportive of the defense, providing expert witnesses etc. particularly when extra non-reimbursable expense is involved. The bottom line is that there is often a considerable discrepancy between the quality of legal services offered to a poor defendant versus that provided to a person who can afford the high cost of private legal counsel.

My proposal is that a Legal Services Corps be formed, comprised of newly graduated attorneys who volunteer to provide Public Defender services at a basic salary level equivalent to that of other professional entry-level staff in government service. In addition, and this would be the kicker, those attorneys who agreed to a fixed four-year term of service would receive reimbursement of their law school tuition, at State university rates, plus any loan interest charges, upon completion of his/her service.

Why might a newly graduated attorney consider such an option? I believe many attorneys are orientated to a public service career in law, not just seeking a high income. A scenario such as I just described in which they receive an acceptable salary, have their tuition repaid thus cancelling out student loans, and build up considerable experience in defense law applicable to a future career in private law has a lot to offer.

Such a Legal Services Corps would provide the same quality of legal defense to poor individuals as rich persons receive through private attorneys. This would go a long way towards negating the public impression, often true, that our justice system caters to the rich and penalizes the poor. We need to do all possible to establish in fact that our American justice system is fair-handed to all citizens regardless of social standing.

A Legal Services Corps should be administered by the State, though funded by the federal government, possibly through return of federal tax revenue as earlier suggested.

Constitutional Issues

The Constitution: Originalism vs. Non-Originalism

Constitutional law – its interpretation and implementation – is an extremely difficult subject for most Americans, like myself, to grasp and remains for the most part the technical domain of the our most elite jurists. That said, most ordinary Americans are conscious that our Constitution is the legal foundation for this Nation and as such is of utmost importance to contemporary issues of governance and society.

So much has been written on this over the course of our history. All I can do here is to mention that a great divide exists today on how the Constitution should be viewed and this divide roughly mirrors our division into broad opposing camps of conservatives and liberals.

Originalism is the more conservative viewpoint – in brief, placing great weight in the actual wording of the Constitution and when in doubt, due to the passage of more than 200 years since it was drafted, seeking to interpret the intent and/or meaning of a passage as related to today's times. In other words, what would the Framers have said on a particular issue if they were here today? Originalists tend to be reluctant to add amendments to the Constitution and resist what they see as loose but precedent-setting interpretations of Constitutional law in decisions by the courts. Originalists tend to oppose increasing the authorities of the federal government and support strong states-rights agendas.

In contrast, non-originalism takes the viewpoint that the Constitution as written, while important, does not reflect the circumstances and realities of today and thus must be broadly and frequently re-interpreted to serve our needs as we change as a country over time. Juridical activism is viewed as a positive effort to keep the Constitution relevant in modern times. Citizens who would self-identify as liberals would most likely side with this view and support more intensive federal government involvement, through the courts, in key issues, particularly those involving civil rights. Non-originalism places great emphasis on legal precedent.

However, many ordinary citizens - mostly on the 'right" but also in the "middle" are feeling that "rule of law", which they firmly support, actually means rule by lawyers, which they reject. They couldn't care less about originalist vs. non-originalist highbrow squabbling. Many feel their Constitution has been taken from them, is no longer accessible to them; is somewhere buried in the mass of law books and precedents managed by the elite class.

For the purposes of this book, I only want to highlight this – the role which the Constitution plays in our Nation today is a huge issue. At one extreme, we have those who believe that the Constitution, as written, is inviolate and must be taken literally with no further interpretation. On the other extreme are those who feel the Constitution is anachronistic – a quaint antique – and therefore must be loosely interpreted to reflect the changing views of our citizens as they evolve.

I believe there is a very solid middle ground between these poles, one which holds the Constitution in the highest esteem – with reverence even – while recognizing that cautious, but modern interpretations are essential. Because so much of today's disagreements on the Constitution are drawn along political party lines, a third party could be helpful in raising this important issue to a higher and more reasonable level of dialogue.

Perhaps it is time for a new Constitutional Convention; not to change the Constitution but to produce an updated, understandable consensus interpretation in which ordinary Americans can find renewed inspiration.

Representation and the Electoral Process

"There is a peculiarity in the federal Constitution which ensures a watchful attention in our majority both of the people and of their representatives to a constitutional augmentation of the latter. This peculiarity lies in this, that one branch of the legislature is a representation of citizens, the other of the States."

Federalist Paper No. 58 (Madison)

We would do well to carefully reflect on the words above. The increasingly strident calls for a popular vote to replace the Electoral College system in the national election does not take into account that we are a very diverse country – geographically, socially, economically, ideologically, ethnically. This is the great beauty and the great challenge of our country. We are divided – thankfully – and we are not a "melting pot". We will always have our amazing collection of different people, different issues, different talents.

The House of Representatives was designed to be as close as possible to the direct voice of the people. The age eligibility is lower, each Congressional District was designed to allow a representative the most contact with those he or she represented. The two-year term was designed to allow the citizens the most opportunity to have their voices heard on particular immediate issues but allow them the opportunity to voice differing views shortly thereafter, in the next election.

In contrast, the Senate was constructed to have the longer-term interests of entire States represented at the national level. Thus, the six-year term and older age requirement. The assumption in our early history and today is that Senators will be the most "enlightened" and seasoned statesmen, a more sober and reflective group as compared to the more "passionate" and youthful Representatives and their constituents. And they represent the States' interests, not the views of the people. An important distinction.

162

The Executive was intended to represent the United States in its entirety – all the people, all the territory. Some of our Presidents have nobly fulfilled that intent. Many have not. A centrist party should make it clear to the American people that any candidate it presents in a Presidential election will serve all the people, all the country, leaving behind partisan interests of party or region, religion or ethnicity. From the very beginning, a centrist party should choose its Presidential nominee wisely. The country wants a President of high stature – in intellect, competency, and ethics. We all want to be proud of our President, inspired, hopeful, and confident.

Popular Vote vs. Rank Order Voting vs. the Electoral College

In recent years there has been a greatly increased push for eliminating the constitutionally mandated Electoral College system and moving to direct popular vote in electing the President. In both the 2000 and 2016 elections, the candidates Al Gore and Hillary Clinton, respectively, won the popular votes but lost the elections because their opponents, George W. Bush and Donald Trump won based on gaining the electoral votes to push them over the 50% threshold. In the view of many, this appears to give Republicans the advantage over Democrats, and to make the majority of the population subject to the minority. Developing on previous points made on the large divide between urban and rural, the Electoral College system also appears to give an advantage to the rural population over the urban.

This one issue was one of the most contentious matters of debate in drafting the Constitution and contributed to a delay of almost nine years in its ratification by all the thirteen original states. The core issue at that time on this matter was whether the most populous states, with the largest urban communities, would dominate the national agenda and control the Presidency and Vice-Presidency of the new United States, thereby effectively reducing the opportunity for the less populous, more rural, and "frontier" states of the time and in the future to hold these offices and to be strongly represented in Congress. The same quandary exists today. How can voters from the rural areas which represent the far larger surface area of the country feel their votes count if urban voters represent the larger portion of the population by several percent? And how can urban voters feel they are competing on an even playing field if rural voters hold an advantage in the Electoral College. Remember that with the electoral college, the number of electors is based on the number of members of Congress per state. The disparity comes mostly in seats held in the Senate as each state holds two seats, whether California, our most populous with about forty million people, or Wyoming, our least populous, with a population of about 600,00.

The current toxic political environment necessitates changes in our electoral system. Amending the Constitution to transition to a strictly popular vote will not solve the problem, and in fact would exacerbate tensions, essentially disenfranchising almost half the population who do not live in or near large metropolis'. Preserving the Electoral College system would be equally divisive as more than half the population would feel, as they do now, that the system is rigged to advantage the minority. Other possible solutions are being vigorously debated and pushed by their separate supporters. None, to me, will fully resolve the issue and give the diversity of voters equal confidence in the fairness of our system. Here are the two principle reforms under discussion for the election of President.

One suggestion is to have a runoff system in which the top three contenders on the ballot compete a second time against each other to determine the winner. The advantage is that voters would have a second chance to reconsider their original vote and to be offered the consideration of the candidate with the third highest number of votes. The drawbacks to this system would be that the election would still be weighted to the two current major parties, given the difficulty for other parties to get on the ballot in most states; because runoff elections are less likely to draw as many voters as the first election; because a candidate could still win with the less than 50% of the vote; and because a runoff would add considerably to the cost and time.

Another suggestion that is gathering a good deal of steam at this time is Ranked Choice Voting (RCV). There are several variations of RCV, but here I will outline the most popular versions. How this works is that there would be only one election, but voters would have the opportunity to rank the candidates one, two or three. If on the first run a candidate receives 51% of the vote they win. If no one candidate received over 50 % of the vote, there would be an instant runoff with no actual second election. The last candidate, the one with the lowest number of votes, would be eliminated and the second-place votes of each individual ballot for this candidate would be added to the appropriate other candidates. If no candidate achieves the 50+ % the process would continue by eliminating the next to last candidate, adding the second-place votes to the remaining candidates, with the procedure continuing until a 51% winner is reached. RCV does address two of the concerns about the runoff system – cost and time. However, it really does not break the hold the two major parties have on the vote. All it really does, currently, is allow voters a chance to vote their conscious on the first run but have a second chance to then vote for their preference of the two major parties, one of which is certain to win from the beginning. Without strong third or more parties, which can have a fair chance of benefitting from the bottom up second-place votes, RCV really will not threaten the dominance of the top two, and therefore cannot change the current political dynamic.

Here is an approximation of how RCV might have worked in the 2016 election. The final tallys were this:

Hillary Clinton – 48.02 %

Donald Trump – 45.93 %

Libertarian – 3.27 %

Green – 1.06 %

Write-ins - .84 %

Evan McMullin - .53 %

Other - .33 %

All of the second-place votes lower than those won by the Democratic and Republican parties would have been counted in upwards. As a guess, divide half the "others', write-ins, Evan McMullin (a conservative but anti-Trump) votes among those two parties. Give all of the Green to the Democrats and all of the Libertarian votes to the Republicans. Here would be the final tally:

Trump – 50.04 %

Clinton – 49.94 %

Trump now wins the popular vote, but by a margin of one-tenth of one percent, or about 137,000 votes. Or Clinton could have won by a small margin with a tiny change in the numbers. Not a resounding success for RCV as a real alternative to the current system. With only two major parties, and a multitude of tiny other parties, the tendency of voters will be to just go ahead and vote for the "lesser of two evils" among the two major parties. Under RCV, they might very well give an alternative, minor party a second-place vote, but ultimately the final outcome of the election will not change.

However, RCV can be very effective immediately in the primary elections. Since all the candidates would be of one party, the ranked voting would not between parties but between persons. So, the ranked ordering of votes, with lesser candidates' second place votes being redistributed until one candidate receives over 50%, would give a much more accurate picture of voters' preferences rather than current winner-takes-all systems. In the 2016 Republican primary, with 17 candidates, it is quite likely that someone else other than Donald Trump would have become the party nominee. Trump effectively "divided and conquered". In an RCV primary this would not have happened. Each of the candidates could have remained actively competing until the primary was conducted. In 2016, most candidates withdrew before votes were cast. They didn't really need to withdraw since they remained on the ballot. Funding was an issue for most of them but they could just as easily have announced to their supporters that they could no longer pay for their campaign, but still sought their votes. If this had happened, the final count appointing the party nominee could have been quite different.

However, for the general election, again because of the entrenched two-party system, I do not favor RCV. I believe we need a more extensive, hybrid system encompassing both the runoff and RCV systems, plus other electoral reforms that give third, fourth and fifth parties an opportunity to form and compete on the ballot. If our goal is reform that improves the confidence of the American public in our electoral system, we need to ignore the cost and extra time a new system entails. Consider it the price for having a democratic representative Republic.

The first reforms will need to involve loosening the requirements for third or more parties to be listed on the ballot. These are state-instituted requirements and vary widely by state. States have that authority under the Constitution. I am a firm believer in States' rights and in a minimalist federal government. However, in this case, I believe there should be a uniform set of rules throughout the country to encourage representation on the ballot by parties and candidates other than the two major parties. While I would hope states would take these steps on their own, sooner rather than later, I believe a pan-U.S. change of this magnitude can only be taken at the federal level, in Congress, with consent of the Executive and the Supreme Court. We need more candidates, from more parties, on the ballot.

We need a strong third party. I would not discourage more parties than that, but again the more votes, other than for the two main parties, are divided the less likely any alternative parties will stand a chance. A third party is not something electoral reform can mandate. It must arise from the grassroots, and it must overcome the current obstacles in state electoral blockages to new parties contending with the two major parties.

As mentioned before, a hybrid RCV/runoff system would better reflect the diversity of the voting population and give voters more confidence that their votes count. Plus, it would enable voters to have more flexibility in their votes up until the first election and through subsequent runoffs. Remember that the allegations that surfaced as to Clinton's mishandling of emails and other possible transgressions occurred after the Democratic primary. The investigation into possible collusion with Russia by the Trump campaign came to light after the Republican primary. By then it was too late for disillusioned voters to change their votes to a viable third party. There was no such party. Voters' only choices were to hold their noses and vote for one of the major parties, or not vote, or waste their votes on the very minor alternative parties, or write someone else in.

I think this scenario would be an improvement.

The top two finishers in all party primaries – Democratic, Republican and all third or more parties – would be entered on the ballot for the national election. Individual parties could still promote the candidate that won their primary, but all runners-up would also have a second chance. Look at how this might have impacted at the state level with the special Senate race in Alabama. Alabamians in the majority are conservative and staunchly Republican but were troubled by the allegations about Judge Roy Moore that surfaced after the primary. If his runner-up in the Republican primary, Luther Strange, had remained on the ballot he might very well have won over Democrat Doug Jones, who won by 21,300 votes over Moore. The final results included 22,800 write-ins – most believed to have been protest votes against Moore by voters who might have voted for Strange if he were on the ballot but couldn't bring themselves to vote for a Democrat.

The first ballot in the general election, under my scenario, would thus have a slate of two candidates for each party. If there are ten parties, then twenty candidates would be listed. If one candidate gets over 50% of the vote they win. If not, RCV would then be applied to narrow the slate to the top four candidates from this first vote. A runoff would be held, after a short period – just enough time to "print" new ballots; no write-ins would be allowed at this point. Again, a candidate with over 50% wins, but if no candidate gets to that point RCV would narrow the field to two candidates – again no write-ins. The final vote would be held and one of the two candidates would inevitably receive over 50% of the vote.

While more cumbersome, costly, and time consuming, such a process would allow voters a real choice, and the chance to have their voices heard. Obviously, those whose candidates lose will not be happy. But, no one will be able to say that the election was not fair and that their votes were wasted or not counted. Everyone will have between two and three chances to vote in narrowing selection fields.

Barring a new system such as just outlined, my preference would be to retain the current Electoral College system. It has worked, if imperfectly, for over two hundred years. I would urge States, however, to look closely at dividing electoral votes among candidates who receive a requisite percentage of votes. The current winner-take-all policies of most States blocks both the losing major party delegates as well as any third-party delegates from having a voice within the Electoral College. Essentially as it stands now the Electoral College is just a rubber stamp of the final by-state electoral count.

States have great latitude in deciding the electoral processes in their State, and thus can experiment with new possible systems, then refine them or find another. However, any proposals for new systems that would change the Constitution must be exhaustively explored by all Americans. Virtual unanimity should be sought within Congress, and with the Executive and with the Supreme Court. After all, such a dramatic change would require a constitutional amendment that would need to be ratified by three-quarters, i.e. 38 of our 50 States.

Our "Aboriginal" Population

As Americans, we should be deeply ashamed of our history as it regards the native populations of the United States. We should call it what it was – genocide. We have no statistics on how many natives lived in the continental U.S and Alaska at the time of the influx of European settlers: estimates vary greatly between historians; however, a median estimate of the native population at the time of the landing of Columbus is about 10 million people. An estimate, maybe low maybe not, of the native population in 1900 is about 400,00 people coast-to-coast – decimation of an ethnic group by 96%. If that is not genocide, I don't know what is. But, after a brief and relatively impotent flurry of concern for Native Americans in the 1960/70's very little is said on the national stage regarding the continuing plight of our first Americans.

Today, there are somewhat over three million people who claim to be Native Americans and another two million who claim to be Native mixed with other races. There are 566 tribes recognized by the U.S. government, and 326 government-recognized reservations under the oversight of the Bureau of Indian Affairs. Only about one-third of Native Americans now live on reservations, which have limited self-governance but for which the federal government serves as "trustee". Federal law has precedence over tribal law, but Native Americans do not have representation at the federal level.

Here are some appalling facts. Native Americans have the highest poverty rate of any ethnic group - 25%. Their median household income is half that of the general American population. They have the highest unemployment rate. Only 30% have health insurance. They have the lowest life expectancy rate of any American group, and the highest infant mortality rate. You would think all good, caring Americans would be jumping out of their seats saying "Enough, no more!" But, we hear nothing about the Native American situation from our national candidates from either party. We might get a little snippet of information or a sidebar from national media such as the recent appalling events in which private companies, backed by state law enforcement and with no federal government opposition, brutally squelched

Native American protests against the Dakota pipeline which was to cross their supposedly protected reservation.

It is time for a strong party to take up the banner, raise national awareness, be a defender of Native Americans. We should not allow this shame to continue. Native Americans deserve to have their human conditions addressed. They deserve representation at the federal level with full political rights. They deserve to have their own State, to be our 51st State. They deserve to retain their collective property rights to reservation lands, even under a statehood system, and to preserve their heritage and ethnic identities. Native Americans who do not live on reservations, understandable because of the lack of jobs and the conditions, should be permitted to have official residency on these reservations even though domiciled elsewhere. This could bring the total Native American population, as a political entity, to five million.

Yes, governing a state with territories and populations dispersed over 50 States would be difficult. But could it be any more difficult than management of 326 reservations and an estimated two million people under the Bureau of Indian Affairs? Statehood - full rights, two senators and maybe as many as five House members are fully achievable with the national will behind it. We can never right the wrong done to Native Americans, but we can make things better through concerted national action. We need to treat these, our fellow citizens, with the humanity, love and respect that really are the core principles behind our Declaration of Independence and Constitution. They deserve the same "life, liberty and the pursuit of happiness" that we other Americans hold so dear. We should not let this blight continue of having "aborigines" as part of our national fabric.

Our Colonies

Here in 2018, we are still a colonial power. Two hundred and forty-two years after shedding our own colonial master, we still hold onto colonies we acquired in the late 1800's and following the Spanish-American War. We call them "territories", but they really are colonies with minimal representation in the federal government, and limited rights as compared to States and citizens of those States. For example, the five territories with a continuous resident population each have only a non-voting representation in Congress. American Samoans may naturalize as American citizens only if they come to a U.S. State. No one born in a territory, and officially resident in a territory, can vote in the general election for President, only in the primaries, even though they are American citizens. No one born in a territory, even if receiving citizenship at birth is eligible to be President, as they were not born in one of the States. All this needs to change. There are only three options, as I see it – their independence, incorporation into existing states, or incorporation into a new State.

Here is a list of our territories and their populations.

Puerto Rico – 3.4 million
Guam – 167.4 thousand
U.S. Virgin Islands – 107 thousand
Northern Mariana Islands – 52.2 thousand
American Samoa – 51.5 thousand
Wake Island – 150
Midway Atoll – 40
Palmyra Island – 20
Johnson Atoll, Baker Island, Howland Island, Jarvis Island, Kingman Reef, Navassa Island, Serrinda Bank and Baja Nuevo Bank have no continuous inhabitants.

With a combined population of almost 3.8 million these territories would represent a 52nd State with a population the size of Iowa. Puerto Rico, the largest territory of all, has the best current argument for regularizing status, following Hurricane Maria which devastated the island in 2017. News coverage of the disaster was troubling. Most of the population was without power, access to clean water, without employment and thus without money for food. As I wrote this section six months after the event, almost 500,000 people were still without power; and it appears now, as this book goes to press a year later, that the true death toll was far higher than that announced officially by the federal government. The two other major hurricanes that hit the U.S. just months earlier, in Texas and Florida, brought an impressive flood of federal, state, regional and private response. The response to Puerto Rico was sadly not of the same caliber. It seemed to many Puerto Ricans, and others like myself, that much more could have been done more quickly. In many ways, it seemed like we were treating Puerto Rico like a third-world colony, not as a bona fide part of the United States. Even before this, our national government did not take situations in Puerto Rico, such as its financial crisis and sea transportation problems brought about by the Jones Act, with the same gravity as they would have with the States. There is a certain second-class status attached to Puerto Rico that can only be solved by Statehood, whether alone or combined with the other territories. Puerto Rico has no senators or representatives, only a delegate, a "Resident Commissioner" with limited voting privileges. If a state, just by itself, Puerto Rico would have two senators, and four members in the House. This would go a long way to ensure that Puerto Ricans have the representation in Washington they deserve.

Our Nation's Capital

The District of Columbia, or Washington D.C., was established by the Constitution and stipulated as a ten by ten-mile square including portions of both Maryland and Virginia and divided by the Potomac River. The Virginia portion was ceded back to Virginia shortly after the Capital officially became the seat of U.S. government. The District has one delegate in the House, like Puerto Rico and the other territories, also with only limited voting powers. For decades, residents of the District have been calling for representation and powers equivalent to that of a state. With 704,000 people, the District is more populous than Vermont and Wyoming.

The Washington D.C. metropolitan area is considered to include 22 counties in Virginia and Maryland. While many of the people in these counties do work in the Capital or depend directly or indirectly on Washington for work, not all of these counties are as comprehensively connected with the District as the ones that are "close in". These counties – Arlington, Fairfax, Loudon and Prince William in Virginia and Montgomery and Prince George in Maryland – are so closely tied economically and culturally to the District that it is not so far a stretch to consider them part of the District rather than part of their respective States. The population of these counties, and the independent cities within their borders, is over four million. Combined with the population of the District, these counties contain about five million people, a population that if a state would rank about 23rd among the 50 states.

I cannot speak for Maryland, but for the State of Virginia, Northern Virginia as represented by the counties I listed is no longer considered "real" Virginia. Economically, culturally, socially they are considered part of Washington D.C and part of the "north". Containing about a third of the population of Virginia and consistently voting for the Democratic party, when combined with the votes of other urban areas in Virginia such as Norfolk, Roanoke and Charlottesville they have succeeded in turning the otherwise firmly "Red" State of Virginia, into a "Blue" state. Again, the urban vs. rural divide has surfaced and it is the source of considerable tension here in this State.

The District by itself is racially diverse, about 40 % white (of whom nine percent are Hispanic), 49 % African American, four percent Asian, and the remaining six percent reporting as Native American, mixed race or other. However, Washington D.C.'s suburbs are much less diverse. Fairfax County for example is 79% white (including 16% Hispanic), nine percent Black, 18 percent Asian, and the rest "other". The median income in the District is $70,000, compared with $112,000 in Fairfax County, and $50,000 for Virginia as a whole. While hardly scientific, these income and racial makeup figures should give one pause. There appears, for Virginia anyway, to be a correlation between a higher urban income and voting Democratic and the less affluent rural areas voting Republican.

We are by no means bound constitutionally to the United States being restricted to 50 states. Why not add another that combines the District of Columbia with its contiguous Virginia and Maryland counties?

A 51ˢᵗ Super State

Here is something I think might be really cool. Rather than three new states to enfranchise Native Americans, the territories, and the Capital separately, how about just one 51ˢᵗ State that includes the Native American Nations, the territories, and an expanded District of Columbia. Such a state would have a population of somewhere around 13.3 million, which would make it the fifth largest state by population after California, Texas, New York and Florida. Such a state would be the most ethnically/racially diverse, the most geographically diverse; including Native Americans dispersed around the country, Hispanics from the Caribbean, and Asians from the Pacific. In association with our nation's Capital, with foreign embassies represented from almost all countries in the world and a significant resident immigrant community, this would be a powerful symbol for our Republic.

Such a state would be entitled to two Senators and seventeen members in the House. A force to be reckoned with. Such a state, under the current two-party system, might well turn out to be a "blue" state given that Native Americans, Puerto Ricans, and greater Washington metro populations have seemed to tilt Democratic, largely because of social issues. However, I believe it quite possible that a strong, centrist third-party would have considerable appeal, as neither of the two major parties have done much of anything for these disenfranchised American citizens.

Dividing Responsibilities Between the Different Levels of Government

State Issues

Today, with our ability to travel or re-locate from one State to another quickly, we do not often think about how the issue of States' rights versus federal government controls was one of the most difficult and contentious issues faced by the Founders and drafters of the Constitution. We came quite close after independence to having 13 independent countries or two or three confederations comprised of several closely linked States. The matter at hand then was whether to have a dominant central government and subsume the individual State authorities to it; or to have stronger powers rest with the States and restrict the federal government to limited areas of authority that could be resisted if desired by the States. Brilliant minds on both sides argued their points at the Constitutional Convention of 1787. Neither side prevailed entirely but they did arrive at what was called the Great Compromise which resulted in each State having an equal number of senators in the upper house of Congress, and the House of Representatives being composed of representatives based on populations of the States. Plus, the Electoral College was created to reflect states-rights by counting two senators into the total number of electors allowed per State, thus giving less populous States a slightly augmented influence.

The point of this is that each of the 50 States remains unique, with differences small or large from the others. The United States is just that: 50 individual and distinct political and social units that have united under one national structure for shared purposes. In other words, we are not all one on every issue or concern. The federal government cannot be everything to every State. Thus, it is nonsensical to think federal control should be pervasive and be involved in every individual State issue.

In terms of this paper, a centrist third party should be active at the State level – evaluating, planning and implementing constructive State-only policies and programs. I cannot undertake here a commentary on the needs of every State in the Union. That will have to come from the people of each individual State. However, in general, I suggest that part of that effort should be to determine what responsibilities now partially held by the national government such as welfare and social programs, infrastructure rebuilding or improvement and so on, should and can be assumed by the State and local governments. In my view, States and the American population in general, have either allowed the federal government to abscond with state powers; or States have been too willing to fob off their responsibilities onto the federal government.

The principle I am proselytizing here is "power down". Responsibility, authority and accountability for an issue or matter should rest with the lowest organized political unit possible. The opposing principle of "power up", in which maximum authority is concentrated at the highest level possible, i.e. the federal government, is just not rationale in a democratic republic, because "grassroots" concerns lose their strength and authenticity if diluted among differing concerns from around this vast nation.

County Issues

The county, variously called shires, parishes, boroughs, census areas in some States or at different times, is the oldest political/geographical entity in the United States, dating back to the Jamestown Settlement in 1617. The Yukon-Koyukuk Census Area in Alaska is the largest by area at 20,052 square miles; Kalawao County in Hawaii the smallest at 12 square miles. Los Angeles County in California is the largest by population with over 10 million people; Kalawao County the smallest with 89 people. New York County in New York has the densest population with 47,000 people per square mile and the Yukon-Koyukuk Census Area the least dense with .03 people per square mile.

Despite the great diversity in sizes and populations and density, the county is the basic political unity for most States in the country. From a national perspective, we often forget or ignore the basic fact that for the majority of non-metropolitan Americans there is a very close tie to the county they reside in, an identification that is often deep, ingrained and emotional. County lines were often formed along natural boundaries such as rivers or mountain ranges which often contained the population within the county lines just because of the natural barriers, but which also reflected the occupations and means of subsistence of the people – grain crops vs vegetable cropping vs timber harvesting vs livestock production etc. And thus, the characters of individual counties could be very much different from those of even an immediately neighboring county. And taking this a step further, the social and political needs of one county can be quite different from those of the adjoining county and much different from a county in a distant quadrant of a State. It is important to note that in large rural sections of the country there has been less mobility to other areas of the State or to other States than with urban populations who relocate to other cities. Family history in these areas often dates back decades or even centuries. There is a lot of pride and affection for the county in rural areas, something perhaps that Americans in metropolitan areas do not really understand.

I have included the county in this discussion for several reasons. One, there is a necessity for residents of a county to retain as much self-governance as possible as it pertains to county-specific matters. Again, there are many governmental functions that can be exercised at the local level that do not need to be imposed by either the State or national governments. There is no "one-size-fits-all" solution to every county issue that can be imposed by higher levels of government. "Outsiders" should resist regulating and imposing laws on people of a county to mirror the thinking in their own county or State or city – as long as there are no violations of nationally held standards of ethics, public safety, or liberties.

Related to the above comment on the importance of liberties specific to a county is that many counties, like my own, have distinct characters in terms of philosophies, religious thinking, and political thinking. We cannot assume that at the county level the general character of the citizens will match that of other counties, or of the State, or of the United States at large. As long as that thinking does not transgress the basic tenets of the Constitution, most specifically the dictums of the Bill of Rights, I see no problem with a county being of a distinct and different ideology, writ large. In other words, a county might be largely evangelical Protestant in terms of religion, archly conservative in terms of standards of conduct and behavior, strict in terms of what they perceive as family and community values. The county might have a cultural heritage passed down from their ancestors of specific national origins; for example, Chinese, German, Scandinavian, Polish, or maybe in the future Korean, African, Middle Eastern etc. In my mind, such diversity is interesting and adds to the cultural wealth of this great country. Again, if and only if it does not lead to bigotry, racism and other negative societal philosophies. There is no reason that a county cannot also be socially "progressive", politically liberal, culturally mixed and so on. Once, again if the general philosophy does not translate into disdain and animosity directed to other groups such as the "conservative" example I just mentioned, two very different counties should be able to coexist peacefully and productively side by side, without an inordinate amount of tension and conflict. The county structure is the "backyard" for many Americans, for the most part like-minded in terms of outlook. Each county should be able to have its own county-specific laws, regulations, and organizational concepts as long as they are not clearly in variance with federal and State edicts. For example, in my conservative county someone attempted to open an "adult toy" and porn shop. The sign was out front with a banner – "Opening Soon". After several weeks without an opening, the banner and sign disappeared. Local government and citizen activists quietly, without fanfare and protests, stepped in and put a stop to this particular commercial venture. There were no counter protests to back the Supreme Court's decision long ago that pornography is legal. Fair enough I say. Each county should have the right to clean up its own backyard, in whatever way within reason, according to what the great majority of its residents – two-thirds at least I feel – define as "clean".

The third reason I raise the issue of counties is related to electoral reform. Rotating Democratic and Republican party administrations each attempt to re-district congressional districts to achieve electoral advantages to their parties for the next election. We call this "gerrymandering". My own congressional district – Virginia Congressional District 07 – is possibly one of the most gerrymandered in the country. It was re-districted in 1993, 1996, 2012 and 2016, each time dramatically changing the geography of the district. It currently includes all of Culpeper, Orange, Goochland, Louisa, Nottoway, Amelia, and Powhatan counties and portions of Henrico, Chesterfield, and Spotsylvania counties. The district lines make no sense in that the character of the particular counties and portions of counties are very different from each other – urban areas arbitrarily mixed in with rural counties. Occupations, lifestyles, and political preferences are very different between these counties. It would take a real stretch to say that any congressional representative elected in this district can really have his/her roots among the people of the district – the populations are too disparate. Meanwhile, other rural or urban counties that could have been combined with contiguous counties in my CD07, in a fashion that melded "like with like" were broken off into other congressional districts that are as poor a mix of different people as my own. I would like to see a centrist third party take the lead on congressional districting, which appears to be a national problem. Districts should be comprised of people who are as similar in concerns as possible. Counties should not be broken up and pieces divided between various districts.

Municipality Issues

Cities, municipalities, metropolises are subject to management challenges and problems that are very different from that of towns and rural localities. This should be self-evident given the large concentrations of people in relatively small areas; however, urban populations seem to believe their issues are national issues affecting the entire nation while non-urban populations generally do not face the same problems and do not want to take ownership of city problems via the use of their taxpayer dollars and via being subjected to laws, rules and regulations that for the most part should be applicable only to cities.

Both perspectives are correct to an extent. The obligation to address city problems rests most heavily on the populations of cities, and on their local governments. The bulk of funding should come largely from the pockets of the inhabitants of the cities, just as implementation of projects and programs should be in the hands of the elected representatives and career local officials who answer to the citizens of the city. That said, non-urban citizens should realize that when over half the population of the United States lives in urban environments, and that the markets and services represented within cities have a significantly positive direct or indirect impact on rural America, the wellbeing of citizens in cities is a national issue.

Members of a centrist third party should be active at the local city level to influence positive change through local means. The federal government should not be involved to any great extent except as issues pertain to constitutional issues. Cities need to make their own decisions on the best ways to address their problems and fund programs with their own revenues, except perhaps if the federal government returns a certain portion of federal tax revenues earmarked for such sectors as infrastructure improvement and social welfare programs. The latter – national revenues being disbursed nationally for State-managed programs from which the federal government would recuse, such as welfare and infrastructure – would probably be acceptable to the majority of Americans. Rural populations would also be receiving their fair share of federal funds and deciding their own best ways to utilize it. Cities, through State allocations, may earmark a greater percentage of their federally provided funds to welfare if that is a priority, while rural areas may concentrate on road improvements given that there are more miles of roads in rural areas and because to many conservative rural citizens welfare is a dirty word. All is fair as long as it is citizens at the local level – city or country - who decide on their priorities and the ways to address them. It would not be fair to expect non-urban citizens to have a responsibility for such serious issues as crime, poverty, low education levels etc. with causes and solutions specific to inner cities, when they do not have inner cities and their own problems, while similar, require different solutions. Similarly, one cannot expect city folk to care much about rural problems such as droughts affecting agriculture, unbalanced farm to market transportation charges, minimal profit margins for farmers on agricultural products but with high returns going to a succession of "middlemen" and retailers. No national policy can solve these issues, ones that affect just a portion of the electorate. Each of us needs to clean up our own backyard.

No-Win Issues

Abortion – Pro-Life vs. Pro-Choice

The abortion issue is still very much at the forefront of American politics. It did not go away with the Supreme Court decision on Roe vs. Wade in 1973 which overturned longstanding legal tradition making all abortions illegal. Pro-life and Pro-choice movements are highly emotional and committed. The annual Pro-life marches in Washington often draw over half a million people. The position on abortion is one of the most deciding factors among voters when choosing between candidates for office at any level. As can be expected pro-life voters are usually Republican and from rural areas, while pro-choice voters are very much Democrat and urban.

A third party and its candidates will undoubtedly have to face the question of whether they are pro or against abortion. The dilemma is that there can be no central, compromise position. An abortion is either performed or not performed. My recommendation is that the third-party response to that question be: "we, as a party, are neither Pro-choice nor Pro-life". To be truly centrist a third party must reject having to take either of these positions and develop a third position that maintains strict neutrality using the following argument.

Pregnancy, child birth and raising a child to adulthood are monumentally serious life decisions that face one woman at one moment in time. This is not a group situation. That woman is completely alone, and the decisions affect her and only her. This is a deeply personal issue, not a communal one. The dilemma of having an unwanted pregnancy, unwanted for whatever reason, is very much an individual situation. No other person is affected to any degree even close to what that one woman faces. The question of whether to give birth to an unwanted child, and then either raise it unloved or put it up for adoption, or to have an abortion is a tragic, heart-wrenching matter for that woman. She will live with the decision for the rest of her life, whatever the decision is. She deserves compassion from the rest of us, not judgment.

A third party can use the following logic to argue why the party will not commit to either the pro or against positions.

No man has the right to tell any woman what she should do with her body.

No woman has the right to tell another woman what she should do with her body.

No man or woman has the right to tell a man what he should do with his body.

Therefore, no government of the people has the right to tell a man or woman what to do with their body.

How would this play out in practice? Roe vs. Wade established that access to abortion is a woman's right, within certain limitations that are still being debated, such as with late term pregnancies. Access to legal and safe abortions is the law of the land. However, this issue is so highly charged socially, politically and religiously that government at the federal level needs to stand back and let other levels determine how the national policy will be implemented at the local level. In other words, the Supreme Court ruled that no woman who has an abortion can be tried for a crime. That is settled, and federal law takes precedence over any State or local laws. The federal government should not get further involved in implementation, including funding groups that perform abortions like Planned Parenthood. Beyond that, abortion policy at the lower levels needs to reflect the viewpoints of the individual hospitals, doctors, and localities. In other words, any hospital or doctor should have the right to refuse to perform abortions. Any employer should have the right to disallow the inclusion of abortion in company funded health insurance policies. Any locality, such as a town or county whose population is vehemently opposed to abortion should not be forced to allow abortion clinics in their locale. The bottom line is that a woman who desires an abortion can go to another county, doctor, hospital and receive a medically safe one. However, residents of a place where the consensus is strongly opposed also have the right not to be involved or to see abortions taking place where they live. Access to an abortion does not mean that clinics can pop up wherever they want, like franchised fast food restaurants. Local jurisdictions should have that right, just as the woman should have the right to make her own decision and have legal access to a safe abortion somewhere in our 50 states. Our third centrist party needs to maintain a neutral position, one that respects both sides but takes neither.

Within the third party, we should be able to have Pro-life and Pro-choice members sitting side by side working on other issues, not fighting over this one. Party members should still have the right to be active as individuals in social movements representing either side but should maintain the discipline not to associate the party in their separate activities.

Sexuality, Gender Identity, Gender Preference, LGBTQIA

While issues of sexuality, under which I am lumping all the categories, have always been present in the United States, these issues have taken on a national prominence over the past two decades. Hillary Clinton brought them to the forefront during her first campaign for the Democratic nomination, and her advocacy continued during both the Obama terms and throughout the course of Clinton's second bid for the Presidency. These issues have been the source of considerable division within the United States and I do not believe a national, centrist third party can win by taking sides on these matters. The only rational standpoint for a third party, in my view, is that government has no business engaging in issues of sexuality, beyond ensuring equitable treatment under the law. In this section, I feel it is important to be frank and not be "politically correct" in describing the strong feelings that divide the political spectrum in this area.

First, what are talking about here? According to one national LGBTQIA organization, about three million people affirm that they are in one of these categories. Another seven million when surveyed reported that they were not LGBTQIA but had "tendencies", whatever that means. Not a huge segment of the U.S. population. And what do these letters mean:

L – lesbian: women who have sex with women.
G – gay: men who have sex with men.
B – bisexual: men and women who have sex with both genders.
T – transgender: men or women who feel their internal identity is not the gender they are born with.
    transvestite: a possible inclusion to this category, people who like to dress as the opposite sex.
Q – queer: those who feel they do not fit any of the previous categories.
I – intersex: those who desire the physical characteristics of both sexes. For men often called she-males.
A – asexual: those who believe they have no gender identity, preference or sexual drives at all.

A large proportion of the heterosexual American population, irrespective of gender, religion, race or national origin believes that LGBTQIA practices are abnormal and unnatural. There has been greater acceptance over the years that gay men and lesbian women are born that way, that they can't help it, and thus there is more tolerance, though only marginal understanding and comfort on the subject. There has not been that same acceptance of the other letter categories and there is considerable discomfort regarding these lifestyles among heterosexuals, who in the great majority find the practices aberrant and disturbing. On political lines, Republicans tend to be the most strongly rejective of LGBTQIA, while Democrats the most accepting. I do not believe it likely that the feelings of Americans, whether strongly against or for, or mildly tilted to one side or the other are likely to change significantly. We have what we have.

Therefore, a centrist third party needs to take the middle road – not take a party stance one way or another. Essentially the message needs to be that government at any level has no business being involved in human sexuality, but that government has an obligation to ensure fair and equal treatment of all citizens. No citizen should be denied the rights accorded other citizens. No citizen should be subjected to abuse and intimidation, whether physical or mental. The law of the land as administered by the judicial system, from national to local, should protect the individual rights of all citizens equally.

Same-sex marriage has been the center of the national debate on sexuality, and in 2015 the Supreme Court ruled that under federal law, and applying to all States, same-sex marriage is legal and couples are to be accorded equal legal rights at all governmental levels. While debate continues throughout the country on specific issues, such as adoption and polygamy, same-sex marriage is and will continue to remain the law of the land for the conceivable future. But the acrimonious divisions, just as with abortion, will not end soon unless an ideological change can be achieved.

My suggestion is simple – take government out of the marriage business. If you look at this logically, from the viewpoint of Americans who desire maximum freedoms and liberties within reason, and minimum government interference in personal lives, then why should government at any level have the authority to approve an intimate union between any two people? Why should government license or authorize or perform marriages for anyone including heterosexuals? The only government function at any level should be to record and register marriages for the purpose of legal rights and benefits such as for social security, health benefits, inheritance, prison/hospital visitation etc.

How would this work? First of all, the following applies to only two people, so let's nix arguments about polygamy – polygyny and polyandry, group marriages etc. Keep it simple – two people only. A couple would appear before any notary public and sign a standard statement affirming that they are legally joined as a couple. They could have been married in a religious ceremony or privately among friends and family or even by just the two of them agreeing between themselves to a marriage or civil union, whatever. Government would have played no part at all. The only purpose of a notary public would be to verify identity (to avoid underage marriages, or malicious pranks of marrying under someone else's name) and to authenticate that the persons signed the affirmation statement in front of the notary. The couple would then provide whatever government institutions applicable with a copy of the signed affirmation and all couple rights would ensue. Taking government out of the approval or licensing business and the words marriage and civil union out of the equation, for heterosexuals and others, should help to some degree in mitigating the highly charged emotional content of the process.

Obviously government would have a legal and administrative role afterwards, such as in cases of divorces and deaths, domestic and child abuse, inheritances, benefits etc., but no more for non-heterosexual couples than heterosexual. A third party should bridge the gap between the acrimonious right/left opponents and as a party not enter the debate beyond removing government from marriage and insisting on equal treatment under the law. Once again, party members may have different views on same-sex marriage, but should be able to sit together and work on other issues if neutrality is observed on this matter.

Another area of debate and acrimony, ludicrous as it seems on paper but not to many people in real life situations, is the matter of bathrooms. Who goes where? Males and females go to the traditional separate facilities – but how about the alphabet soup described before. As a white, middle-aged male

I couldn't care less where I go or who sees me or what I see of others performing their natural functions, not that I relish it. But I do understand others do feel uncomfortable or even fearful and that is entirely legitimate. Women very well might not want to have any others around at this private time who are not of their gender. Parents, understandably in my view, should be very cautious of who is joining their children in restrooms. There are evil people out there – hetero or non-hetero. What about just silly pranks? I could imagine boys at school, just to be funny, trying to use "gender identity" as a way to shower with the girls, or ambitious female reporters using this as a gimmick to finally gain access into professional male athletic team restrooms!

The left embraces, promotes and even celebrates the LGBTQIA lifestyle. The message from the right is too often filled with hateful, inhuman, ignorant verbiage. A third party in its platform should represent fairness, equality, and kindness to all Americans, regardless of their differences. Beyond that, to be truly central, a centrist party should just be circumspect on this issue – be neutral, not get down into the weeds with the others. At the end of the day, individual sexual issues should not be considered part of the national agenda, except as they are related to basic American civil rights.

Slow-Win Issues

Veterans Affairs

We Americans have an ethical obligation to guarantee that citizens who have served in our military and defended our freedom and liberties are treated with the greatest of respect when they return to civilian life. This has been a major and unresolved issue since the earliest days of our Republic, when after the Revolutionary War former soldiers were denied pay and bonuses promised and marched on the Capital to demand them. This happened once again following World War I, and returning soldiers, denied what was due them, organized into the American Legion, the first American veterans organization focused principally on advocacy for veterans rights. World War II saw an improvement, with the GI Bill which gave veterans four years of paid university tuition and 100% financing of home mortgages. Medical care for service-related injuries was provided at veterans hospitals free of charge. Much of this system remains in place, administered by the Veterans Administration, our second largest, and second most expensive executive department. The VA and its employees are often pilloried in the press for failing our veterans. This is largely unfair, as the VA does magnificent work in a great number of areas that are not known to the public – in veterans hospitals, with disability payments, with VA home loans, in mortuary affairs (every veteran being entitled to free burial in a national cemetery) and many others.

Where a third party can be constructive is in helping to clearly identify what problems specific to veterans are not being adequately addressed and press for viable solutions to those problems. I will mention a few areas in which our national program falls considerably short.

1. Care for those disabled in combat. In my mind, if a soldier, sailor, Marine, or airman is severely wounded in war and unable to resume a fully productive life in the civilian world, we owe him and her fully paid, accessible medical care and a living income for the rest of their lives.
2. Care for those with Post Traumatic Stress Disorder (PTSD) and Traumatic Brain Injury (TBI). There should be a full-bore effort in both the government and civilian medical sectors to address these

debitating conditions – developing new treatments, new drugs, new rehabilitative strategies. At no cost to the veteran.

3. The homeless and unemployed. Too many veterans leave service with no prospective employment or home. There should be publicly funded transition programs to reintegrate these service people back into civilian life.

4. Insufficient education. The education component of the WWII GI Bill was removed sometime after the Vietnam War and the replacement program in which service people paid into an education account and received a matching amount from the government was largely a failure. How many 18-year-olds, making a minimal salary in the service have the foresight to contribute a significant percentage of their pay to a future education, when many of them joined the service because at the time they didn't want to go back to school? I propose restoring the 100% tuition benefit for four years of post-service education, whether at a university-level institution or a professional trade institution.

5. Incarceration. 20% of the inmates in state and federal jails and prisons are veterans. Imagine if 20% of those incarcerated were teachers, or lawyers, or checkout clerks? Wouldn't there be a general public outrage? We need to look at the underlying cause of this dismal statistic and turn it around. Something is very wrong here.

I am in a bit of a quandry here as to solutions. I advocate small, minimalist government at all levels, and thus a reduction in government expenditures. But veterans' programs such as listed above will significantly increase expenditures, unless a serious effort is undertaken to streamline veterans programs and eliminate waste. I believe the federal government should do all possible, but also State and local governments; and the civilian public at large. Veterans and veteran advocacy groups need to be deeply involved. This is a shared obligation, a sacred duty for us all. We can make a difference if we all join together and make it happen.

HealthCare

"Public health service should be as fully organized and as universally incorporated into our governmental system as is public education. The returns are a thousand-fold in economic benefits, and infinitely more in reduction of suffering and promotion of human happiness."

President Herbert Hoover

The healthcare issue has been one of the most divisive national issues dating back to the Clinton administration, which tried to develop a national system that would provide coverage to all Americans. The Obama administration tried again, but even while controlling both the House and Senate it was unable to arrive at a consensus, bi-partisan plan that both Democrats and Republicans could buy into. The Obama plan was ramrodded down the throats of congressional Republicans using the numerical superiority of the Democrats. Very unpopular among Republican voters and their congressional representatives, this one issue became a rallying cry that to a great deal propelled Republicans to the White House and to control of both houses of Congress. But, even after taking control of the Presidency and both houses of Congress in 2016, Republicans were unable to repeal and replace the Affordable Care Act, better known as Obamacare.

I do not see a new healthcare plan being designed and passed anytime soon. No one seems to be able to come up with a plan that is better than either Obamacare or the previous system. The root to the problem, as I see it is that we have a for-profit healthcare system, controlled to a large degree by large corporations. Hospitals are largely under corporate structures as are pharmaceutical companies, franchised health clinics, health insurance providers, and medical equipment manufacturers, wholesalers and retailers. Corporations, by law, are beholden to their shareholders – not to patients. The goal of any corporation is to make as much money as possible without "killing the golden goose", i.e. keeping rates as high as possible but not so high that they seriously erode their patient base.

There is insufficient national support for a national, socialized health system with free or almost free healthcare for all. This would require a significant increase in taxes and many Americans are apprehensive that a government-run health delivery system would be inefficient, costlier, and deliver inferior healthcare than the systems we have now or had in the past.

There is considerable interest among Americans, even moderate Republicans, to provide coverage via an expanded Medicare to lower income citizens who are unable to afford the healthcare insurance premiums and thus are getting little to no care. Americans, as I've said before, are a compassionate people and it does not sit easy with most that there are many millions of men, women and children who suffer without care or die early because they cannot afford to see a doctor or go to the hospital. The question is who will pay if they can't? Republicans, and many fiscally conservative Democrats, are very opposed to increasing the national budget and the national debt any more. People are saying enough is enough, we need to get our financial house in order.

Realizing that solutions will not be coming soon, this is the time for a third party to provide the stimulus to bring minds together to work on a plan that will bring all opposing factions together to achieve a long-term solution, even if it is not enacted for many years. With a third party seeking common ground and educating the voters on the issues, and independent groups of experts providing the knowledge and working on details outside party politics, the major parties can step back a bit and reflect, rather than stirring up their bases with nonproductive diatribes and butting heads with each other. The medical community, particularly physicians and other healthcare providers, should be taking the lead on national healthcare policy. They know the needs of the public, the healing tradecraft, and the business of medicine. They are also the best placed to work with the corporate entities involved to reach solutions that serve the needs both of the public and the industry. Here are a few of my ideas, for what they're worth.

The healthcare conglomerate of profit-based corporations will not change soon if ever. That said, there is nothing to prevent baby steps towards creating a non-profit sector within the industry that would provide care for those within our country who cannot access the current system. By non-profit I do not mean either free or based on volunteer healthcare providers. I mean clinics and hospitals, with physicians and other providers who are paid well, at competitive salaries; with equipment and facilities that meet industry standards. However, with the profit aspect removed and the medical operations operating under non-profit regulations costs could be brought down significantly without reducing the quality of care or the attractiveness of this sort of medical system to the providers. There are many non-profit organizations that operate effectively without the profit motive attached. Some examples are relief and development organizations such as CARE, Save the Children, the Red Cross and many others.

Such a non-profit health system, starting from ground up, also has the potential to change public and provider attitudes towards how healthcare should be delivered. For example, General Practitioners (GP) – MD's – once provided the bulk of healthcare. They have the training and expertise to handle the majority of health issues. Times have changed, and the medical industry has shifted a great deal towards specialization, at a greater cost to patients and to insurance providers, the latter increasing their premium rates to cover the increases. Years ago, a GP would set broken bones, based on an X-ray taken in-house; now a patient is referred to an orthopedist who quite likely will send the patient out for an MRI, then treat accordingly. Overkill in most cases. Part of the reason is that we have become a litigious society, and malpractice insurance is prohibitively expensive for GPs, as well as for all physicians. GPs do not want to risk a major lawsuit, and often their own insurance companies insist that many common conditions be referred to a specialist. In the course of any effort to revamp our current system, and possibly create new non-profit systems, the legal implications will have to be heavily evaluated and possibly protective legislation would be required. Another reason for the diminishing role of GPs is the high cost of specialty equipment which an individual doctor or small clinic cannot afford. A larger non-profit institution could have the client base to provide evaluative facilities with MRIs, laboratories etc. for in-house and even cooperative use by smaller non-profit clinics. The attitudes of medical practitioners and patients would need to change – focusing on necessary care rather than elective care. Unfortunately, with the current profit-based system, patients with good health care coverage tend to overuse their access, going to see a doctor for negligible problems that may not warrant any visit at all. For example, when in the past if a child fell off a bicycle and skinned his/her knee, a parent would dab on a bit of iodine and slap on a Band-Aid and that was it. Now, if it is just a matter of a co-pay, the parent might take the child to a doctor anyway, then the doctor might send the child for an X-ray or MRI. Lots of wasted time and money for the patient – but extra profits for the corporations! Meanwhile, those without insurance coverage or with poor coverage, high co-pays, high deductibles will avoid going to see a doctor even when it is a serious condition. We need a re-focusing of philosophy on medical care, non-profit systems, and patient needs. We need to be more pragmatic, concentrating on the truly serious and triaging the petty situations to last place. Consumers would need to learn and take seriously what are real medical needs and what is frivolous.

Still, even a non-profit system will cost, and who pays? Always the big question. Possibly there could be non-profit insurance companies too. Wouldn't that be novel! Obviously, insurance is based on the principle that a large number of people paying premiums but not utilizing services at this moment cover those who do require the services now. This would not change with a non-profit insurance company, but the profit motive would be gone and presumably there would be more emphasis on frugality within the non-profit health-providing institutions as well. If the profit motive is taken away, there would be little incentive to pad medical charges with such ridiculous line items like nine-dollar Q-Tips!

Lowering the cost of the provision of health care and lowering the cost of health insurance would help many citizens, but there would still be those who can afford neither. There must be some safety net for those people. Again, who pays? Throughout this book I am trying to make an argument for minimalist government at all levels. In the case of healthcare, I believe the federal government needs to have only minimal responsibility, except for oversight and broad regulatory controls over medical institutions and insurance companies. The federal government cannot legislate a one-size-fits-all program for the whole country. States and counties must assume the task of providing whatever health coverage systems best fit their citizens and these governmental levels and the elected representatives of localities at these levels must be accountable to their voters. With the current system, all blame is put on the federal government, which really does not have one answer to what are really many different problems. Each State and county has unique issues and thus must take a much greater role in solving them. The federal government should provide maximum legislative and regulatory support but should not try to achieve one uniform system. It will not work.

Again, this issue needs a great deal of study. It needs a great deal of cooperation and coordination between the institutional players. Time and thought is needed, and a centrist party can be very helpful in setting such an effort into motion.

Gun Control

"Little more can reasonably be aimed at with respect to the people at large than to have them properly armed and equipped: and in order to see that this be not neglected, it will be necessary to assemble them once or twice in the course of the year."

Federalist Paper No. 29 (Hamilton)

I am writing this one week after the horrific killing of 17 persons, mostly students, at the high school in Parkland, Florida. The national outcry has been tremendous, with the majority of citizens calling for steps that would prevent such a tragedy from occurring again. Once again, our principle national divisions have appeared: urban/and or Democratic vs. rural/and or Republican. The the former calls for gun control measures ranging from total abolition of firearms to significant reduction in the availability of types of weapons and extensive controls on individual access to weapons. And the latter either rejects any control measures or at most agrees to very limited controls on types of weapons and restrictions on individuals.

The meaning of the Second Amendment to the Constitution, as usual, takes central place in the polarized arguments of the two sides. We cannot expect the extreme fringes of either faction to understand Constitutional history or respond to reason. However, it is certain that those citizens towards the center of the national viewpoint can arrive at constructive measures that will help ensure that firearms remain in the hands of responsible citizens, but out of the hands of murderers, criminals, and the insane. I say "help" because there are no absolutes ever in this world that good will always prevail over evil. Crimes of all types in which firearms will be involved will always be with us despite what measures are taken. We can, however, reduce them with prudent measures.

First, it is important to understand the period and context in which the Constitution and Second Amendment were drafted.

1. The Union just barely won its independence from England following a bloody and costly conflict.
2. Future conflicts with England, France (though an ally during the Revolution) and Spain were possibilities.
3. A number of the States engaged in armed conflicts with each other or threatened so.
4. Internal insurrections within the States took place.
5. Native (American Indian) tribes engaged in frequent attacks on the European transplants.
6. Banditry from criminal elements was present.
7. Predators: bear, wolves, mountain lions, coyotes and other animals raided homesteads.
8. Hunting, in this still wild and virtually untamed wilderness was a vital component of feeding one's family and providing meat to town dwellers.

Very little thought at that time was given to banning firearms, except among some pacifist groups like the Quakers and among a minority of townspeople. Firearms were an essential tool in the settlement of the American wilderness.

The principle argument at the time of the Constitution was whether to maintain a permanent standing army or to rely on a citizen soldiery that could be called upon in times of crises to supplement a small national force or to react to crises at local or national levels prior to raising a larger, temporary federal force. These were to be local" militias", under States control, but also responsible to orders from the federal government if needed. The militias were to be locally disciplined and "well-regulated" to distinguish them from the ragtag, barefoot volunteers early in the Revolution who could not have won the war if they were not better equipped and trained later on. But, they were not to be a standing army, nor groups like today's Reserves and National Guards. These were ordinary citizens, farmers mostly, who could not be taken away from their farms and livelihoods except for local assemblies "once or twice a year" as stated by Hamilton. Again, little consideration was given to disarming the citizenry: even those not in a militia needed their weapons for survival. For the most part, men, women and children at that time were excellent shots.

Today is a different story. We have strong standing military branches (Army, Air Force, Marines, Navy and Coast Guard). Plus, Reserve forces and

National Guards. There is no immediate need for additional State-based militias, except perhaps if the U.S. engaged in a major contact where the standing militaries needed to be augmented. If we did have such a need, I am sure it would be greatly preferable to have weapons-familiar persons volunteer than inexperienced ones. And guess what? Chances are the great majority of volunteers would come from rural regions of the country, regions that already provide the majority of permanent military members. Such citizen-soldiers already exist, and I have implicit trust in their trustworthiness and skill when it comes to firearms of any description.

So why, in 2018, do Americans feel they need firearms – ask mostly urban people? Here's why.

1. A significant portion of American citizens, myself included, do believe that an armed citizenry is necessary as protection against a despotic national or State government taking control. Yes, this is unlikely in the United States of America today. However, it is not impossible, and it is well known that one of the first steps taken by despotic regimes of the not so distant past – fascist or communist – was to disarm the general population.
2. Self-defense: even urban dwellers are gun owners, primarily to have a credible defense against criminals. I note that in rural areas like my own, violent crime is minimal. Criminals are unlikely to invade a rural home, carjack, assault a pedestrian when they know chances are quite likely that the intended victims are armed.
3. Hunting: this is not only a time-honored pastime and sport, but also still an important source of meat in rural areas. I know a significant number of families that rely on hunting for the majority of their yearly meat – deer, duck, dove, quail, turkey, bear, rabbit, squirrel. Given the high prices for meat in supermarkets, hunting serves an important economic need. Remember that median incomes in the country are substantially lower than in cities.

How can we reach agreement then on the gun control issue? What can centralist Americans come up with that will satisfy the concerns of most? Here are some thoughts.

1. First, we need to think about the concept of "clean up your own backyard, not mine". We have many different gun control issues here.

Guns in the hands of criminals and gangs in Chicago and other big cities is one issue. The horrific school massacres and other mass shootings is another issue, and it is again noteworthy the majority of these have taken place in or near urban settings. Other gun violence in urban or rural areas or small towns is another issue. I am not trying to justify any of them or to claim that gun violence is not pervasive throughout the country. I just want to highlight that there need to be different solutions for different problems for different regions of the country. The solutions, to be effective, cannot be one national policy – one size fits all. Each jurisdiction needs to produce solutions specific to its own situation. For instance, a county or city does have the authority, Second Amendment notwithstanding, to legislate its own policies and controls. One county or municipality might want to ban all possession of firearms and ban all gun shops and gun shows. If that is what the residents want, they should be allowed to do so. Remember the Wild West stories, some true, of the tough sheriff who makes the cowboys back from the range surrender their guns while in town? The next county or municipality might want no controls at all. They should be allowed to have more liberal gun policies, but only up to a point. The reason societies have government is to establish order, seek peace and stability and protect its citizens from harm. Controls are essential to achieving these goals and guns are no exception. There was never an intention among the Founders to allow unreasonable and dangerous use of firearms. This logically means reasonable and responsible efforts to keep firearms out of the hands of those who would misuse them.

2. Building on the precept of "reasonable and responsible efforts", it makes sense that those most familiar with firearms and most passionate about keeping them should be the ones to make those efforts and formulate effective policy. This is not happening. It seems the far right wants no controls at all which is irresponsible, and the far left wants a total ban on guns, which just will not happen. The extremist fringes are certainly the most vocal and most intransigent. I know there must be middle ground there and moderate centrists in each camp who disagree with the absolutism and hyperbole of their political parties. Again, a centrist party might be more effective in

achieving good compromises by allowing pragmatists and reasonable persons, currently too silent, to work on the gun control problem.

3. The first step is to identify the parameters of the issue. Currently, it seems, the anti-gun lobby does not even know enough about firearms to make cogent arguments in support of their positions. Ban all guns; or ban all "assault weapons"; or ban all semi-automatic weapons; or ban AR-15's: or ban all magazines larger than for five rounds; and on and on with such drivel! Here is a brief primer for these types who speak passionately but are too lazy to even read up a bit on the more common types of firearms out there.

Single shot: these could be muzzle-loaders - black powder rifles or pistols; bolt-loading hunting rifles; breech-loading shotguns. The main point is that one cartridge with one projectile, or one shotgun shell is loaded manually, fired, the spent case or shell manually ejected (except with muzzle loaders which have no cartridge or shell left behind after fired), then a new cartridge or shell manually loaded.

Semi-automatic: this is a firearm in which multiple shots can be fired before new cartridges or shells need to be replaced in the weapon. I am being very broad in this definition so there are distinctions within this category that some might not feel merit semi-automatic status. These are revolvers, in which five to ten rounds depending on the caliber of the cartridge, are loaded into the cylinder of the pistol and fired with each trigger pull until expended, then manually ejected, then reloaded. Shotguns which have a sub-barrel magazine that holds five shells which are manually injected into the breech with a slide of the handgrip also fall into this grey area of not quite semi's but have multiple shot capability before reloading. There are lever action rifles too that have built in magazines holding five or so cartridges, but which require manual cocking after each shot to load a new cartridge into the breech. True semi-automatics would be the rifles and pistols in which a separate magazine with cartridges is inserted into either the receiver or butt, respectively, and with each trigger pull a shot is fired, cartridge ejected, and a new cartridge inserted into the breech. In other words, one trigger pull, one shot, with no other action required by the shooter until the magazine is spent. Semi-automatics include an extensive and varied range of rifles and pistols of so many different calibers and capabilities that to call for a ban on all semi-automatics would eliminate the majority of rifles and pistols in private ownership today. The effort calling for such a ban is futile, it will not happen. People are wasting their time.

Automatics: These are rifles and pistols in which one trigger pull, when held, fires a burst of several rounds or expends an entire magazine while the trigger is pulled. In other words, the weapon continues to fire while the trigger is pulled. The rifles in this category are standard issue for the military, with both a semi-automatic and automatic toggle switch to choose from. Automatic pistols, not really pistols, are generally what some call "machine pistols", such as we see in movies used by gangsters and drug cartels. There are also military-type, in-between automatics that people will generally identify as a "sub-machine gun", such as an Uzi. Automatic weapons are illegal to private ownership in the U.S., except under a special, hard-to-get license. Most of these weapons are available to the civilian market in a semi-automatic version, thus legal. These semi-automatic versions of military weapons have provoked the greatest outrage, having been used in some of the worst mass shootings. To clarify further, an AR-15 or Bushmaster is the semi-automatic version of the military M-16 or M-4 rifle. Also, while addition of a "bump stock" modification to an AR-15 does not make it technically an automatic as engineered, this is a really stupid argument. The "bump stock" makes the rifle fire all the rounds in a magazine with one trigger pull, so it is a de facto automatic.

Given the above, I believe it is essential to narrow this extensive field of firearms to really determine which ones present the worst threats to public safety and thus focus the debate between the two widely separated pro and anti-camps on just these areas, not on every firearm out there. Possibly then agreements can be reached. Here is the way I see it.

1. All semi-automatic rifles that were originally designed as military weapons with an automatic firing function should not be available for private ownership, except under special license. The ones currently available on the American civilian market include: The AR-15, Bushmaster, M-14, Mini-14, AK-47, G-3, FN-FAL, Uzi, Galil, among others from around the world that were originally designed automatic. None of the weapons in this category are essential or even appropriate for hunting. None of them are appropriate for personal self-defense.

All of them have rapid fire capability even in semi-auto configuration along with magazine capacities of 20 to 30 rounds. In other words, they are people killing machines. Pure and simple.

Remember that in the history of the U.S. military, automatic rifles were not in service until Vietnam, with first the M-14 then the M-16. Soldiers used the M1 Garand semi-automatic rifle, which has an eight-round clip, in both World War II and the Korean War. Most of the Civil War was fought with single shot muzzle loaders or with single shot bolt action. Henry and Spencer repeating rifles – lever action – entered the conflict towards the end in limited numbers. The Revolutionary War was fought with muzzle loaders. Look at the deaths in these wars. Not dramatic enough? The point being that citizen-soldiers do not need semi-automatic and automatic military style weapons to protect our Republic, for self-defense, or for hunting. Nor do we need large capacity magazines. Other rifles now available are sufficiently potent for all purposes and if the M-1 with its eight-round clip could win WWII and Korea why do private citizens feel they need more? However, gun enthusiasts and shooting competitors will still want military-style semi-automatic weapons. There should be a possibility to design a special license, backed by a more in-depth background check, that would allow such persons to purchase and retain such weapons. Plus, there should be a methodology that could be developed so that resales of these weapons are monitored and tracked. There is nothing in the Second Amendment that prohibits all controls for all firearms. Can we go out and buy .50 cal heavy machine guns or artillery? Of course not. Moderate, thinking gun owners need to realize that logical controls are necessary, and stop letting the radicals – left and right – control the agenda and policies.

2. Handguns need a separate policy. All guns can kill, even those taking the smallest caliber cartridge and even single shot weapons. However, we need to calmly evaluate which weapons of this type are the most likely to be desired for hunting, target practice, and self-defense separated out from those that are most likely to be used for criminal activities or mass killings. This is a very difficult task, as again all handguns can and are used for many purposes, legitimate and legal as well as illegal. I would say the greatest distinguishing factor needs to

be magazine size. Here's why. Anyone who wants a handgun for self-defense does not need more than six rounds, the standard capacity of a medium bore revolver. This could be set as the standard for semi-automatic, magazine-fed pistols as well. If a homeowner or attack victim cannot kill or incapacitate an assailant with six rounds they are unlikely to do so with 12 or 20 rounds, the current magazine capacity of some handguns. Those people who feel they need that many rounds should be spending a lot more time practicing on a firing range. Similarly, any hunter who cannot kill their target with the first two or three rounds is unlikely to do so with more. The animal will be long gone. Such a hunter also needs to spend more time at the firing range. Target shooters who might want more shots just need to reload. This only takes seconds. How would this help reduce deaths and injuries from criminal activities? It won't help much, but every little bit helps. Any reduction in the number of shots fired could mean fewer killed/hurt in the first moments of an attack. The time needed to reload, however brief, gives a few seconds in which the good citizens can react – disable the shooter, or run to cover. Any bit helps.

3. Non-military style rifles. These can be anything from a .22 cal. plinker/rabbit gun to a big bore .50 cal big game gun. These are not self-defense weapons. They are hunting rifles or used for target practice. Again, any self-respecting hunter who cannot kill a deer with one well-placed shot from a bolt-action 30.06, followed by reloading one more shot for a kill shot if the animal is still alive, is not worthy of the title "hunter". That said, there are semi-automatic hunting rifles currently configured to hold several rounds – either in an internal magazine or an external removal magazine. A six-round magazine should be more than enough, except possibly for a .22 cal rifle, some of which can hold up to 20 rounds in a below-the-barrel tube magazine. I think we can take .22's off the table. Yes, they can kill, and yes only adults should purchase them, but it is not all that likely that criminals and mass shooters will choose these weapons.

4. Shotguns. Again, six rounds should be enough for any hunter. And, again, yes, they can kill and severely injure. But, thankfully the size, lack of concealability, and lack of range have not made these weapons of choice for criminals or mass shooters. They are weapons though, and a shotgun was used recently in a school mass murder. These are

not children's toys and should only be purchased by adults. Which leads me to the next point – age to purchase weapons.

5. I believe, given the horrific evidence of the past two decades, that purchase of ANY firearm – rifle, handgun, shotgun, should be limited to those 21 or older. Even .22 cal plinkers. Now, a great number of people in the country will say this is wrong and excessive. They have been shooting since they were children. I know I, like many others, started shooting at about the age of five. So did my sons. This is how we learned safe gun handling and good marksmanship. Generally starting with something like a 22-caliber rifle and handgun, and a .410 bore shotgun. As age, expertise, and size progressed we would work our way up to bigger firearms. There is a tremendous advantage in starting young and learning shooting skills as well as responsibility and safety. We need to be very careful here that with the current anti-gun atmosphere that the anti-gun people do not try to make any gun use by those under whatever age they set is illegal, and then try to charge parents or other adults with criminality for letting underage people shoot or handle firearms. This is not paranoia on my part. I can see some anti-gun people pushing for this sort of thing. From the other standpoint, I just don't understand why the pro-gun lobby is so against setting an age limit of 21 on any and all firearms. This would not prevent people under 21 from handling, using or hunting with firearms when accompanied by or under the supervision of an adult such as when on one's own property or in a hunting party elsewhere. I'm trying to reason with the pro-gun group now. Yes, your children or young adults under 21 are probably fully responsible and accomplished in handling firearms. But how about the teenagers in the city? Did they start shooting when they were five or six years old? Did their Dads or Moms "whup their butts" when they mishandled the guns in an unsafe manner? Did they teach their children responsible and safe use of firearms? Highly unlikely. So why should those teenagers, now 18 years old be able to just go out and purchase weapons when they do not yet have the maturity or good judgement to handle them correctly? Think about it. In this effort to come to agreements between anti and pro-gun camps there need to be tradeoffs. Some ask: "why can a young person go into the military and fight for our country at 18, but not purchase a weapon until they are 21"? Well guess what? If they go

into the military at 18 they will be trained and disciplined in the use of firearms, and when they get out they will be 22 years old and be then able to buy one! If they don't believe in going into the military and doing national service, why then should they somehow then have a right to buy a weapon before 21. Doesn't make sense to me.

6. Finally, background checks. Pro-gun people should be the very first people to want extensive background checks and should be the very first ones to develop a good system before the anti-gun/city people force a really bad policy down our throats. The national background check system as it stands now has not worked. We just saw that with the last few mass killings. That said, we shouldn't get rid of it, just try to improve on it and use it as just one step in the purchase approval system. I would add a requirement for a local police check too. Remember with the Parkland school killings local police had gone to the house of the killer 39 times in two years on complaints of domestic disturbance and violent behavior. But he still legally purchased 10 weapons. I would also add, as part of the packet requesting approval for the very first time under a new system, a requirement to submit a minimum of five notarized affidavits by persons who certify that the gun buying applicant had no known disqualifying reasons, known to them, for buying a weapon. These affidavits should include ones from neighbors, medical personnel, employers and family. This affidavit requirement would be only required once every ten years and be registered both in the local police and national databanks, essentially resulting in a "license" to purchase firearms, barring any later disqualifiers in the local and national law enforcement background checks. Many Second Amendment supporters will think these requirements are too stringent and would infringe on their rights. Why? I don't understand it when pro-gun people consistently argue that it is not the majority of gun owners who are the problem but the criminals and insane who are the threat. If so, why should not the law-abiding citizens take those steps necessary to separate themselves from those who are potential threats to public safety?

7. I am very suspicious about the current public demands for mental health being a criterion for firearm purchases. This could be a very slippery slope, including unprecedented government and law enforcement access to health records and a really muddy definition of

what mental health issues are disqualifying. For example, personal medical records, now inaccessible to government entities, could be required to be accessible for background check purposes. Medical personnel could be required by law to report any possible medical problems they encounter when treating patients. And who would define what mental issues would disqualify someone from purchasing or owning a firearm? I could see the list of conditions multiplying rapidly – over time including everything mental such as ANY depression whatever the cause; grief, loss of a job, menopause, physical injury or deteriorating health, breakup in a marriage or relationship, workplace problems etc. The list could go on and on. On the law enforcement side, disqualifying factors would also have to be carefully delineated to avoid adding every offense to the list. For example, would repeated traffic violations be disqualifying? Would driving under the influence (DUI) be disqualifying? Disrespect to an officer? Disturbing the peace? Failing to license one's dog? We need to be very careful in both the mental health and the law enforcement areas and there needs to be broad public agreement on the parameters. However, there needs to be a better background check system put in place immediately.

8. ALL sales and transfers of weapons must require an extensive national and states-wide background check before a new owner takes possession of the firearm. This obligation needs to be put on the seller or person who is transferring, even between friends and family. Again, many strong Second Amendment advocates will say this is excessive. Why should a parent not be able to give a rifle to an offspring who is of legal age? In 99.9% of cases there will not be a potential problem. However, it is the .1% of cases that are a very big problem. Putting the onus on the seller or transferor, even if a relative or friend, puts them on notice that they are accountable to some degree if anything goes wrong, unless they follow the rules by letting the background check process decide in the matter. This is no different than the accountability of a parent if they let their unlicensed, underage child drive their vehicle. Or an intoxicated person drives their vehicle. Why should sales at gun shows, public auctions, in the newspaper, at estate or garage sales be any more relaxed than sales at licensed gun shops? Where do you think criminals or others with bad intent will go to purchase firearms?

Wherever it is easiest and with less chance of detection – make sense? Just as a note, any of the background check or "licensing" steps outlined above should not be an excuse for government entities to make money through increased permit and processing fees or taxes. If governments, representative governments, are serious about gun control they need to make the process cost free to the consumer, and with a minimum of paperwork, time and delay involved.

9. Finally, to repeat – pro-gun and Second Amendment supporters need to take charge of the gun control agenda. It is not sufficient or acceptable to say "no" to all controls. Change will come and if it happens that the urban anti-gun lobby, with their three percent superiority in number of voters nationwide takes charge and forces really draconian measures on us – we have only ourselves to blame.

ANATOMY OF A THIRD PARTY

"We hold these truths to be self-evident, that all men are created equal, that they are endowed by their Creator with certain inalienable Rights, that among these are Life, Liberty and the pursuit of Happiness."

The Declaration of Independence
July 4, 1776

A new national centrist party, to be effective and capture a significant following among the population, will need to be dramatically different than either the two major parties or any of the current minor parties. A real third party will have to smash the templates of the other parties, reject many of their political formulas, and start anew from the ground up. This applies to structure, to philosophy, modus operandi, to ethics, to expertise. This new party must be audacious, daring to challenge many of the "sacred cows" of many partisan groups. This also means we, each and every one who seeks a viable third party, must adjust our own thinking – each of us will have to give up a "sacred cow" or two. This must be a party with a minimalist platform solely based on constitutional principles rather than on the flood of differing interests that emanate from groups or factions whose focus is not on national requirements but individual concerns. This party should adopt the principle that if two-thirds of Americans support a policy or action, it should be a "go". If not, then an initiative, law, or other government action should not be adopted until reformulated to secure two-thirds acceptance. Obviously, we cannot have the American people voting on every government action to see if two-thirds agree! But, voters can insist that its elected representatives abide by this principle. Partisanship – so often seen now in the 49 against 51 percentages in Congressional votes – must be overcome. Only a strong third party with enough votes in Congress can force the other parties to a central position.

A new powerful party must have its roots deeply embedded in the political and social fabric of ordinary, mainstream America. In other words, this needs to be a "grassroots" movement that propels forward a national ideology from those convictions, aspirations, and needs held in common by the great majority of our citizens. In other words, to be successful, this cannot be a party that is rooted just in the North or South or East or West. It cannot be a movement that reflects just the beliefs of urban or rural citizens. Or one that is just white, or black, or Hispanic or another race or ethnicity. It cannot be just Christian or Muslim or have a following that is predominately one religion or another. It cannot be just working class or white collar. It cannot be dominated by the young or the old. This party must arise from common purposes, goals and humanity. This party must be purely American, reflecting the foundations that precipitated this experiment, one unique in human history.

Second, this party, at the national level must be fully cognizant that starting up, solidifying, and assuming a prominent national position will be a hard row-to-hoe. There will be significant opposition from those political and social forces who currently hold or continuously jockey for power: the two major parties, corporate and other economic interests, special interest groups, racial and religious communities, regional proclivities. It will be difficult, but this new party should refrain from engaging on all issues, addressing all factions, trying to have a position on each and every problem or concern in the country or the world. The firm emphasis should be on matters that pertain to the country at large, to the great majority of its citizens. Party efforts should not be directed as opposition to the major parties, factions or other forces, but take the higher ground and seek to bring those groups into common agreement on key tenets of our national political agenda.

Third, the party must realize that individual party members will still have differing specific interests and passions in a multitude of areas. And the party should not denigrate or punish members for undertaking efforts in those areas – as long as there is a clear distinction between their personal convictions and efforts and the consensual platform and efforts of the party. To explain further. Every effort should be made by the party to ensure its platform and precepts are agreed to by the great majority of Americans and stand back from taking sides on deeply polarizing issues which will only further divide the citizenry and party membership – and ultimately fragment and destroy the new party. As an example, the issue of abortion is a no-win issue for a new third party. Passions are viscerally strong in both the pro-life and pro-choice camps. Undoubtedly if a new centrist third party is to be as broad-based as I suggest, there will be members with deeply held beliefs from both positions. Ideally, political party members from either camp should be able to sit side by side and work constructively on issues and positions which they hold in common and lay aside the issues which divide them. The only way to do this, as I see it, is for the party platform to be as minimalist as necessary to function properly internally and for the common national good. This would require agreement, and discipline, so that individual members separate their personal activities from party activities. In other words, the pro-life and pro-choice members can participate in activism from their personal viewpoint outside the party context, refraining from associating the party with their personal positions on issues the party has agreed will not be within its purview.

Fourth, every effort should be made to include among party membership expertise of the highest order in every field of knowledge that is relevant. To me, a "grassroots" movement does not mean one arising just from one group or another – young, working class, academic or blue/white collar - no one group has the knowledge on all subjects to be relevant in all. Nor does it mean just harnessing the passions and populist fervors of the discontent. We need "grassroots" passion, but we also need experts in all areas, and each of us has expertise in some facet of a particular area that is relevant to the whole picture. For example, the Wall Street financier will have knowledge on the petroleum market that you and I do not have. The petroleum engineer will know the ins and outs of extraction and production. The environmental engineer will understand the impact on the environment. The skilled tradesperson on the offshore drilling platform will not only understand the work-a-day technology but also have a personal understanding of what this industry means to the millions of working class Americans engaged in this industry. We need them all to form a complete, cogent, practical policy in the energy field. This need for comprehensive synergy drawing on expertise from all informed persons on a particular issue is one that is essential when presenting a party position to the voting public on any of the critical subjects the Nation faces. We should by no means assume the American public is dumb, nor allow a party to fob out shallow clichés and sound bites. Party positions need to be backed up with substantive, empirical knowledge from the very beginning. Our representatives should not have to "learn on the job" after being elected.

Fifth, too often it seems that those we believed and hoped would be responsible government representatives are motivated more by personal power and gain than public service. Ethics in our new party must be an integral and uncompromising standard for those persons we choose to support in bids for government office – at all levels. A new third party will quickly destroy itself by putting forward candidates for office who are unqualified, self-serving, unreliable, immoral, untruthful or otherwise not of "statesman-like" attributes. Very often, new parties trying to get a beginning with just a few members, will want to put forward candidates for as many elected positions as possible, just to get the party name "out there". In some instances, a person who has strong, appealing convictions and charisma, but is possibly inexperienced and maybe very young may be a very positive force in counterpoising less attractive candidates from other parties. Or, this same person may serve to reflect negatively on the party if competing against mature and better qualified candidates from those parties. There is no one-size-fits-all answer here; but it is almost certain that a disagreeable, dishonest, polarizing candidate will not serve a new, centrist party well. The major parties have enough of those and I believe the great majority of Americans are tired of that. All I can do here is advise caution on whom the party chooses to support. Better to take a measured pace, seek top expertise on all areas of concern, develop policies and platform that are as incontrovertible as possible, then identify candidates from as deep a pool of talent as possible.

One serious concern I have is that any political party, major or minor, will certainly be most "branded" by its most visible leaders, and most definitively by whoever is chosen to be its presidential candidate. This presents a dilemma. Any party, to be taken seriously on the national stage, must have standard bearers, banner holders, poster children who represent the "face" of the party to the voters. Name recognition is important. We need active support from persons of prominence in every sector – politics, business, entertainment, whatever. The hazard is that persons of prominence generally have influence, power, wealth and quite often above average egos; thus, the risk is that they may want to brand the party in their own image and in essence create their own personality cult at the expense of the "grassroots". They may very well want to have party members follow their platform and agenda rather than themselves follow and represent the will of the members. We should not get starry eyed with prominence and capitulate if our basic party values are threatened.

Long-term National Planning – Team America 2050

Our third party should become known as the "planning party", a forward-thinking party. It is a virtual truism that today the American political psyche is fixed on the short-term, basically on the periods of four-year presidential terms in office. The activities of the two major political parties, the national leadership, and the media are focused on immediate fixes to national issues as perceived by those in power or those seeking power. The aim is to achieve "wins" that will translate into votes in the next presidential or congressional election cycles. Very little thought is given to methodical, measured planning strategies to assure success for the country decades in the future.

I am arbitrarily choosing 2050 – 32 years ahead - as a planning landmark because our population at that time is estimated to be 450 million; a nice round number that should make everyone sit up and take notice. Thirty-two years will also encompass eight presidential terms – presumably including both Republican, Democrat and even maybe a third-party President. Our third-party goal should be to develop long-term plans of action that are not so much designed to win elections, but to provide goals, strategies and concrete operational steps that will produce worthwhile improvements in our national "health". To be useful and relevant these plans must be in line with the common goals and aspirations of the great majority of the American people – I will again use the rough figure of two-thirds of the population. We should not be jealous of our work in the important areas of national concern, but seek to pursue consensus positions, backed by our best national brainpower, and be happy if whichever party happens to win the Presidency or dominates Congress enthusiastically pursues the plan – year after year, administration after administration. Obviously, each administration will have its own personality and emphasize certain aspects of a national plan more assiduously than others. But, if we can move forward as a people with the strong support of our national leadership on proactive steps to solve national problems, regardless of party affiliation, this would be a significant achievement.

Certainly, a national plan would need to be broken down into shorter planning segments – five, ten, fifteen years etc. We shouldn't want to stop at my arbitrary 32-year mark either – a plan could be carried out 50, 75, 100 years even, though logically future thinking becomes much more imaginative the further we push our goals outward. Also, planning even in the short-term must be practical and flexible. Our country, and the world we live in is constantly changing. That said, a national agenda designed to address current as well as future national needs is essential.

Let me take one of many issues and describe how in this one area long-term planning could make a positive difference. In 32 years, our population will increase by 25%. Therefore, all of our national needs – housing, energy, transportation, food production, medical services etc. will need to be increased by roughly the same percentage. For the sake of discussion, let's just focus on transportation. Currently it seems our approach is piecemeal, hodge-podge. Even though infrastructure projects may take years, even decades to finish, the prior planning is based on immediate needs. For example, traffic around a metropolitan area increases to the point that traffic congestion, gridlock, has become such a misery for the commuting public that public outcry stimulates local government to take action. This action will involve years of planning and securing federal, State and local funding. Then years of construction, by which time the population has already increased to the point that the road expansion is outdated and overloaded by the time it is completed. And the cycle of planning, funding and building new roads begins again. This road-building phenomenon repeats throughout the country, in city after city.

Wouldn't it be better if a long-term national plan on transportation was put into action that both kept pace with immediate needs and addressed future ones as well? A plan that made maximum efficient use of already short funding resources? I am certain that we have the technology experts – engineers, IT professionals, transportation careerists – who could develop transportation grids and technologies which would serve us well; far into the future, to 2050 and beyond. Would a metropolitan, above-ground monorail such as the one featured in the original Disneyland 50 years ago be a possibility? Would a national grid or high-speed rail be feasible and practical? The Japanese and Europeans have had such for decades; why are we so slow? We have the experts in our country who can answer these questions and develop solutions, if there is a national will, backed by our representatives in government. We cannot fund and build such massive infrastructure all at once and overnight. But we can start the process, plan stages, and move forward to achieve intermediate milestones. A plan for a national high-speed rail grid could look something like this: New York to Los Angeles by year-five; Minneapolis to Houston by year-ten; Seattle to Miami by year-fifteen etc. Isn't that roughly how our rail system began and moved forward starting 150 years ago? We can do it again, but much better given current technology. We cannot rely on the current political parties and their representatives to press forward on this issue or any other one that may risk them a vote or two. We need a third-party, supported by ordinary Americans who ultimately are those most impacted, to drive transportation improvements forward. This holds true with every other infrastructure endeavor, every other national reform. The history of the United States has been one of extraordinary drive, energy, innovation. We never sat back and said we cannot do something because it was too hard. We just did it, and we can do so again.

Our Many "Backyards" – Small to Large

I know I seem fixated on the "clean up our own backyards" analogy to the political dynamic. But I like it; because hypocrisy bothers me. Political or social activists appear, too often it seems to me, to want to change the national or even global dynamic but do almost nothing at the local level. For example, activists may become totally passionate and dedicated to addressing at the national level the discrimination and abuse directed towards women, as with the "me-too" movement of recent months. But, they do not apply the same energies and passions to helping out in their county, town or city with real women who are victims of this abuse. They are reluctant to clean up their own backyards, get their "hands dirty", have a personal association with the problems; preferring to keep pristine and righteous in vociferously fobbing off the problem to "Washington".

There is also an annoying tendency for activists to want to correct perceived deficiencies of others in parts of the country far away from them. They want to "nationalize" all problems elsewhere in the country, have national policies and programs to "solve" others' problems, but are quite unlikely to want others to come in and dictate solutions to their own. Just think of this imaginary scenario. Rural and small-town America does not have an inner-city crime problem. Logical because they don't have inner cities, right? But how about if Judge Roy Moore from Alabama and Sheriff Joe Arpaio from Arizona took it upon themselves to solve the horrendous gang violence in Chicago. Wouldn't Chicagoans take umbrage? Of course they would, that's their backyard.

There are so many examples I can offer as to this willing disassociation with problems that are very real and inescapable, right there in our face, down the street from us; while so many people expend lots of fruitless energy on protesting inequities seen as national problems. There is an unwillingness here to have "skin in the game".

One of the real beauties of starting anew with a centrist party could be to reverse this dynamic. Again, adopting a 'grassroots" ideology that builds from the local, to the State, to the regional, to the national, and then to the global. Rather than the reverse – top down programming – as seems to be the case with the two major parties. And actually, so much can be done without making a particular issue a matter of party politics at any level.

Take for example the issues of global warming, climate change, environmentalism, conservation – all polarizing in the current political environment. Rather than protesting, marching with placards, writing congressmen – all unlikely to affect much of anything – why not on our own properties consume less energy, recycle, use less pesticides, herbicides, chemical fertilizers, use a fuel-efficient car, grow more trees? Then go locally and clean up streams and rivers, work with manufacturers and the city/county to reduce pollutants and encourage energy saving and "clean" practices. Then participate at the civil society, not political party levels, to improve conditions at the state level. Then, if we still have excess time and resources in our hands, which is doubtful, go nationally and globally.

If all of us were to do so – become active at home and locally even in just one area we are passionate about – I believe we would see much more positive outcomes on larger scales. Again, I do not believe a new political party should be active in all areas, on all issues. But outside the parameters of a party, there are so many things we as individual citizens can do at a personal and local level.

However, within the bounds of government and politics, there is still so much that can be done. How many people, speaking honestly, can say they are active at the local government level? How many people attend the meetings and hearings open to the public in their town, city or county? The ones that decide on zoning and development, on social programs, on expenditures? I can say honestly that I am very delinquent in this area, much to my embarrassment as I write this. However, members of a third party staying within the parameters of the party platform, or individuals acting as individuals outside the party, can make positive contributions locally.

How many people consider running for local county or city office? Or for a State office such as delegate? Too often it seems that people focus on the national offices – Representative or Senator to Congress – as if Washington is the only place things can get done. Actually, there are a tremendous amount of actions taken at the county, town or city levels – ones that most immediately impact on the individual. And at the State level – delegates and senators to State legislatures work on many issues of specific concern to citizens; ones that are not likely to be taken up in Washington. Again, there is such a national predisposition to focus on Congress, Washington D.C., the federal government, as if these few representatives have the power, time, or disposition to address the minutia of our daily lives. A futile exercise for the most part. The lower down the political chain we go to influence the process and address our own individual needs, the more we can accomplish.

Grassroots Activism – Party vs. Political Interests vs. Social Interests

A viable third party must be created from the ground up – by the people who are most concerned and willing to devote time and energy to creating change. They need to give full expression to their beliefs and somehow they need to band together to combine and formulate their ideas and beliefs into a consensus framework, platform and agenda that will be effective. This will not be an easy task, given the diversity in people in our country – diverse in so many ways that it is impossible for them to coalesce into agreement on all subjects and in all areas. That said, a new party must reflect agreement and consensus in as many key principles as possible.

Currently, the two major parties formulate their political platforms through their existing party committee structures – essentially pulling together political policies at the top and then imposing them on the rank and file through the descending layers of the party apparatus. There is very little real upward movement of ideas and beliefs from the base of ordinary people. This is why so often we will hear canned party precepts being expressed mechanically and with very little variation between speakers at any level of the party strata. Staying on message is the strategy. The ordinary party followers are just supposed to follow the party lead and spread the message in that all important "ground game".

For a third party to take root in the Americana political arena it must be different. The 40% or so of voters who now call themselves "independents" will not be looking for a slightly different clone of one of the major parties, or a party narrowly focused on certain issues to the exclusion of others also of importance. Voters will want to feel they "own" this party; that they created it and control it. Any whiff of autocracy in the party structure and they are certain to walk. Back to one of the main parties or over to a different new party that is more inclusive.

To achieve and maintain consensus a new party must be transparent, "democratic", flexible and responsive. Equally as important, to maintain coherence and prevent discord, this party must have a minimalist platform that focuses on the most important issues and seeks consensus on those issues, while avoiding partisan issues on which no common ground can be found among the greater proportion of the populace. At the same time this party should be careful to avoid heavy handed efforts to squelch the natural desire of citizens to express themselves and be active on political and social issues that the party cannot subscribe to consensually, whether it be at the national, State or local level.

There needs to be a degree of independence at each level, that allows for consensus on level-specific issues. For example, a national platform should not include a position on the rehabilitation of the Chesapeake Bay watershed. This is not an issue that anyone in California, Texas or North Dakota is really personally interested in although they may be generally sympathetic. They will be most concerned about their own watersheds, which are not of immediate concern to those of us in the MidAtlantic. So, a new party should leave this item off its national agenda. However, the state party committee, backed by state members, could pursue their state specific issue within the state. Similarly, a local committee in Virginia might want to pursue conservation measures regarding the Rappahannock River, which is local to them, and part of the Chesapeake Bay watershed. But this should for the most part remain a local party issue, as other regions of Virginia have equally as important rivers, also part of the Watershed but which to them are more personally important.

In other words, each State and local party committee should have the license to develop its own character and portfolio – as long as the precepts, agreed to consensually on higher-level issues are not violated. For example, if the national party platform has reached consensus on language supporting secularism of government, then a State or local party chapter should not be permitted to pursue a government agenda at those levels that is clearly religious. But individuals have the right, and this should be respected, to pursue religious issues they feel strongly about, such as participate in their religious organizations.

But, they need to do so outside the party umbrella and make clear that on that issue they are not representing a party position but a personal one. This party ethic should be applied liberally, but within bounds. Obviously, anyone who strongly disagrees with party principles, should find another party; but, we would hope that new party platforms could be devised to include support by as many persons as possible, while allowing them the freedom to develop State and local chapters with their own character, as well as allowing individuals to pursue personal political and personal interests outside the confines of the party.

More examples may be necessary to make the preceding clearer. The national party platform may contain no reference to the legalization of marijuana, because there is not an overwhelming consensus nationally to do so. But the State committee, with the agreement of its members may decide that there is a very strong consensus within the State to pursue this issue in State legislation. Fine, as long as it is made clear this is a State party effort. But how about if a member feels strongly about the issue, when it is not contained in party platforms at any level? Then he or she should have every right to participate actively in organizations that are promoting this particular issue, as long as the party member keeps the party out of it. Also, the party at any level should be very careful not to accept endorsements from any organization that is partisan – whether "good" or "bad". Best just to have a policy that it does not recognize endorsements at all, which will enable the party to remain clearly steadfast in its platform and not have it complicated by outside groups, even if sympathetic. Thus, a State chapter could pursue legalization of marijuana in that State, but if given an endorsement by the National Organization on the Legalization of Marijuana (NORML), stand back and say it does not accept endorsements from anyone or any group - period. This will avoid misperceptions as to the party stance on issues, and help the party avoid getting mired in the details of another organization's policies, which may conflict with another group working that issue too, or conflict with some policy points of the party. Just saying no to endorsements cuts all conflict of interest, real or perceived, right out.

This stepping back should apply to endorsements of candidates from other parties in elections for which the third-party is not competing its own candidate. The reasoning behind this is that the third-party should not be regarded by the public as an offspring of any other party. Currently, politicians will dance between the major parties to minor third parties, then trot back to the main party when convenient to them. A Republican may become a Libertarian in-between elections, then revert back to competing as a Republican for election time, knowing full well that he/she cannot win as a third-party candidate. "Independents" generally come from the Democratic party but will compete as an independent when they feel they stand a better chance of winning under this identifier against Republican and Democratic candidates. But these "independents" will invariably side with the Democrats in elections they have not entered or in Congressional caucuses. Bernie Sanders for example, won his Congressional seat as an independent, but competed for President as a Democrat.

To take this one step further, if a third-party gives a blanket endorsement even just once for a candidate of either major party it will be identified with that major party for the future. There will be no credible stepping back and its centrist identity will be forfeit. However, this third-party should voice its position for or against specific policies of candidates from other parties. In other words, the endorsement would be of a position or policy not the candidate. For example, if one major party candidate voiced a cogent position on controlling immigration the third party could agree. And if the other major party candidate voiced a reasonable policy on compassionate treatment of longtime illegal immigrants, the third party could also agree. Again, the emphasis should be on endorsement of policy stances, not overall endorsement of candidates or a major party.

A new centrist party should also foster an ethic of not engaging in personal attacks on opponents, whether someone within the party or from another party. Also, members, party officials and candidates should foster a strong ethic that they will not respond to personal or hyperbolic attacks on themselves. Just step back and not get enmeshed in "twitter wars", slime attacks and all the nastiness that characterizes partisan politics today. Just ignore those who relish the mudslinging, including the press. Let's be a "thick-skinned" party. If you ignore them, deprive them of that attention, they will go away eventually. Probably feeling a bit childish and silly.

In my mind, a centrist party should not be a protest party but one actively working on concrete issues. Thus, I think it important that the party make it a policy not to participate in marches, demonstrations, sit-ins, rally's and other such group efforts to gain public and media attention on specific issues. Again, this is not to say individual party members should not participate, just that the party should be kept out of it. Another example: say there is a march on Washington calling for gun control measures. Those individuals who feel strongly about this issue should go but leave the party out of it. In other words, don't gather together members from the party chapter, all wearing party tee-shirts, stand in a group in the demonstration waving signs with the party name, chanting etc. The reason for having an embargo on group party participation in such events is that public opinion will identify the party with the protest position, when in actuality the party may not have a consensus position on the issue.

Our Youngest Voters

A new centrist party should direct considerable attention to the young, particularly those in the 16-18 age group. Among the young there is an idealism, passion, fervency; a gut-based focus on what is good and clearly wrong. They have the capability to visualize how the future should look like, while all too often we who are older may have surrendered the hope for a brighter and kinder world ahead. We need to listen to them.

But also, these teenagers will be eligible to vote in not so distant elections at the local, state and federal levels. We should want them to believe that their views matter and their votes will count.

I am not at all sure of the legalities involved in outreach to people below the voting age of 18. I do not know if it is legal or even proper to provide them with campaign literature, or involve them in the "ground game", or utilize their considerable expertise in IT and social media. Maybe such involvement needs to come indirectly via their parents. Maybe it would be possible for a third party to be included in school presentations on our political system, joining representatives from the two main parties and others. Again, I am unsure of what is allowed, or what is proper. I do think it would be well worthwhile, however, to explore this further.

We want our young to get involved in government and social activism as early as possible, before discouragement and disenfranchisement sets in. When all they see is the squabbling and dysfunction in Washington and the polarization throughout the country, it will be very easy for them just to say they want no part of politics or government. They will not believe they have any power or influence over the processes. They will not vote or work on issues. That is the fact now for the most part, however, a third party that includes them, listens to them, feels their input and skills are valuable, can change the dynamic and help revitalize the overall atmosphere. We need the young for the good of the country; the new party needs them from the beginning because they really are the "grassroots"; hopefully we will have them as third-party members for their full voting life.

The Millennials

The Millennials came of voting age in 2000, so range in age between 18 and 36 today in 2018.   They include a wide range of people – from those just starting their careers or still in college, to those who are solidly established in their professions.   They may be young parents, with children still in primary to high school.   They were raised in the digital world and are savvy on information technology and social media.

Those in this age group who live in urban environments have often been dismissively called "snowflakes", for their seeming over-sensitivity to criticism particularly from their peers, love for group-hugs etc.   Those of this age are often seen as much behind the times in terms of a broad education and national/global awareness.   In urban areas, particularly the north, this is the group that will be glued to their smartphones for any news, information, social media etc.   In the South, if you see someone driving around with a big civil war battle flag waving from the back of their pickup, the person is most likely in this age group too.   While the social divide between urban and rural is just as acute as with other age groups, what they have in common as millennials is that they are not as a group very politically or socially involved.

Forget any such disparagements of this group, however true.   Millennials hold the potential to be the most potent political force in the country today, both now and for the next two decades.   They meet the minimum age requirements for federal office: 36 years for President, 30 for Senate and 26 for House.   They are attuned to the news of the day – local, state and national – however "fake".   They appear to be very concerned about their current situation, and their future prospects.   They want a voice, they want positive change, and quite likely they have the most energy and motivation of any age group to effect such change.

Any new party, to be viable, must take this age group into serious consideration.   Millennials must help develop the party platforms and agendas for all levels of government.   They will be an important source of officials at all levels of the party apparatus.   They will be the most likely source of volunteers to conduct the "ground game" in any election.   And they will be potential sources of candidates for public office – again at all levels of government.

They are a "must have" for a party, and by every indication a centrist party would appeal to them if it reaches out to them.

University campuses should be a prime objective in party outreach. College students are generally eager to embrace new ideas, particularly if they provide alternatives to what many of the younger set see as negative and disturbing factors in our society. I would like to see a new party establish a student chapter at each and every college or university. These could very well become the source points for a rapid "bloom" in party membership.

Gen X

Those Americans born in the twenty-year period between approximately 1962 and 1982, bridging the generations between baby boomers and millennials, have often been called Generation X. They were born into and grew up at a time of significant societal shift in America. Two-income families became a norm, a necessity, so many became what were called "latch-key kids", coming home to an empty house while both parents were working. This was the period too when children, rather than being "latch-key", spent considerable periods of time in day care or in supervised after school activities. This generation is now, in 2018, between 36 and 56 years old.

Often described over the years as disaffected and cynical, they have been seen as dismissive of the generation that came before, the baby boomers, and hearken back to earlier times such as the 1950's and 1960's when American life seemed much more simple and straightforward. They tend to place "normalcy" at the top of their personal aspirations: financial, social, educational, political. In general, they do not favor radical positions, and shy away from significant activism. Whether urban or rural, they are very status quo oriented and less likely to challenge authority – as long as they themselves are doing well. In many ways, they appear to have assumed a lot of the perspective of their grandparent's generation – work hard, study hard, save money, educate the children, "don't rock the boat", "keep your nose clean", conform.

That said, this is the most entrepreneurial generation. They created the digital age. They made personal computers, smart phones, and social media important components of modern American life and culture. Their impact on our country – and globally – has been revolutionary. They are now well established in the business world, often the new senior executives of small and large companies. These truly are the movers and shakers in America's economic world today.

But, I do not see much motivation within this group as a whole to precipitate social or political change in the country. That said, this age group is the one that has the most power to make such change happen. We need them to come around to the viewpoint that changes are necessary, and that while they might not see an immediate personal benefit, the future of their children and grandchildren and the country depends on their active engagement. My hope is that a very centrist party will appeal to them and provoke an engagement that will pull all the combined energies of the generations together in common causes. They are in our demographic middle and have all the assets to make positive change come about.

Our Seniors

This is a huge demographic, that includes the youngest baby boomers who are still actively working and may still have children in college, all the way through to the most elderly. Ages would range from 56 to over 100! This group includes the generation that knew the Great Depression, World War II and the prosperous post- war years of the 1950's and 1960's when financial security existed, the middle-class was the largest group in American society, and hard work, frugality, patriotism, belief in the American system and dream were ethics and realities. However, this group also includes the baby boomers, what some call the "me generation". This group rejected many of the ethics of their parents' generation; they found fault with the "political-military complex", with rampant commercialism, with environmental destruction, with organized religion, with social injustices, with a perceived police state, and of course America's wars abroad. But then the baby boomers made another shift and turned towards "self-actualization", non-traditional religions, and disengagement from the broader society. Then, it seems, they melded back into the mainstream.

Thus, it would be very difficult to generalize as to such a diverse group's willingness or ability to participate actively in bringing forward a new party and new centrist political philosophy. But, I am certain that these Americans represent a very important political demographic that we must pursue assiduously. Given the general disenchantment in the American population with the current situation, it is not unreasonable to expect a centrist third party would have appeal.

The insights, experiences, and wisdom that can be gleaned from this age group will be invaluable. As most are now retired, they also represent a significant potential asset in terms of volunteer support. Plus, many have the financial means to be helpful if they choose.

"The Sweet Spot"

All American citizens, regardless of age, are important to our social fabric and thus must be regarded as such by any new centrist party that hopes to be successful. This obligates the party to foster collegiality, mutual respect, and consensus among all groups. And in terms of candidates for elected office, the "enlightened statesmen" are certainly present within the full range of ages.

However, I feel the real "sweet spot" from which to hopefully draw new leadership will be in the 45-60-year-old group. I do not want to draw too fine a line on this, as again "stars" are out there from young to old. But, I feel that too many of our elected officials are just too old to perform the full functions of their office effectively, and that their entrenchment in these positions for sometimes decades, is counterproductive to beneficial change.

Someone in the 45-60 age frame will be balanced in the rough middle of the American adult population. They will generally still be actively working, senior in their profession, at the peak of their career, whatever that career may be. They will be experienced, likely to be healthy, still intellectually curious and motivated. They will be current on the feelings and aspirations of their age group. They are likely to have young but adult children, so therefore have personal insights into the needs of this age group. They are likely to still have parents in the "senior" category and thus be sensitive to their needs. In other words, I believe this middle-aged group holds the most promise for peak talents and abilities for our most senior positions – local, State, and federal.

Seniors, as a group, generally do not have the most current real-life perspective necessary to represent the needs and political will of younger groups. Nor do they have a real-time knowledge of the state of the Union or the realities of global issues. Too often, if politicians, they have started out in office younger, in the "sweet spot" themselves, been active and effective. But then they hold on, term after term well into obsolescence. They just do not want to step out gracefully, with dignity, and pass the baton to younger and more able leaders. There seems to be a vanity there quite often. They become "legends in their own minds", feel the country or the state or the local government cannot function without them. They want to stay relevant. Political power at whatever level becomes an addiction. I do not believe in age limits or term limits, because exceptional talent is still present among the oldest citizens. I just believe voters should carefully consider the age factor when electing officials, and that political parties, particularly a new start-up such as I am proposing, seek to present younger candidates.

But not too young! All generations have "stars", real standouts in terms of ability, intellect and conviction. However, experience – work, life, political, economic, social – comes with time. This is unavoidable. Young people have not acquired the degree of experience I believe is essential to be truly effective in tackling the many complex national issues that face us in today's United States and around the world. Enthusiasm and passion can only carry one so far. A new party should be careful not to present candidates for elected office whose immaturity will be apparent and thus not be helpful for the person or the party. Young people need to be included, feel needed, feel they belong. But somehow realize that there are many options beyond just running for office, particularly a higher office. Too many people, and not just the young, believe they have to run for Congress to make an impact, forgetting that local elected offices and party positions are important in and of themselves plus build helpful experience for higher positions later on.

Communications – Mainstream Media, Local Media, and Social Media

No political party can survive if it is unknown to the voting public! This is where a third party will face its biggest challenge initially. The party needs to utilize all means to gain recognition and voice its message. Mainstream media will be the hardest to penetrate. Television networks are clearly identified with one of the major parties and thus will be reluctant to cover a third party unless it has independently become visible such as with a well-attended rally. Major newspapers are also unlikely to cover third party events or stories unless it appears to them that there is substantial public support. Local media, television, print and particularly radio, is probably the best option for a third party to pursue.

I do urge maximum attention be given to radio and here's why. Although most people do not listen to radio at home, they do listen to radio when driving in a car whether commuting, running out to shop, or travelling. Some people listen to news, most probably to music, others to commentary, but there are ample interludes in radio programming for ads, interviews, or just brief reporting. Developing a rapport with radio stations could be very productive.

I've been doing a lot of driving from Virginia down to North Carolina, Georgia and Alabama. When bored with the music channels, I search for talk radio. I find it striking that the only talk radio stations I can find are alt right-type programs – Rush Limbaugh and others. I have not heard a single program that could be called anything but rightwing. I think this is a vacuum that a centrist party could really exploit to get its message out and to hopefully draw interested voters into the fold.

Social media is perhaps the most promising communications vehicle for a new party. It is the least expensive media, has the most reach, and has become a national phenomenon in terms of popularity for the public. Here is an area in which the skills and energies of the younger set will be invaluable. Quite frankly a lot of us older folk are not so savvy in this area, so cannot be expected to develop and implement a social media strategy. But we do recognize its importance and a third party should take full advantage.

Mail, in my opinion, is the least attractive avenue for outreach. I believe it is outdated now and that many, like me, look at flyers of any kind in the mailbox as junk mail and rarely pay attention. For political outreach and campaigning, mailings are time consuming and costly and not effective. For a party where cost and volunteer labor are a factor, mailings should be considered down on the list of good options.

Finally, the very best outreach for a new party should be face-to-face contact with potential voters. This could involve manning a stand anywhere possible – university campuses, supermarkets, trade fairs, car shows. Anywhere possible. This offers an opportunity to discuss party principles directly with the voter and provide printed literature for them to take home. This is where the new party can really come alive, connecting people with people.

Funding

Unfortunately, politics today, particularly national politics, is a game of big money. And the ill-considered 2010 decision of the Supreme Court to allow corporate entities to be "people too" and contribute to campaigns through super PACs has allowed business interests to assume a major role in political campaigns at both state and national levels. Is this what the Founders of the United States meant by representative government? Do you honestly believe that big corporations represent your interests? I say no to both the preceding statements. Big money and big business now in essence choose the candidates that you will be allowed to vote for. Strong and viable candidates without the financial backing from corporations are doomed to failure if they cannot overcome the funding issue and this is a major problem for a third party. The public may just barely learn their names, and usually only if they can gain some prominence and visibility through other means – personal wealth or professional success or even notoriety. Excellent, possibly superior candidates who are identified by citizens in their communities, whether competing in State or national elections, do not stand a chance unless they can find sources of very significant funding.

Look at these rough figures for the 2016 General Election. The Republican and Democratic presidential campaigns spent about 2.65 billion dollars, of which 600 million came from super PACs and outside sources. 2016 House and Senate races cost 4.26 billion. Politicking through the two main party primaries cost about another billion. This is a total of 7.8 billion for the congressional and presidential races. It's a bit obscene really.

However, a new third party will need funding. And to set itself apart and be credible to centrist Americans it really will need to eschew corporate and individual megadonor funding. In other words, it will need to rely on the support of ordinary voting citizens. This can be done. For the 2016 campaign Bernie Sanders raised about 220 million, mostly through small donations. Approximately 119 million Americans voted in 2016. If each voter had divided just $67 dollars between Presidential, House and Senate campaigns the total collected would have reached the 7.8 billion actually spent. However, current limits under electoral law are much higher than $67.

239

Individuals may donate $2,700 to a federal candidate's committee, plus up to $33,400 per year to a national political party committee, plus unlimited amounts to super PACS. In 2016, some individuals – I repeat, individuals - donated over 20 million. Can we really be so naïve to think the individual who donated this amount of money has the same standing in a campaign as the million people who donate $20 each? How many ordinary Americans can donate these amounts? Not many, so it is clear that political influence via funding is disproportionally weighted to the wealthy.

This excessive and uneven use of money to effect federal elections is something that voters should rail against. But, a third party should not waste too much energy on this element of electoral reform as it is not likely to change anytime soon, and there are even more important issues to pursue as priorities in a third-party agenda. That said, a third party can set an example, reaching out to ordinary voters stating that on principle not only will it not accept corporate contributions, but that it will also not accept individual contributions of over $100 to the central party committee, or sanction contributions of over $100 per candidate per individual who is eligible to vote for that candidate. In other words, I could donate $100 to the central committee, $100 to a Presidential candidate, $100 to a senatorial candidate, and $100 to a candidate for my congressional district. Why shouldn't this $400 be enough? If multiplied times the number of voters in the 2016 election this would amount to 40.6 billion dollars. Mega-obscene, five times what was spent in 2016, unlikely to be reached, but still more reflective of the will of the people than the current system which is open-ended for the wealthy.

A new third-party should possibly establish its own limit of $100 per individual, divided among party and candidates as the person sees fit. If a third-party were to develop a constituency representing one-third of voters, or roughly 40 million voters using 2016 figures, each contributing $100, the total would come to four billion dollars! Obviously, many voters would not contribute at all, and most much less than $100, but the point here is that sufficient funds can be raised through small individual donations for a third-party to be a viable contender. The onus will be on the party and the candidates to make their messages appeal and resonate with ordinary voters so that they feel their 10, 20, or $100 donation is worth it.

Looking Ahead – The 2018 through 2024 Elections

There was no break in the campaign season following the 2016 election. In the past, there was usually a one-year hiatus after a presidential election before campaigning began for the mid-term elections, and two years before the start of rumblings about the following presidential election. This time around there was no break. Politicians and a lot of the public became focused on both 2018 and 2020 even before Donald Trump was inaugurated!

My sense is that most Americans, regardless of political persuasion, do not like the perpetual political campaign. They would like to elect an official, then go back to their own personal lives with some confidence that that official will doing his/her job as their representative in a responsible and acceptable manner. Most Americans, even if disappointed their candidate did not win, would regard the winner as the elected representative and accept the result. Today, the distrust by the public of government in general and of the party they oppose particularly is so visceral that I see no hope for the majority of Americans standing behind our institutions of government with a sense of common interest, once a hallmark of the American political spirit. Unless the dynamic changes.

A third party, if centrist and mature, has the possibility of reviving the American spirit of common national purpose and goals. Over the course of our history this national sense of being all Americans working together was one of the fundamental strengths of our Union. We should foster whatever steps necessary to bring this feeling of patriotism to the forefront again.

The 2018 mid-term election is very important, and any third party with ambitions for both local and national standing should strive to be widely known to the public now. If not, it is likely to fade into obscurity in the following two years, leading up to the next presidential election in 2020. It is unlikely that a new third party will win any seats in Congress this go-around. However, it would be very influential if this third party could enter the fray, not as a 2018 contender, but as a future one; voicing its policy positions in advance. This would certainly attract national attention. There are hundreds of seats up for election at state and local levels – state legislature or executive, county, town or city. Third party members should participate actively at all levels – again not necessarily as candidates, but as alternative voices to the now two-party reserve. The more visibility at all levels the better, but again the caution for the party to only present highly qualified persons that can represent the centrist philosophy effectively and be palatable if not attractive to the majority of voters in that particular jurisdiction. It might even be useful for the third-party persons who intend to be candidates in 2019 and 2020 to become visible now in 2018.

I think all of us can resign ourselves to the mid-term Congressional elections being just the usual competition to see which of the two major parties wins control of the House and/or Senate. However, a third party, if it were to gain national attention as a valid entity with a significant following, and even if not competing a single candidate, can modify the dialogue during the campaign and influence the agenda of the new sitting Congress.

If a third party were to capture a modicum of national prominence now and maintain this through 2019 and to the end of 2020, it could very well become a gamechanger in terms of the national picture. Again, in 2020 like 2018, all of the House seats and one-third of the Senate seats would be up for reelection. Plus, hundreds of State and local positions will be open. It is by no means impossible that a third party could win a significant number of seats at the various levels. It is unlikely that enough seats could be won to have a major influence on control of the various political bodies, however, again party influence and participation in political debates at all level may very well be within reach.

For the 2020 general election, for President, it would be excellent if the third party could present a candidate on the ballot who had the consensus of all state party chapters. Again, my caution that this candidate be of superlative qualifications, one who would be recognized by the broad American voting public as meeting a national standard. In other words, this candidate should not be a throw-away – someone who is just competing to get the third-party name on the ballot. This should not be a "niche" candidate – one who is essentially focused on a few limited issues. We do not need another Libertarian, Green, or Constitutional-type candidate that will only appeal to a small segment of the national voters. A lot will ride on this candidate, and the party will be identified with him/her for a long time afterwards, so we must choose wisely. Such a person is out there, we just have to search deeply and make sure our platform and agenda is such that the "best and the brightest" will want to come on-board. My assumption is that Donald Trump will win his second term in 2020. However, with the results of the Special Counsel investigation looming nothing is certain. Who the Democrats will field is just as uncertain. 2020 promises to be an important year in our electoral history and a third party needs to make certain it is visible, providing a rational alternative to the two major parties which are so mired in divisive politics.

The 2022 and 2024 elections will be the pivotal elections for the third-party. These are years in which we could see a third-party entering in full balance with the two major parties. These years are where I could envision this party capturing a full third of the seats in the House. Maybe less in the Senate given the term lengths, but any presence would be significant and have to be taken into account by that body. A strong run for the Presidency by this third party is not inconceivable, nor an electoral college split that would throw the decision into the House.

Party Candidate Qualifications

A new centrist party should compete for as many local, State, and federal positions possible. That said, every effort should be made to avoid endorsing individuals under the party banner who will not reflect well on the party. Losing elections is not so much the issue here but maintaining the party's reputation is critical. If the party runs just one candidate in a particular race who is unqualified, or unethical, or at odds with the party platform, rest assured that the voters in that voting block will remember and brand the party accordingly in future elections. Again, this could apply to local elections such as for county government, or elections for State legislatures, or federal House and Senate elections, or the Presidency. The quality of candidates presented in the very beginning of a party's engagement will make or break its reputation.

First and foremost, any candidate should meet the highest standards of ethics. Regardless of their other qualifications, I feel that the party should have zero tolerance for a candidate who is known or believed to be a racist, bigot or xenophobe. We should not support a candidate who is known to be a habitual liar. We should have no part in supporting a person who has committed crimes against persons, whether physical such as assault or financial such as fraud or psychological such as intimidation or other abuse. A party is not bound by the same legal standards as a court of law. We do not have to abide by the principle of "innocent until proven guilty". However, a party should be fair, consider rights of due process, and be circumspect as to whether allegations are just mudslinging or credible. Such a party policy would be a significant departure from current major party policies which go on the basis of all party members being eligible to compete in primaries, with the party leadership not playing an active role in vetting candidates. Instituting a party policy in which party leadership vets candidates before allowing them to compete under the party banner presents a quandary, is a double-edged sword, which must be astutely managed. We do not want to have a situation such as with the Democratic National Committee, in which the committee not the voters chose Hillary Clinton as its candidate four years before the 2016 election and essentially blocked the chance for other qualified candidates to compete on an even playing field. However, we also do not want to turn a blind eye, as has seemed to happen so frequently in recent elections at all levels, where candidates are known to have serious character deficiencies but are supported, win an election, then are publicly exposed, fight the allegations for extended periods into their terms, then resign in disgrace.

Candidates should be the first to do "opposition research" on themselves, be their own most strict judges and determine whether any of their "skeletons in the closet" are likely to surface and be of sufficient import to hurt their chances with the voters or prevent them to serve effectively in the office if elected.   But, the party itself needs to be vigilant and take the cynical approach that a candidate will not always be objective regarding their own shortcomings. How many times in recent scandals have we heard the person protest vigorously that allegations were a lie; then when proof mounts change the story to something like the public doesn't know both sides of the story or that an event happened long before and is no longer relevant; or that persons and investigations are "witch hunts"? Do any of us believe that no one in their party was aware of the candidate/official's baggage? In my view, any party that does not conduct a modicum of due diligence into the character and qualifications of its candidate is also culpable if he/she is found grossly deficient.   A party should do its own "opposition research" on its own candidates before presenting them to a possibly unwitting and trusting public. The party goal should be to ensure candidates embrace the broad viewpoints of the party membership, not leadership, and establish that candidates it is placing on ballots will most likely meet basic ethical standards. Every citizen has the right to compete for election to public office. However, no candidate has the right to compete under the auspices of the party of his/her choice.

A new third party should also take a different approach to identifying candidates than the major parties do. For the most part, those parties wait for candidates to select themselves as hopeful competitors in an election. Presumably the party power elite does have its own private outreach mechanisms in "smoky backrooms", but for the most part candidates, particularly for higher office, already have their own power structures and funding sources, then declare themselves. A third party should not prevent such individuals from coming forward and competing, if they meet ethical standards as described above; however, a new party should aggressively seek out "the best and the brightest" throughout the United States, via the party's "grassroots" base. Another way to describe this different approach would be power up rather than power down. I firmly believe that we have a great wealth of talent around the country that are better qualified than many of our current elected officials. The problem is that they have neither self-identified, nor been sought out by the parties. I think it would be well worth the effort for a new party to just ask its membership: "who do you know in your community who would be someone bringing great credit to an elected position, and what position do you see as the best fit". We are in the information age. A national party, comprised of State committees, can ask for input on particularly stellar individuals who might better serve our citizens in some capacity than ones chosen by the two parties and pushed down for the party base to swallow.

Proactive efforts by the third-party base to identify exceptional individuals, then convince them to join the party, and then to convince them to compete in elections at some appropriate level holds promise for drawing in lots more talent, talent that has a closer connection to the voting public than those chosen by the major parties from existing power bases far removed from the ordinary person.

A Launching Strategy for a Centrist Party

First impressions are critical if a new third, centrist party hopes to break strongly from the starting gate and present a credible challenge to the leaders. First of all, it must be truly democratic in seeking out the views of its members on policies and directions. The convictions, energies, and talents of "real, ordinary people" must be strikingly visible in the overall character of the party. It is also crucial that a new party offer more to the voters than the major parties do with well thought out policies, a clear direction, and viable strategies. A new party should be different than the field of major and minor parties active today. If not, why bother creating an organization that is just old wine in a new bottle?

Look closely at the platforms of the major and minor parties. The bulk of key policies are not that different from one to the other - whether right or left. All of the parties see the need to tick off the same key subjects – defense, veterans, free trade, justice, the economy, "jobs", equality. But none of the parties really get into how they will make substantive, positive changes in these areas. They really have just checked off the mandatory boxes and hope that is enough to attract votes. But at the end of the day, these other parties and their candidates don't really have the slightest idea of what to do. They just tick the boxes, repeat the same tired old sound bites, and hope people trust them to bring improvements. Voters are pretty cynical now though. They want something more solid than campaign promises, clichés, slogans. A new party needs to aggressively present a new face, a new brand – backed by solid facts, programs and plans – if it is to have even the slightest chance of competing with the major parties on their own playing field. But how does the party make itself known to more than 200 million voters of which it will need at least 20 million people as members to really be considered a viable party? Obviously, all the outreach mechanisms such as direct contact, social media, emails, mainstream media will need to be utilized, but I want to offer an idea for a supplementary initiative that I believe will help.

Assume a new party is serious enough and active enough by this time to have established a national committee and separate state committees in all 50 states. If the party hasn't it will probably not be able to make much of a showing until after the 2020 election. Too much groundwork needed. But for a party that has already made significant progress in setting up a national structure, the following outline of a program may be helpful.

1. Take maximum advantage of the remaining two months until the 2018 elections. Use this book, or another, or several as springboards to stimulate feedback and interest from the "grassroots". Get the party known to the public. From the party national committee to the state chapters to current party members advertise the book(s) as "must reads" as a catalyst for membership dialogue on the party platform, ideological direction, and strategies. No endorsement of the contents of a book is needed or even advisable. We want to hear from the "grassroots" as well as subject matter experts, but there must be a starting point and structure to channel debate constructively.

2. Set up a separate discussion forum on the national and state party websites inviting/urging comments on the book in general, but better yet on specific issues. The goal would be to use the input of members to formulate a party platform that will win consensus from the membership and be of interest to the wider public.

3. Urge members to spread the word on the book(s) to their own non-member contacts, in the hopes of attracting new members to the party who will also contribute to the discussions on the websites.

4. A useful device, using a book as a theme, would be to print thousands of bookmarks that candidates and supporters, and party organizers, can pass out at events or door-to-door so that interested people can have an inexpensive "take-away" and explore the party further. One side of the bookmark would advertise the book and the other side would have the name, picture and website of the candidate or the website of the state or national party committee. This would give the candidate more substance to a voter than just a handshake and a smile. The voters we want are the thinking voters, the ones who do want something more than just slogans.

5. The national committee should ask state chapters to compile their state membership input on a platform into a state recommendation for the national platform, then a representative group from the states

should meld all the 50 state recommendations into one that can be presented to the entire membership for a digital vote at the national convention. A big job and one that needs to take place immediately so that party candidates can have a degree of political "backbone" at hand when they compete in the 2020 elections. Using an existing, current book as the stimulus for arriving at a platform will help focus member discussions on key issues and philosophy and thus considerably reduce the time needed to arrive at a consensus platform. Again, if a party has not established a known presence in 2018 it is doubtful it will be ready for 2020. The pressure is on now.

6. Once the main subjects of a national platform are accepted, the effort should be to "flesh them out" with individual, detailed position papers on each of the subjects. These papers should each be prepared by a group of experts, who have respected credentials pertaining to the subjects. These position papers should be available on party websites linked to the main platform summaries. Quite possibly the finished product – platform with position papers – would be worth publishing as a separate book to take the place of whatever outside book had been used as the initial springboard. The point of all this is to establish the party as one very different from the others – pragmatic, well-prepared, knowledgeable, responsive to those it represents.

7. This is a suggested timetable for 2018 - 2019:

September 2018
The party central committee sends out information on this and other current books on third parties/centrism to all state chapters.
The state chapters forward this information to all members, inviting comments and platform submissions to be submitted to the state website.

December 2018
State chapters compile member submissions, drafts State versions of a national platform.

January – May 2019
The national platform committee completes its work combining state platform submissions into one, sends the completed draft platform to the state committees for review, revision and finally "ratification" –

seeking two-thirds agreement. State committees conduct a digital vote among their members in this process. If concurrence of two-thirds of the States is not achieved, the areas of disagreement are worked out until this level of concurrence is achieved.

June 2019
A national convention is held to formally adopt the official platform. At the convention, those members interested in running for the Presidency or Congress would be given an opportunity to speak.

August 2019
State primaries would be held to choose party candidates for State positions, as well as for a presidential candidate. This early date would enable all candidates to begin collecting signatures on January 1, 2020 to be listed on the ballot.

A Strategy for a Presidential Election

While it is unlikely – not impossible, just unlikely – that a third party will be able to mount a presidential bid in 2020 that will threaten the power holds of the two major parties, it is very possible that the third-party efforts can capture significant national attention. While I believe it is vitally important for a third party to maintain "grassroots" solidarity through concentrating on local and State issues and elections, it is just a fact of life that no third party can become a "household word" at any level, unless it does present a strong candidate, under a strong party platform, in the general election.

Building on my previous suggestion that the party solicit input from the "grassroots" as to sympathetic and stellar "pillars" in their own communities, I would recommend that the effort continue unceasingly from now until mid-2019 to identify potential presidential candidates who can be strong representatives of the party on the national stage, then compete in a party primary that precedes those of the other parties – in other words move up the timetable to "scoop" the dominant parties with an early party candidate decision and a strong and comprehensive early campaign.

The party primary would be an excellent time to test innovative mechanisms for voting such as the Ranked Choice Voting procedure, a short low-cost campaign period, and an electronic vote for the party nominee by all members regardless of location, to take place as the final event of a party convention.

In our current political "circus", the personalities who win the respective primaries of the major parties become the focus of the campaigns – they take the stage as the would-be heirs-apparent to the enthroned "king. Their spoken and written words become the party gospel, parroted up and down the line by party officials, "surrogates", and media supporters. Obviously, public scrutiny of the candidates is essential, however it is clear to me that any President is just the tip of the iceberg. Yes, their views, character, charisma, knowledge are very important; but it is really their administration that will be the iceberg. And we never seem to have an inkling of what persons the candidates will carry with them into the White House to fill the most key positions and formulate and execute the new administration policies.

I believe it will be a very powerful innovation and trust-building initiative if the third-party presidential candidates would begin their campaigns, continuing through the party primary, during the main campaign, and into the Presidency with an already committed slate of key officials who would form the foundation of their administration. Let me explain further. Candidates competing for the party nomination would name who their Vice-presidential running mate would be. Then name persons who would fill all cabinet posts - Secretaries of all the Departments and key agencies. Then they would name who would be moving into the other key White House positions – Chief of Staff, National Security Advisor etc. By doing so, the candidate would show the voting public that they have credible, experienced supporters on their team already; persons who would have already given considerable thought to the new administration's agenda in the most key areas of the U.S. government.

These highly-qualified persons would write detailed position papers that would be included as addenda to the national party platform. These persons would be able to articulate to the voting public the policies proposed by the candidate and his/her team. They would be an integral part of the campaigns, primary and general, as active on the campaign trail as the candidate. With a small new third party, it is quite possible and practical, for candidates competing for the primary to consider "sharing" a good number of the same key officials. If exceptional individuals in specialized fields are identified and willing to serve under the third-party banner, why should party candidates seeking the party nomination not be collegial and draw on the same pool of experts? Again, I believe public confidence in a candidate would be greatly enhanced if there was an awareness of who were backing a candidate and who had already committed to hitting the ground running with the newly elected President.

Look at the situation today, in 2018, in which there seems to be a revolving door of key officials in cabinet and other key positions. The government at top levels is in disarray. Thank goodness for the intrepid career public servants who are keeping the administration running, but I know this is a challenge without stability at the top. A third party can break the mold and create a new dynamic and modus operandi.

Just practically in terms of campaign logistics, there would be a great advantage to having a large slate of credible pre-chosen officials out in the field. One candidate, being one person, can only cover so much geography per day and in today's two-party system, it seems so ludicrous, particularly in the last few weeks of the campaign for the general election, to see the two candidates shuttling back and forth to "key" States for quickie visits in the hopes of winning the electoral vote. States with less electoral votes or who are considered shoe-ins for a candidate are virtually ignored in the latter days of a Presidential race.

With a new third-party initiative to field already chosen key officials, it would be possible to have these persons out in different States simultaneously delivering authoritative speeches and commentaries on how the new third-party administration would function. Not one of our United States would be ignored or forgotten as is the case today. Important policy speeches could be delivered by the persons who would administer the policy, possibly in the States that are most concerned about a particular policy. For example, a would-be Secretary of Energy could concentrate on speaking in energy States on specific issues of concern to them: to coal miners about the future of coal or alternatives to it; to people in the Gulf States about offshore drilling; to people in the Northeast about fracking; to voters in the central States about pipelines.

Most Americans, I believe, want our government to be run by the best people possible. After an election, they want their involvement to end so they can return to their daily lives confident that the business of government is in good hands. They are disturbed and apprehensive by what they are seeing now in the Presidency – erratic, authoritarian behavior at the top, dysfunctional Departments below. Americans are not happy with Congress either – seeing their representatives of whichever party as dysfunctional and lacking spinal fortitude. A third party can restore confidence in our system by fielding a Presidential candidate and his/her team of whom all Americans can be proud of and support. I am certain this would be a great relief to the American public.

A Model National Centrist Platform

Having reviewed the national platforms of the Republican, Democratic, Libertarian, Constitution and Green Parties – the latter three currently being the strongest minor parties - it is clear to me that in the generalized responsibilities of the national government as described in the Constitution there is relative unanimity among the parties as to core goals and objectives. The differences between the parties appear in their differing views by party as to the scope of federal government involvement and methods of implementation. But here, in core principles, we should find it encouraging that there is sufficient agreement among these parties, which range from far left to far right, to allow for healthy debate, compromise, and decision-making.

What each party has done, however, is append a multitude of additional policy stances to their core platforms which are not constitutionally ascribed to the federal government, even by broad interpretation. Thus, most of the party platforms are too lengthy in line items, too specific, and as a whole not representative of the views of a sufficient majority of the U.S. population to represent a national consensus. I believe a new centrist party platform should be concise, bare-bones, reflecting only core Constitutional principles. That said, each stated principle should be backed up by a comprehensive explanatory position paper developed by nonpartisan experts. These supportive papers should be kept current to reflect changing conditions and they should also be action plans for implementing programs over an extended period, such as to the year 2050 – 32 years into the future. Here is my outline for a minimalist centrist party platform.

1. **Overarching Party Philosophy**. This centrist party is neither "left" or "right". Its aim is to be "middle-of-the-road" with an emphasis on pragmatism, moderation, and consensus governance based on core Constitutional principles. The party strives for a minimalist Federal government, with full powers to effectively govern the Nation, but which does not intercede on matters that are clearly best governed by

the States or constrict basic freedoms and liberties of our citizens. A baseline principle of this party is that all policies implemented at the federal level should have the support of two-thirds of the American people, recognizing that the current dysfunctionality of our national government stems from the sharp divisions created by our two national parties.

We believe that a strong third party can challenge the 50/50 hold of these parties on the electorate and thus move the political discussion away from divisive and partisan issues towards the core and central issues that face the nation. Similarly, this party is certain that the wealth and wisdom of this Nation resides in its citizens and believes a true democratic political system must reflect the will and concerns of all its people. Thus, the platform of this party must reflect the consensus views of its membership.

Our philosophy is that we strive to have 100% of our membership in agreement with at least 80% of party positions and at least 80% in agreement with 100% of our positions; unlike the situations within the two major parties which are factionalized between extreme and moderate viewpoints. We consider ourselves the one and only planning party – looking ahead to the future and formulating intelligent but measured steps to implement improvements over the short, medium and long-term. We reject precipitous, ill-conceived positions and actions that are provoked by radical and extremist components of the American electorate.

2. **Minimalist Government**. We believe that the purpose of government is to provide for the needs of its citizens that are beyond the scope of individuals to undertake on their own. In other words, the reason we need government is to ensure as a nation that our individual liberties and collective well-being are protected and enhanced. As Americans, we do not want or need to be controlled. We do not want to be over-governed. With this as a starting point, our party seeks as small a government as practical at Federal, State, and local levels. We do not seek arbitrary, poorly conceived reductions in government personnel or budgets; but we do strive to reduce government's footprint

wherever possible. As an extension of this precept we seek to transfer authorities of the federal government to the States where this is effective and cost efficient; and of State authorities to local levels when this would be most legitimate.

3. **National Defense.** This party believes that defense of the Nation was of paramount importance to the drafters of our Constitution; that national self-protection remains vital today; and will be critical far into the future. We recognize that national defense requires a complex interaction between a number of government entities and that all these entities must remain robust.

We believe in a strong intelligence function to provide the information necessary for other entities to perform their duties. We believe in a strong diplomatic effort to avoid wars, to aid in our successful pursuance of wars, to constructively engage in efforts to terminate wars and intelligently manage the period following cessation of hostilities. Diplomacy should be at the forefront of managing American relations with its foreign friends and allies

We believe in maintaining strong military forces to ensure that if military action is warranted, we can win quickly with a minimum loss of American life. We believe that military engagements should be last resorts for our country and that only Congress has the Constitutional authority to declare war. Our party is troubled by the progressive concentration of power within the Executive to initiate military actions and continue them over long periods of time without the consent of Congress.

Our party seeks immediate nonpartisan analysis and long-term planning to guarantee that the intelligence, diplomatic and military functions truly reflect the optimum level of performance; not just now but well into the future.

4. **The Economy.** This party recognizes that for the majority of Americans it is "bread and butter", quality-of-life issues that are first and foremost in their minds, particularly when times are hard, and

their daily life is a struggle. We believe that the United States cannot long remain just a consumer nation but must restore a good portion of its production capabilities that have been lost to other nations. We are the largest economy in the world and as such have the capability of being virtually self-sufficient in providing for our own needs. We need to restore our lost industrial sectors here back home and ensure that our economy is as diverse as possible.

"Made in America" needs to once again be a source of pride for us. We need to foster an environment where our people pursue careers, not "jobs", in the vast range of occupations available in this era, and everyone should have the opportunity to attain the financial stability of a solid middle-class standard of living. We should not have a lower class of Americans. To rebuild industrial capabilities in the United States we need to consider all means necessary, including tariffs on foreign exporters who through state subsidies and/or low wages are able to undercut our American producers by selling low quality products and commodities at low prices against which Americans cannot compete. That said, we are in support of strong international trade agreements and actions that favor all parties and undermine none.

Our party argues for a national/federal flat-tax system – conjecturally set at 25% for the present, that applies to all individuals and business entities, and that all deductions except legitimate business expenses be eliminated. We believe that the only way for a tax system to be "fair" is for every worker, every business to pay exactly the same percentage and have no access to loopholes and deductions.

We propose as well that a portion of federal tax revenue – possibly 10% - be then returned to the States for their use in specific sectors which the federal government will relinquish back to the States – infrastructure projects, social assistance programs, education, programs alternative to welfare systems and other areas that are not clearly federal responsibilities under the Constitution.

5. **A Balanced Budget and Elimination of the National Debt.** Our party believes that the federal government should be required to develop and approve an annual balanced budget, covering every sector

and expense, and then be obliged to stick to it. We should never again borrow money to cover our national expenses, except in dire emergencies. We should eliminate the national debt over time in a measured program that is covered as a line item expenditure in each annual budget.

6. **Planning for America 2050.** Our party will take the lead in marshalling the wealth of American knowledge, expertise, ingenuity, and motivation to develop credible, practical plans to achieve national goals over the next 32 years. We want these goals, and the measures established to attain them, to have virtually universal support from our citizens as well as strong support from each succeeding President, Congress and State government as well. We want to assure the United States of America in 2050, when the population will be at 438 million, 111 million more than today, will be well-prepared to offer its citizens the prosperity and quality of life they deserve. There are several crucial areas we must address.

Infrastructure. Our infrastructure is not meeting the needs of today, is far less than what will be needed in 2050, and what we do have is crumbling. Our party believes in addressing our problems immediately, but intelligently and in a measured forward-looking fashion. We do not need to just repair what we have and build more of the same. We will certainly need to repair some of what we have now so that we can sustain our operations, but we should never lose sight of the fact that we should be planning to provide the optimum needs of what we envision for 2050.

In other words, if our failing or inadequate transportation systems of today need to be addressed we need to spend our taxpayers' dollars on systems that meet our best projections for the needs of the not so distant future. We know that our people, 111 million more of them projected in 2050, will need to go from home to work to school, to shopping, to visit friends and family, to vacation. But, just building more roads makes no sense; we will never keep up with the demand and, in the end, we will just have a country covered with a spiderweb of asphalt, snarled with traffic as now. We will have airports that are over-taxed and railways that are inefficient and dangerous. We need high-tech solutions to transportation that include more efficient, safe pathways for private vehicles, local mass transportation, long-distance high-speed transportation. We need to think realistically, but with a great deal of futurist, cutting-edge technology involved.

The majority of infrastructure amelioration and new initiatives need to devolve to the States. The federal government must step back from its current role of being the benefactor, distributing largess project by project to the States. Congress has no business deciding the merits of individual projects for which States seek funding. This "pork" has clogged up too many Congressional bills, unrelated to the very real national issues being weighed. Individual "bridges to nowhere" are not national issues; they belong at the State level. With a 10% return to the States of federal tax revenue, States can decide what projects they will fund, and their own State citizens can hold the State governments accountable.

Housing and Development. Cities are swallowing the countryside. Development is destroying the forests, waterways, farmlands, wildlife. People are the cause and people must be the solution. Part of the American Dream has been to have a single-family home on a decent-sized lot. There is nothing wrong with this – except that we can no longer afford to just keep spreading outwards, destroying the environment, requiring more roads, power and water lines, shopping centers, schools and so many other infrastructural needs of human populations.

We need to plan now to build upwards and downwards – utilizing all the high-tech, futuristic knowledge we can summon – to accommodate a much larger population. We should not forget that with more people we will need more food - thus more arable farmland.

Water. We take water for granted, but for human populations here and around the world the availability of potable water for consumption and personal needs as well as agriculture is approaching a crisis situation. Our party places a high priority on assuring that our citizens throughout the country have access to the water they need. Again, we seek a maximum effort on the part of our best scientific and social planning minds to achieve this goal.

Energy. Demands for energy will only increase in the future. Environmental damage from extraction as well as utilization will also increase. Our party will press for action at all levels – federal, state and local – to maximize use of what we have now, develop new technologies to replace energy sources that we seek to replace, and plan ahead to prevent future crises or avoidable damage to the environment or the health of our people. We do not seek precipitous and rash efforts to eliminate certain sources of energy – coal, petroleum or nuclear. We are conscious that we will need these sources for the foreseeable future and that we need the people involved in these industries. Any action we would espouse would be well-considered, well-planned and incremental so that we would not face harmful deficits or leave millions of Americans in these industries without a replacement source of comparable livelihood.

Education. The United States once took pride in having one of the most educated populations in the world; and this education level had a significant bearing on our being at the forefront of developing new technologies and in having one of the highest standards of living. Sadly, education has slipped in our country; we are quite far down the list compared to other developed countries. Part of the reason is that American youth no longer have the same incentive to learn as they once did because there are far fewer opportunities to translate the education into an occupation. We have outsourced so many of our occupations that there are fewer reasons to study and train as a basis for a livelihood.

Our party seeks to return as many of the industrial and manufacturing functions back to the United States and, as part of this goal, seeks to invigorate the learning environment so that American youth can once again learn trades and academic skills that will directly translate into productive careers. We believe that equal access to quality education cannot be achieved when there is inequality in school funding between school districts – richer districts providing better education than poor ones, widening the divide between the haves and have-nots. However, we believe education is the purview of States, not the federal government, and thus discourage establishment of nationally mandated per-student funding levels. But, we do encourage States to look closely at equal funding of school districts as a State option. National education policy cannot reflect the needs of all regions of the country; only State and local governments are close enough to the needs of their citizens to provide the appropriate education in their regions.

Science and Technology. The United States was once the world's leader in science and technology. Not so anymore and this must be addressed before we become "second-echelon" to emerging scientific and technological phenomenon such as China and India, once considered "third-world" developing nations.

To restore our lead in science and technology we must be able to give our youth and our current scientists and workforce a reason to pursue careers in these areas. This can be done if we draw back from becoming solely a consumer nation and restore our industrial and manufacturing capabilities. Private business, large and small, provides the engine for scientific and technological advances. Government – federal, State, and local – must provide the inspiration and our party will be at the forefront to create a new and positive atmosphere in which science and technology resume their status as high-value endeavors. We need to focus our brain-power – scientific genius, technical excellence and production knowledge into building for the future.

7. **Justice.** Americans need to have their confidence in our justice system restored; this is vitally important. Justice needs to be viewed as protecting all law-abiding citizens, as a fair and essential public service to ensure that American society functions in an atmosphere of stability, peace and liberty. A new direction is needed to cease the current state of mass incarceration, particularly of those convicted for victimless crimes, and that the prison industry must be changed from

261

a profit-making system to one that is non-profit. Solutions must be found to end the disproportionate levels of arrests, convictions and incarcerations of racial minorities.

The War on Drugs must officially end; persons currently or at one time incarcerated for simple drug possession charges freed and their records cleared; marijuana legalized; future drug use convictions decriminalized; and bona fide addicts remanded to effective drug rehabilitation programs rather than prisons. Persons convicted of crimes, once their sentences or penalties are completed, should be considered to have paid their debt to society and be protected from discriminatory practices which exclude them from securing employment or places of residence.

We believe the death penalty should be abolished nationally.

This party has enormous respect for law enforcement agencies and personnel at all levels. However, we believe there has been an unhealthy shift in attitude nationally in which law enforcement is perceived as intrusive and adversarial to a significant portion of the population. We need to seek solutions to restore public confidence in law enforcement. The United States of America is not a police state and a key element in assuring this democratic principle continues is to ensure that law enforcement always remains under tight civilian control.

The great majority of law enforcement officers are exemplary citizens, hard-working, courageous, self-sacrificing – while underpaid and often unappreciated. However, a small minority of officers have not enhanced the reputation of their organizations and in the cases of egregious abuses of human rights – such as the killings of unarmed civilians – the federal government should assert senior authority over the judicial processes to ensure justice is served fairly and perceived as such by the entire citizenry of this nation.

We believe the Supreme Court, as the highest judicial authority in our tripartite constitutional government has not sufficiently evolved over time as have the Executive and Legislative branches. It remains underpowered and passive, an unfortunate weak link in our national system of "checks and balances". It need not be so as the Constitution clearly stipulates that Congress has the authority to increase the powers and authorities of the Supreme Court.

We believe it is time for a Constitutional Convention to address, debate, and reach national consensus on constitutional issues that need to be updated and adjusted to more accurately pertain to our current era. The drafters of our Constitution recognized that over time certain elements contained therein would need to evolve and this party believes we should begin that comprehensive process.

8. **Electoral Reform.** The Constitution is specific in outlining our system for electing a President. States establish the methodology for choosing electors from that State who will join with electors from all other States in the Electoral College to choose the Executive. This was intended to present a reasonable balance between a national popular vote and the rights of those in the least populous States. The current two-party dominance has created a mockery of what the drafters of the Constitution intended.

Our centrist party seeks electoral reform at State levels to proportion electors by votes received by any party. We believe that the Electoral College should be a truly functional mechanism in which electors from three or more parties choose the President, rather than rubberstamp the State "winner-take-all" assignment of electors between the two major parties.

Our party does not support a national popular vote, as we are very conscious of the dominance of the urban vote and believe it would be destructive to our national fabric to permit the populations of large metropolitan areas and cities to control national governance, thereby excluding the populations of rural areas from an effective voice.

This party is firmly opposed to re-districting of Congressional Districts to manipulate voting blocs to the advantage of whichever political party is in power. We believe that counties are the primary political entity in our national structure and that in determining the boundaries of Congressional Districts no county should be broken apart to redistribute fragments among different districts.

9. **Separation of Powers**. Over the course of our history, the Executive has become much more powerful than our Founders intended, while the Legislative has become much weaker and dysfunctional, partially self-induced through the two-party system. Our party believes in the co-equality of our three branches of government, each in their separate areas of responsibility. We will strive to more clearly delineate these responsibilities and seek adjustments to ensure a viable separation of powers is restored.

We believe that the concept of separation of powers is the primary basis for democratic governance via a republican/federalist structure. To be effective in accomplishing designated responsibilities, each layer of governance must retain the authorities to accomplish them. Each must remain accountable for its actions, and our system of checks and balances must remain intact and even strengthened.

Thankfully, in our great United States, there is the fourth and most powerful check and balance. Let us not forget.

We the People.